TWAYNE'S WORLD AUTHORS SERIES

A Survey of the World's Literature

Sylvia E. Bowman, Indiana University

GENERAL EDITOR

THE NETHERLANDS

Egbert Krispyn, University of Florida

EDITOR

Macropedius

(TWAS 218)

TWAYNE'S WORLD AUTHORS SERIES (TWAS)

The purpose of TWAS is to survey the major writers —novelists, dramatists, historians, poets, philosophers, and critics—of the nations of the world. Among the national literatures covered are those of Australia, Canada, China, Eastern Europe, France, Germany, Greece, India, Italy, Japan, Latin America, the Netherlands, New Zealand, Poland, Russia, Scandanavia, Spain, and the African nations, as well as Hebrew, Yiddish, and Latin Classical literatures. This survey is complemented by Twane's United States Authors Series and English Authors Series.

The intent of each volume in these series is to present a critical analytical study of the works of the writer; to include biographical and historical material that may be necessary for understanding, appreciation, and critical appraisal of the writer; and to present all material in clear, concise English—but not to vitiate the scholarly content of the work by doing so.

Macropedius

By THOMAS W. BEST

University of Virginia

Twayne Publishers, Inc.   ::   New York

Preface

Though some well-known scholars, especially Johannes Bolte, Wilhelm Creizenach, and Karl Goedeke, have thought highly of him, the sixteenth-century Dutch dramatist Georgius Macropedius remains generally no more than a ponderous name. His plays have been caught in a vicious circle, sucking them into oblivion like a maelstrom. Because he wrote in Latin, his potential audience has steadily shrunk, making editions of his works bad risks financially. Their resultant scarcity has further discouraged acquaintance, even by students of his period. Unlike Erasmus, Macropedius cultivated no extra-literary importance that might have caught the eye of historians. It remains for someone to rescue him from the vortex for an introduction to modern readers in their own language. Only after we have met him can we rate him fairly as a playwright of the early Renaissance.

However presumptuous, I am volunteering to make such a presentation, grateful to the editors of Twayne for their support. In keeping with my purpose, I have described the plays of Macropedius at some length but with an effort not to be tedious. Considerable description seems particularly advisable since most of these works are not generally available, even in the original. As part of my detailed account of them I have included ample commentary, however, and I have not minced criticism. Lest the brevity of my bibliography cause consternation, I should stress that I have listed only the few publications which I consider really important for the study of Macropedius.

Material for this little book had to be gathered from a host of libraries in this country and in Europe. Without exception I have found cooperation wherever I have turned. Remembering my dependence on outside assistance, I wish to make a warm expression of my thanks to the librarians with whom I have dealt and to the staff of the Interlibrary Loan Service at the University of Virginia.

Without specifying all the institutions which gave me help, I would like to single out the following: Bibliotheek der Rijksuniversiteit in Utrecht, Bibliothèque Nationale in Paris, Bibliothèque Royale de Belgique in Brussels, The British Museum, Centrale Bibliotheek van de Rijksuniversiteit in Gent, Gemeentelijk Archief of Utrecht, Koninklijke Bibliotheek in The Hague, Niedersächsische Staats und Universitätsbibliothek in Göttingen, and the libraries of Chicago and Harvard Universities. With Professor J. Ruwet, Chief Librarian of the Bibliothèque de l'Université in Louvain, who wrote to inform me of the destruction of Macropediana there in 1914, I share sincere regret, and I am grateful to Professor R. C. Engelberts in Utrecht for his friendly letter regarding *Bassarus*. Not to be forgotten is the Research Committee of the University of Virginia, which supported this project with badly needed money.

THOMAS W. BEST

Contents

Preface

Chronology

1. Introduction   11
2. The Prodigal Son   23
3. The Erring Schoolboys   42
4. The Farcical Villagers   67
5. The Epicures   110
6. The Models of Virtue   136
7. The Impatient   159
8. Conclusion   169

   Notes and References   171
   Selected Bibliography   179
   Index   183

Chronology

1486   Macropedius was born in Gemert.

1502   He became a Brother of the Common Life.

1517   The Reformation began in Wittenberg.

1521   Charles V was crowned German emperor.

ca. 1530   Macropedius became school rector in Utrecht.

1535   *The Rebels* and *Aluta* were published.

1536   *Petriscus* was published. Calvin's *Institutes of the Christian Religion* was first published.

1537   *Asotus* was published.

1538   *Andrisca* was published.

1539   *Hecastus* was published.

1540   *Bassarus* was published. Macropedius probably traveled to Rome. The Society of Jesus was officially sanctioned by Pope Paul III.

1541   *Lazarus the Beggar* was published.

1544   *Joseph* was published.

1552–1554   Macropedius' revised plays were collected in two volumes, including the initial printing of *Adam* (1552) and *Hypomone* (probably 1554).

1555   Charles V abdicated as ruler of the Low Countries.

1556   *The Pupil Jesus* was published.

1558   Macropedius died in 's-Hertogenbosch.

CHAPTER 1

Introduction

FOR most of Europe the revival of Plautine and Terentian plays in Italy during the fifteenth century presaged the decline of dramatic forms prevalent in the late Middle Ages. In the homeland of the Renaissance respectable vernacular imitations of Roman comedy arose relatively early as a consequence of this renewal. Near the beginning of the sixteenth century Ludovico Ariosto (1474–1533) was already composing so-called *commedia erudita* at Ferrara. Soon the Spanish theater began to manifest Renaissance influence, whereas in France and England vernacular productions fashioned after classical or neoclassical models did not appear before 1550. After 1530 in Germany and the Netherlands Latin comedies smacking of Plautus and Terence became common. Though most of the Latin works on Netherlandish and German stages were written by teachers for performance by their pupils, in general they were superior to vernacular plays prior to the Dutch Golden Age on the one hand and the Silesian Baroque drama of Andreas Gryphius (1616–64) on the other. Among the many humanist and Jesuit productions of these sister countries are some with merit and spirit enough to interest our own era, but with few exceptions the authors of them did not consistently demonstrate outstanding ability. The foremost Latin dramatist of Germany was the Jesuit Jacob Bidermann (1578–1639). His Dutch equivalent was Macropedius.

I *The Life of Macropedius*

Young George was born of a noble family named Van Lancvelt in Gemert near 's-Hertogenbosch.[1] He may have attended the Latin school in the latter town. There at any rate he joined the Brethren of the Common Life in 1502, became a priest, and functioned as a teacher, without having studied at any university. The Brethren professed the simple, almost mystical piety of Geert

Groote (1340–1384), as classically expressed in *The Imitation of Christ* ascribed to Thomas a Kempis (1380–1471). Though not monks, the Brethren lived in communal houses, priests, clerics, and laymen together, renouncing ownership of property, and working for joint support. Macropedius (having so latinized his name) became schoolrector in Liège and in Utrecht after being in 's-Hertogenbosch. We have no definite dates for his stay in any of the three cities, but it is likely that he was in Utrecht as of the year 1530. He remained there until 1556 at the earliest and besides being rector of the St. Jerome School was in charge of the house for poor boys maintained by the Brethren. In the preface to one of his plays, *Lazarus the Beggar (Lazarus mendicus)*, he indicates that he spent some time in Rome, though he says neither when nor why he was there.[2] Since *Lazarus* was first published in March 1541, the trip probably occurred in 1540. Presumably Macropedius went on business. After leaving Utrecht he returned to 's-Hertogenbosch, where he died in late July 1558, afflicted with gout, as he had been for most of his life. He was buried there at the church of the Brethren.

II *Macropedius the Man*

As a priest and an educator he shows himself in his plays to have been preoccupied with morals. At the same time, he tempered his didacticism with humor and couched it in dramatic portraiture of compelling realism. When we examine his dramas we will see that he was a dedicated teacher and Christian, but we will also find that he had a sharp eye for people and a mind open to their sometimes comic failings. While naturally frowning on fornication, for instance, he did not shrink from the frank portrayal of well patronized prostitutes or lecherous priests. He shared the satirical bent of his age, which united in ridicule both its penchant for laughter and its passion for correction.

Like many humanists of the Netherlands and Germany, particularly earlier ones such as Erasmus (1467?–1536), Macropedius remained a Catholic. He was always concerned with ethics, but after 1535 he seems to have become more deeply religious. While he abandoned secular themes at least partly under pressure,[3] he voluntarily qualified the worth of humanistic education in the first edition of the Everyman allegory *Hecastus,* published in 1539. There God's messenger deprecates the sole pursuit of worldly knowledge. In a scene added after V, 7 in the revised edition printed in 1552, Acolytus, a boy assisting the priest Hieronymus, argues down the pedantic Philomathes, a young enthusiast for the classics. Teachers of grammar, dialectics, and rhetoric, Acolytus says, do nothing for the soul. He himself was once devoted to "elegant letters" but bade them farewell when he saw that only devoutness conduces to salvation. Is it not wiser, he concludes, to seek Christian piety than Ciceronian latinity, which will not preserve one from the horror of the grave? He is vindicated as Philomathes flees in panic at the spectacle of Death, come with spike in hand to stab his father Hecastus. Macropedius did not forsake humanism, like Acolytus, but during the last twenty years of his life he became more intent upon spiritual matters than he appears to have been before.[4]

In his general chariness he adopted the attitude of most intellectuals of his day regarding authority. Faithful servants in his plays encourage obedience, and for the sake of law and order we are enjoined in the chorus to the fourth act of *Petriscus* to render unto Caesar what is his and to do so without demurring. Even corrupt officials deserve respect as bulwarks against anarchy, that most abominable of abominations. Because of his conservatism Macropedius concurred in the hanging of adolescents for petty thievery, as we will see in both *Petriscus* and *The Rebels* (*Rebelles*). With the chorus to Act II of *Asotus* he expresses a low opinion of youth in general. If not disciplined, lads will become little different from animals, he assures us. They must be coerced because they are naturally licentious and given to boasting their vices. At the same time Macropedius probably tolerated a certain amount of boyishness good-naturedly. In IV, 6 of the first edition of *Petriscus*, a sheriff, when told of how two juvenile delinquents tricked an innkeeper out of wine, comments "By golly, that's amusing cleverness! It could be condoned if it weren't frequently exercised."

The only sounds emanating from Macropedius' school were not the stentorian drone of the lecturer and the piercing yelps of the chastened, for this votary of the Muses loved to sing and had no slight knowledge of Polyhymnia's arts. In the late 1520's he dictated some music theory to his pupils.[5] His plays abound in canticles—not only choral odes between the acts but also songs within some acts as well. Music, like a little wine, the blessings of which

Macropedius lauds in the chorus to the third act of *Petriscus*, cheered his ascetic life.

Certainly there was no woman to brighten it. Not only did he live in strictest celibacy. With the gnarled misogyny that he repeatedly evidences he held the whole female sex in contempt, as prone to miserliness, drink, bitchiness, and lust. In the chorus to Act III of *The Rebels* he opines that a woman is more dangerous than fire, ocean, wild animals, or an evil spirit. "A man is worthier," he roundly declares in the second chorus to Act IV of *Andrisca*. There he also shows himself agreeably sensible, however, in advising husbands to guide their wives firmly, without tyranny, and mildly, without cowardice.

Finally, Macropedius was humble and self-effacing. This is a plausible reason for the dearth of information about him. He did not seek publicity, nor did he flatter the great. He dedicated his plays to wealthy patrons not for his own reward but for charity to aid the paupers in his care. In spite of his reticence, however, he did secure a certain esteem. He was known and respected both as a playwright and as an educator. His reputation rested not only on his dramas but also on several strictly pedagogical tracts. Before considering the sort of play which he wrote, let us briefly survey all of his *oeuvre*.

III   *The Works of Macropedius*

For his pupils the Utrecht schoolmaster published eight textbooks.[6] Four deal with Latin and Greek grammar, and one each with dialectics, prosody, and letter writing. The eighth primer is a compendium of calendrical information, containing an appendix on computation. In addition we have four odes *(cantilenae)* which Macropedius composed for his schoolboys to sing. Though written in classical meters, all are religious in content and have even a medieval flavor. The first, which was printed November 6, 1539, is a reminder of Christ's Judgment. It was perhaps inspired by *Hecastus*, released that same year. The second, written for St. Martin's Day 1540, is a *memento mori* subtitled "Ode on the Image of Death." It exhorts us to deal with both good and bad fortune by remembering the transience of life. The third and fourth *cantilenae*, printed 1551 and 1552 respectively, are Christmas hymns, relating the story of the Nativity and comparing us to Jesus.[7] All of these poems are rather ploddingly pedestrian and confirm what the choruses to Macropedius' plays almost invariably suggest: Despite his love for music he was scarcely a lyricist.

His dramas, twelve in number, were written over a period of approximately fifty years and published from 1535 to 1556. Besides this dozen, three other theatrical works have been ascribed to Macropedius, but mistakenly. Known only by their titles, they are *Susanna, Passion of Christ (Passio Christi),* and *Dimulla.* The first to attribute *Susanna* and *Passion of Christ* to him was the Swiss Conrad Gesner (1516–1565) in his *Bibliotheca universalis* of 1545.[8] Since both works must have appeared before that year (though Gesner gives no publication dates for them), they would have been included in Macropedius' collected plays, issued 1552–1554, if he had in fact been the author of them. They are not to be found in that two-volume edition, however. There is another reason for doubting that Macropedius wrote a *Passion of Christ.* In the prologue to his *Lazarus the Beggar* he states that it would be indecorous to present the Savior on the stage, whether as infant or man. Not only did he not include the figure of Jesus in any of his plays before the last one; he also did not permit the performance of other dramas in which Christ appeared. When he wrote *The Pupil Jesus (Jesus scholasticus,* 1556) he had apparently changed his mind (see Chapter 6, Section II), but that was very late in his life. R. C. Engelberts (*Bassarus,* pp. 31–32, note 19) shows that the title "Dimulla" arose simply through an erroneous reading of Gesner. Thus repudiating the three alien eggs deposited in Macropedius' literary nest by scholarly cuckoos, we will limit his dramatic canon to *Asotus; The Rebels* and *Petriscus; Aluta, Andrisca,* and *Bassarus; Hecastus* and *Lazarus the Beggar; Joseph* and *The Pupil Jesus;* plus *Adam* and *Hypomone*—treating them in that order. All twelve are specimens of Renaissance Latin school (or education) drama as it was produced in both the Netherlands and Germany. We need consequently to acquire some concept of this genre, which Macropedius was instrumental in shaping.

IV   *Latin School Drama*

It derived mainly from the comedies of ancient Rome, and academic playwrights commonly plundered those venerated models. Even one of the best education dramas, the influential *Acolastus* of Gnapheus (to be discussed in the next chapter), is a cento of Terentian and Plautine expression. In his first play, *Asotus*, like *Acolastus* a version of the prodigal-son parable, Macropedius also usurped many lines from Plautus, but he afterwards foreswore so much dependence.

The character types of Roman comedy enjoyed a rebirth in the Renaissance apparent even to readers of only the vernacular plays of England. Suffice it to mention *Ralph Roister Doister* (1552) and *Volpone* (1606). A counterpart to Merygreeke and Mosca is the Colax of *Asotus,* although he is no manipulator like them. Subsequently Macropedius included parasites, as well as other Plautine and Terentian stock figures, only in minor roles and in modified form. He continued to use Greek names, however, and most of them describe the personage whom they denote, just as "Asotus" (from Luke 15:13 of the Greek New Testament) means "prodigal."

Some of the conventions of Roman comedy also recrudesced in school drama. In the plays of Macropedius the emergence of someone from a house is heralded by a creaking of the door. When a character not present is needed on the stage, he opportunely happens along. Monologues and asides are frequent, and of course eavesdropping also occurs. Time can be stretched or contracted elastically. The action in *Petriscus,* for example, lasting from early morning to late afternoon with no pauses between scenes and only brief lapses between acts, is reduced to the two or three hours of performance. In Act V of *Andrisca,* by contrast, Byrsocopus waits outside his house just long enough for his wife to shed her wet clothes. This would normally take only a brief moment, but he lingers through two scenes comprising thirty-five lines of dialogue before he rushes in with the hope that she will be stripped by now. Like both Plautus and native farce writers, Macropedius occasionally breaks, or at least threatens, the dramatic illusion with remarks or appeals to the spectators, and in the final scene of *Petriscus, Andrisca, Bassarus, Hecastus,* and *Joseph* one of the participants announces the conclusion of the action, sending the audience home.

A further convention, characteristic of Renaissance literature in general, is the incorporation of allusions to classical literature and mythology, however unclassic the subject matter. The God of the Hebrews in plots taken from the Old Testament is more likely to be called "Jupiter" or "The Thunderer" than "Jehovah." "By Hercules," "by Castor," and "by Pollux" are regular expletives in the lines of school plays. In *Aluta* a sharper native to Utrecht invokes Mercury, Roman god of thieves, as he sets about despoiling the semiconscious protagonist. Bassarus, a sexton in a Dutch village, uses as an analogy for his relationship to the local pastor the gladiators Bithus and Bacchius, whom Horace mentions in his satires (I, 7, 20). Inappropriate though this mining of antiquity may seem to us in such a context, the strange alloys which resulted were common currency to men of the sixteenth century.

The prologue, used by Terence to argue his defense against a hostile critic, by Plautus to explain the situation of characters at the beginning of a comedy, and by both to solicit the goodwill of audiences, regularly precedes the Latin plays of the Dutch and German schoolmasters. Macropedius, who must have had a problem with noisy audiences, always ends his prologues by enjoining silence. In the case of *Adam* he even calls upon maturer spectators to control the more obstreperous. Education dramas have a plot summary, as well, and many have an epilogue, in which the author normally specifies the message to be carried away. The plays are divided into five acts, among which choruses are often inserted, intended as musical interludes. These are usually moralistic, serving as a commentary upon some aspect of the preceding action and on occasion treated by Macropedius as part of the plot. All of his dramas have intermezzi, a number of which paraphrase Biblical passages, and the 1552–54 edition of his works includes a melody for each chorus. Just how such entr'actes came to be used in school drama is a matter for speculation, though Macropedius took over the practice of including them from the German Johann Reuchlin (1455–1522), whose two comedies will be mentioned in connection with *Bassarus*, Chapter 4. Johannes Bolte [9] has suggested that the idea derived from Greek comedy as described by ancient grammarians. Regardless of its origin, Macropedius welcomed the chorus out of his love for music.

All the segments of Latin school drama, from the prologue or plot summary through the epilogue, are normally written in unrhymed, quantitative verse. The meter might vary from one scene to another or even within a single scene. Macropedius always states at the beginning of a scene the names of the characters who speak during it, and in the main he specifies the type of verse utilized. The majority of his scenes are in iambic trimeters, though

[17]

many are in iambic tetrameters, sometimes catalectic. Act V of *The Rebels* contains an assortment of verse forms, a couple of which are rather surprising, as we will see. Also with his choruses Macropedius customarily designates the meter, mostly iambic dimeter. The reason for such labeling leads us to the purposes of education drama.

It was undertaken primarily as a teaching aid in the schools. Naming the verse form helped young readers to scan, and performances sharpened language proficiency if not also memory. In the prologue to *Andrisca* Macropedius argues at length that play production is the most effective of all instructional exercises. Renaissance schoolmasters throughout the Netherlands and Germany valued the staging of comedies (and tragedies, beginning later in the sixteenth century) not only as a help in mastering Latin but also for the improvement of speaking ability and poise. A statement in *Julius Redivivus* by the Swabian Nicodemus Frischlin (1547–90) serves as a nice illustration for the latter point. In II, 2 Cicero, returned to Renaissance Germany with Julius Caesar in order to discover what progress has been made since ancient times in that formerly benighted wilderness, meets the poet Eoban Hessus (1488–1540), who is bearing a book of verse to the emperor. Cicero asks him to read some lines, saying "I'm eager to hear—or rather to see—you speak." By taking part in play production, schoolhouse thespians were expected to master the art of elocution, learning to make the proper gestures with the proper intonation and to control their stage fright in the process. Acting was little more than recitation.

Closely related to the pedagogical aims of humanists who taught from the stage were the ethical concerns of all Renaissance educators. Boys were thought to better their morals by observing evil punished and good rewarded. A Christianized Thalia might turn them from the devil, like the title figure in the fifteenth-century Dutch miracle play *Mariken van Nimmegen*. Even debauchery and lewdness were not always considered harmful if purity prevails. To insure that it did in their theaters, school dramatists preferred to use Biblical stories for their plots, but they still sometimes included scenes which might be called "for adults only" today. Though Victorians may wince at the incongruity of parading improprieties before innocent eyes under the banner of edification, playwrights guilty of this paradox were not always hypocrites. Like Hamlet they followed Cicero in treating comedy as a mirror of life, necessarily reflecting vice along with virtue—both for the profit of the beholder. No less an authority than Martin Luther is reported to have said in the early 1530's that comedies should not be barred because of dalliance or even occasional obscenities in them, since the Bible contains these, too.[10] After all, how is one to know danger unless the pitfalls of seduction are disclosed? School drama was supposed to enable its practitioners to deal knowledgeably with life. In the preface to the 1535 edition of *The Rebels* and *Aluta*, Macropedius sets forth the matter this way: "What is more conducive to learning for boys, to noble studies for adolescents, and to virtue for the more advanced—indeed for everyone in general—than erudite comedy, which is rightly defined by some as an imitation of life, a mirror of custom, an image of truth, and by others as a harmless compendium of public and private affairs?" The authors of school plays regarded their proscenium as a microcosm in which young citizens rehearsed for the stage of the world.

Serving the utilitarian ends of these pedagogical dramaturges were all the artistic means which their talents could muster, for they sought to please. Macropedius begins the prologue to *Petriscus* by stating that his purpose was to entertain his audiences as well as to train his charges. The speaker says "When our teacher perceived that nothing is more suitable for his pupils or more pleasing to you spectators than comedies, he wrote this one, extempore and for the temper of the times, so that our young boys might have some practice and that you might have some amusement simultaneously." Those schoolmasters who wrote for the theater knew that Horace calls for a combination of the useful with the sweet, yet they also had an ulterior motive for making their productions as enjoyable as they could. Larger audiences afforded a little more badly needed cash. In the prologue to *The Rebels* Macropedius has the speaker call unabashedly for money. He could stoop to such audacity because the proceeds were for his poor boys and not to line his own pockets.

With this cursory description of Latin school drama in the Netherlands and Germany we have nearly all the background information essential for an understanding of the works which we are to examine. It must be augmented, however, by some brief consideration of how these pieces were presented.

V *The Staging of Macropedius' Plays*

A detailed explanation is impossible, because like school dramatists in general Macropedius followed Plautus and Terence in omitting stage directions. We can be confident that he used no front curtain, no scenery, and only minimal props. Like Plautus and Terence again, he set most of his action outside, in front of the houses belonging to the principal characters. These buildings were probably indicated by structures with real doors, which were sometimes belabored as in Roman comedy and medieval Dutch plays. Each entrance seems to have been recessed in a vestibule, like that used by the ancient Romans.[11] Bassarus, for example, likes to lurk unseen in his doorway, eavesdropping on his neighbors, and in Act III of *Petriscus* the spitfire Mysandra, armed with a stick, ambushes her husband at their threshold.

Macropedius did not alter the stage during the performance of most of his works. With the exception of *Aluta, Lazarus the Beggar, Adam,* and *Hypomone,* all the action of any given drama takes place in a single locality. For *Aluta,* as we will see, the different settings may have been represented together, from start to finish. Only the final scene of *Lazarus* involves a change.

Interior scenes do occur in Macropedius' plays, despite the preference for outdoor action. In Act IV of *The Rebels,* for instance, we see both outside and inside a tavern. How was this made possible for audiences? A Latin morality, *Homulus,* completed in Maastricht in 1536 and used by Macropedius for his *Hecastus,* has some stage directions in the form of marginal notes. Several of these refer to an elevated throne of God within a curtained area which is opened and closed after the fashion of vernacular plays given by the popular "chambers of rhetoric." Another stage direction describes an interior scene as follows: "This having been spoken, Homulus goes away to confess his sins to the priest. A place shut off by curtains is opened. There sits the penitentiary, who, after hearing the confession, gives Homulus the eucharist." Using a curtain for a wall was one way of engineering interior scenes. Another was to have them viewed through the entrance to the house in which they were set. In V, 7 of Macropedius' *Joseph* the comment is made that Pharaoh can be seen on his throne inside the palace because the door is open. Double doors may have been needed when something was to be observed through an entrance.

Without giving any explanation or documentation, R. C. Engelberts (*Bassarus,* p. 29) indicates that Macropedius' plays were performed in front of the Utrecht town hall. At times school dramas were indeed staged outside, but in the prologue to *Aluta* the audience is warned against flatulence or halitosis "lest the theater reek with a bad odor." Would such a remark have been made in the open air? Until evidence is mustered against it, the assumption that Macropedius gave his plays indoors seems preferable.[12]

His actors were costumed, though in the dramas involving biblical figures (*Asotus, Lazarus, Joseph, Pupil Jesus, Adam,* and *Hypomone*) any attempt at historicity was probably not more than slight. Scant mention is made of dress in these works, and no precise descriptions are included to dispel uncertainty. We are told, for instance, only that the prodigal Asotus is presented with a robe (*stola*), a ring, and sandals on his return home or that the title figure in *Joseph* is to be clad in Egyptian attire (*vestis Aegyptia*) when he appears before Pharaoh. On this occasion he is also said to be robed (*stolatus*). In *Adam* two Levites at the time of Moses are recognized as Hebrews "by the color and even the cut of their clothes" (*ex colore ipsoque cultu vestium*), but the style is again not specified. In school theater generally costuming tended to be contemporary.

Several remarks can be hazarded as to when Macropedius' plays were acted. *Petriscus* and *Andrisca* end at supper time with a call to the spectators to go home and eat, implying that performances took place in the afternoon. This was customary with education drama, and the cost of lighting the theater at night was prohibitive. In the prologue to *Bassarus* a lengthy explanation is advanced for why no drama has been produced for a year, suggesting that ordinarily the stage was more in use. The speaker of the prologue to *Andrisca* says that no actors have appeared during nearly a semester. That Macropedius liked to have plays performed at least semiannually stands to reason in view of his high estimation of the pedagogical worth of the theater. For the staging of school drama in general Shrovetide was the favorite time of year, and Macropedius wrote four comedies actually set during carnival.

He apparently had the good fortune to see all of his dramas acted, if only by inexperienced boys (who also took the female roles), but he did not supervise the production of all his works. The prologue to *The Rebels* is spoken by the director, who specifically states that he was sent by the author to give the message. At least Macropedius did not intend to oversee the performance of this play. He was doubtless too busy. In the preface to *Joseph* we read that he was so overburdened with duties that he scarcely had time for his personal needs. In the preface to *Bassarus* he avers that it took him a year to find an occasion for revising this work.[13]

That being the case, one is led to see the real artistry embodied in most of his plays as the result of creative frenzy. *Aluta*—short, to be sure—he composed in only four days, during moments snatched from routine chores. Being pressed for time, he dashed off *Lazarus* and *Hypomone* extempore, he maintains, and we have seen that he makes the same assertion regarding *Petriscus*. He seems always to have written quickly, depending on inspiration for success. He did not have time for the meticulousness which properly complements the Muses' whisperings. At least in the case of *Aluta* he also lacked patience enough, for he frankly admits as much.

His first drama, to be treated in the next chapter, is a good example of faulty workmanship left largely unmended, even though it was touched up for publication. It documents the author as a theatrical apprentice. Besides inconsistencies, which might result from the revision, we notice there misjudgment of dramatic effects and slavish imitation. At the same time we are impressed with the promise of talent. The fact that Macropedius still left *Asotus* in imperfect form when he had it first printed is actually to be appreciated. As a result, we can observe how he progressed as a dramatist.

CHAPTER 2

The Prodigal Son

THE first comedies which Macropedius published were *The Rebels* and *Aluta*. They were printed together in 1535, when the author was nearly fifty years old. In the preface to this edition he introduces himself to the world as a dramatist, stating that he began to compose some of his "trifles" twenty years earlier for the benefit of his young pupils. He is starting to publish them now, he avers, because some of his friends and his printer (Gerard Hatard of 's-Hertogenbosch) have been importuning him to do so and especially because these works would be helpful to studious boys. If *The Rebels* and *Aluta* should find a gratifying reception, he later adds, he will release four other plays—*Asotus, Petriscus, Andrisca,* and *Bassarus*—with perhaps several additional ones "worked out a little more elegantly." Thus by 1535 Macropedius had completed half of his dramatic production and may have begun some further plays.

In the preface to *Asotus*, printed in 1537, he states that it was his first dramatic effort, undertaken when he was still a young man, some thirty years previous. Considering the result useless, he put the manuscript away at that time, retrieving it and altering it now as a present to Goeyert van den Boll, the mayor of Utrecht (where Macropedius had then been living for some time). Though apparently unaware of doing so, he presents us with a discrepancy of eight years. In 1535 he stated that he had begun to create plays twenty years earlier. In 1537 he wrote that he had started to do so thirty years before. We have a difference, then, between 1515 on the one hand and 1507 on the other. This inconsistency suggests that Macropedius was only approximating the composition date of *Asotus* and that he may not even have remembered exactly when he wrote it.

For roughly twenty-five years, if not thirty, the play lay untouched. When the author finally decided to take that crucial step of offering the produce of his talent to the taste of all Europe, he began not with his first fruits but rather with the later and riper *Rebels* and *Aluta*. Subsequently, in 1536, he released *Petriscus*. *Asotus* was only the fourth drama to be printed, probably because Macropedius did not consider it publishable until he reworked it. When he finally did attempt to polish *Asotus*, he no doubt had in mind another Latin prodigal-son play, the *Acolastus* of a fellow Dutch schoolmaster, Willem de Volder, called Gnapheus (1493–1568), whose comedy first appeared in Antwerp in 1529. It was winning such favor that by 1537, when *Asotus* went to press, it had been printed sixteen times and by 1585 was to run through forty-seven editions and to provoke a number of translations and imitations. A review and analysis of both treatments of the biblical parable (Luke 15:11-32) will highlight the relative merits of *Asotus*, along with revealing some similarities shared by the two works in their handling of the subject matter, even though Gnapheus was more concerned with the allegorical level of the story, and Macropedius, with the moral.

I *Acolastus*

In his preface Gnapheus deplores the neglect of comedy. "This age of ours has its Ciceros and Livys; it has its Virgils and Demostheneses—not to mention Solons, Hippocrateses, and Chrysostoms —but of Menanders and Terences it has none," [1] he declares. To break the ice, he has tried his own hand, he continues, apologizing for having disobeyed Horace by including tragic outcry in a comedy. He considers this a lighter crime than departing from the sense and dignity of the subject matter. "I preferred to honor piety," he says, "rather than some literary nicety." He adds the interesting comment that the humanist-physician Reynier Snoy from Gouda (ca. 1477–1537) was rumored already to have composed a prodigal-son play. The suggestion has been made [2] that a Latin archetype, now lost, was followed in part by Gnapheus, Snoy, Macropedius, and Burkard Waldis (ca. 1495–1557), who published a Low-German prodigal-son play in Riga in 1527. If there was a Latin original, however, would Gnapheus not mention it, just as he mentions Snoy?

In his prologue he assures us that he is not posing the threat of a dangerous, newfangled teaching but has only dramatized the well-known Biblical story. Though deferential toward Plautus and Terence, he is disdainful of more local dramatists, whom he accuses of having made bad plays by rehashing good (i.e., ancient) ones. He himself nevertheless rifled the Romans without altogether rivaling them. The customary admonition to silence, attentiveness, and ultimate applause brings Gnapheus' introductory remarks to an end.

The first act opens with a jeremiad by the prodigal's rather wooden father, Pelargus, who is grieved that his pampered younger son is rebelling against parental authority. Acolastus we discover to be an empty-headed egocentric intoxicated with conceit, who petulantly demands his inheritance and jubilantly departs with it, urged by a nebulous friend of whom we know only his name, Philautus ("self-love"), and his passion, hatred of Pelargus.

Gnapheus' play succeeded in the Renaissance and is enjoyable today thanks in large part to the parasites and the prostitute of Acts II–IV. In a cast led by patently two-dimensional figures, these heartier, full-bodied malfeasants stand out in welcome relief. The parasites, Pamphagus ("omnivorous") and Pantolabus ("catch-all"), also furnish most of what is comic in this comedy. With their ravenous hunger, their scheming flattery, and their triumphant satiation they function as sinister clowns, amusing but dangerous. As such they are kin to the ludicrous devils familiar in medieval plays and not unknown to Macropedius, as we are soon to see.

Pantolabus, once a wealthy debauchee himself, balances Acolastus. He is penniless when Acolastus is monied. When Acolastus loses his property, Pantolabus acquires some of it. As Acolastus' bad luck (his fortunate fall) effects his salvation, so Pantolabus' good luck assures his damnation. He reverses Acolastus also in seeming fairly natural, since he is not burdened with the allegorical import that Pelargus' son (whose name comes from the Greek for "undisciplined" and "immoderate") has to shoulder as the embodiment of man's selfish recalcitrance. Pantolabus has the advantage of not being flatly symbolic.

Because Gnapheus' scenes in the foreign country where the prodigal squanders his possessions make for basic differences between *Acolastus* and *Asotus*, let us summarize what takes place after the protagonist leaves home. As Act II begins, we find that forerunner of Acolastus down the rose-strewn but thorny paths of vice emaciated from a month of near starvation. With his money disbursed and his reputation ruined, Pantolabus has hidden from the public eye like a snail that cowers in its shell. Now driven out by hunger, he tells us that his stomach barks, his cheeks hang withered, and his scabrous teeth are itching from neglect. He pleads with Pamphagus for instruction in the art of parasitism, since he knows no way to earn a living. Because it was primarily Pamphagus who impoverished this sybarite, the master condescends to initiate Pantolabus in the mysteries of sycophancy, which he construes as a school of ancient philosophy with principles formulated by that model toady Gnatho in Terence's comedy *The Eunuch*, II, 2 (where the figures of Gnapheus' parasites are adumbrated). Pamphagus imbues the proselyte with dubious precepts just as Philautus has tutored Acolastus.

In accordance with an auspicious dream which Pamphagus had the night before, Acolastus arrives, bedizened with gold and girdled with a money-belt. The two flatterers quickly insinuate themselves into his favor, playing on his self-esteem like pipers on a hollow reed. They exalt him as their lord and extend their services. Pantolabus conducts the "king," as Acolastus is pleased to be called, to an inn, while Pamphagus goes grocery shopping, supplied with some of the royal cash. Sannio the pimp will see that the kingly bed is warmed by the choicest quean. When Act III opens, the carousal is about to begin. Lais the comely courtesan arrives, surrounded by an entourage of maids. To the profound relief of the cook dinner can finally be served. Later Acolastus takes a stroll, doting on his doxy while his chamber is prepared for a night devoted to Venus.

The next morning, at the outset of Act IV, we are first met by Pamphagus yawning in a hypnopompic stupor, woefully crapulous from the previous evening's excesses. He who was ever omnivorous, endowed with the stomach of an ostrich, feels the need for a purge. His belly, fired with indigestion, heaves with the lava of Etna. Despite his indisposition, he and Pantolabus exult, swapping compliments on each other and eulogies on the feast. Sounding the knell of doom for Acolastus, Pamphagus declares that he will proceed to slim their patron's purse with loaded dice. As he does so, Pantolabus describes from personal experience the chicanery which Pamphagus employs. His account lasts only twenty-three lines when Sannio dashes out, proclaiming with wonderment that Acolastus has been ruined. Pamphagus himself then bursts forth to confirm the report. The bankrupt wastrel has fled to Lais' lap for consolation. In a scene almost worthy of a tale by Sacher-Masoch, the soured sweetheart imperiously demands payment, orders her customer stripped of his clothes (although he gave her his golden necklace the previous evening), and leaves him contemptuously with a parting slap in the face. The lamenting and lamentable Acolastus accosts a farmer, begging for a job. In spite of a crippling famine in the region he is given work as a swineherd. "Oh, what a comedown!" he cries, calling Fortuna faithless as the wind.

In Act V he further bewails his misfortune before starting to regret his misconduct. Only after a long monologue plangent with abysmal depression does another bespeak humble contrition. Thereupon Pelargus talks of pardon, and Acolastus becomes inspired with hope of acceptance and determination to return. Drawn by some irresistible force, to be identified as grace, he hurries home, where he is forgiven and attired in new clothes, symbolic of his new nature. The elder son does not appear.

Acolastus' allegorical quality has already received comment. Pelargus, the pedantic friend Eubulus, and Philautus are, no less than the protagonist, concepts masquerading as characters. Philautus does not exist apart from Acolastus, and Eubulus lives only to assist Pelargus. Philautus is Acolastus' conceit; Eubulus (from the Greek for "good advice") is Pelargus' rational faculty. Philautus persuades Acolastus into error in demanding his freedom; Eubulus dissuades Pelargus from error in handling his son. Gnapheus employed these appendages to the two central characters not only in superficial imitation of Terence but also in the interest of better dramatization. Development through dialogue instead of soliloquy is hardly laudable, though, when use is made of personages who are neither fully human nor frankly allegorical. Rather than being *homo sapiens*, Eubulus is only *sapientia*. Philautus is, as Pelargus suggests in line 174, nothing but *philautia*.

The case of Pelargus himself has a little complexity. He stands for fatherhood, and in this capacity he is also God. As if being indefinite were not problematical enough a condition for him, he is embroiled in a contradiction, as well, since one moment he can only be the earthly father, while the next, he is supposed to be also the heavenly one. This inconsistency can perhaps be exemplified with a single sentence. In lines 97–98 Pelargus expresses both the bewilderment of a man and the grandioseness of God when he inquires "Should I really let my son leave home, the heir that I have destined for my kingdom?" He consists of two images that cannot always be focused together.

Acolastus is an intriguing and even intricate play, but characterization in it does not match dramatic technique. Like Aristotle, Gnapheus probably did not consider the former to be a playwright's primary concern. Most modern readers, however, would disagree. Happily, good characterization is in the main exactly what we do find with Macropedius. It is clear when he presents an allegorical figure that this personification is not also intended to be an ordinary person. In his better plays he endowed his principal characters with more personality and individuality than did Gnapheus and most other dramatists of the early Renaissance.

II *Asotus*

It is only through characterization that Macropedius surpasses Gnapheus in treating the prodigal-son theme. Because it is limited to strict unity of place, even though unity of time cannot be maintained, *Asotus* suffers from the omission of scenes like those in which Acolastus squanders his substance abroad. By leaving out the protagonist's reversal of fortune in exile Macropedius sacrificed the most poignant moment of the plot, and part of his attempt at compensation worsened this error.

The prologue opens with the assertion that *Asotus* contains nothing foolish or offensive, like the ravishing of virgins or the guile of pimps. Instead, Macropedius explains, he is presenting "a mystical parable drawn from the fount of purity." He begs our indulgence for treating a biblical subject comically and, like Gnapheus in the epilogue to *Acolastus*, he urges us to be mindful of the hidden meaning. The old man in the play, we are warned, will represent God the Father, who will pardon our sins as the sire forgives his son, if like the son we are repentant. Addressing those who might object to his disregard of the unity of time, Macropedius asserts that he is more concerned about fidelity to his story than about any poetic device. As we have seen, Gnapheus expresses the same idea in the preface to *Acolastus*. For a precedent Macropedius refers to Plautus' *Captives*, where a lapse of at least several days appears to occur while the character Philocrates goes abroad and returns. Actually, though, Plautus takes such liberties here that the trip lasts only several hours. Assuring us again that this play will be beneficial and clarifying the meaning of the name "Asotus," Macropedius ends the prologue with a call for silence.

As in *Acolastus*, Act I begins with a protracted soliloquy by the father. Eumenius ("well-disposed") relates that he has spent his life providing for his children. He has traveled widely, at great risk and with great effort, aging prematurely, in order to give his sons everything. Their house is large, their servants are numerous, their fields are fertile, their land is extensive, and the herds are huge. By the grace of the gods there is nothing which the children lack. Though Eumenius is now retired and wishes to spend his last days in leisure, not everything is as it should be. His elder son is frugal—even to a fault—but the other is willful and wasteful. Because a number of slaves are encouraging the younger scion in his vices, Eumenius is sorrowful and worried. To make the situation worse, those rowdies are damaging his reputation, he fears. He is at a loss to account for Asotus' behavior, since like Gnapheus' Pelargus he considers his own actions to be standards of moral excellence and he has never coddled his children. From their infancy, in fact, he has chastised them with the rod and the whip. Anticipating the subject matter of *The Rebels* and *Petriscus*, he states that he has had his boys educated by a tutor who was not forbidden to beat them; but "in vain," he sighs, "has my younger son been lacerated." His startling explanation for Asotus' incorrigible depravity is a verse from the Vulgate (Ecclesiastes 7:14): "No one can correct whom God despises." [3] Thus Eumenius portrays himself as a hard and narrow disciplinarian, in spite of his name. He says that he has lived to make his children happy, yet his dealings with them seem to have been more through welts than words. The youth who does not respond to this maltreatment he holds to be unsalvageable. Initially even less likeable than Pelargus, Eumenius makes us antipathetic toward himself and sympathetic toward his offending son before the latter appears, though undoubtedly Macropedius intended for this opening monologue to have the opposite effect.

At the end of Scene 1 the father goes off to the country with the older boy, Philaetius ("faultfinding"), committing the supervision of his home to a slave named Comasta ("merrymaker"). Despite the fact that it is now morning, he does not expect to return until the next day. Like the old men in most Roman comedies, Eumenius has a home in town and a farm in the country. Throughout *Asotus* the stage is meant to represent the street in front of this town house. Out of sight are a brothel, a prison, and probably the barn which is several times mentioned as being close by, even though the setting is in the city. Which city this is, we have no way of knowing. As in *Acolastus,* it is an unspecified port.[4]

After the master has left with Philaetius, Comasta reveals in a short soliloquy that he is not the just steward Eumenius thinks him to be [I, 2]. The "silly old man," as he calls his owner, is unaware that he is actually the person responsible for Asotus' dissoluteness. In the master's absence he will send the loyal servants away and arrange an orgy for the son, he informs us.

Opportunely Colax the parasite happens along [I, 3]. Whereas in *Acolastus* Pamphagus is an unprincipled and cruel deceiver who does not scruple at dishonesty, and Pantolabus, though not quite so unconscionable, is himself a brazen opportunist, Colax is a well-meaning gourmet in straitened circumstances. Like all of Plautus' parasites but Artotrogus in *The Braggart Warrior (Miles gloriosus),* he is not a sycophant, though his name does mean "flatterer" in Greek. Instead, he is a famished glutton so desperate for food that he is willing to perform demeaning and compromising services, provided he is rewarded for his efforts with something to regale his palate. Unlike Pamphagus, he would not do anything criminal, but after an amusing and lengthy exchange of banter with Comasta he readily agrees to fetch the courtesans Planesium (from Plautus' *Curculio*) and Margaenium ("little fury") along with several tipplers. To speed him on his errand, Comasta permits him a bite from the larder first.

There is but a momentary interval before one of the slaves, Tribonius (probably "thresher"), flees from the house in panic [I, 4], like the servant in *The Captives,* IV, 4. Colax, who speaks of himself in I, 3 as a hunting dog, has attacked the victuals like a starving wolf, to use Tribonius' (and Plautus') simile, and the slave fears for his own safety. The parasite's edacity moves him to complain bitterly of Comasta's mismanagement, but his indignation gains him only indignities. After being scolded, he is packed off to thresh wheat in the barn, as Colax emerges from the house and sets out to earn what he has eaten. Comasta retires, emptying the stage for the chorus, which sings of parents' self-sacrifice and urges sons to be appreciative.[5]

In the first scene of the second act Tribonius and another faithful domestic, Merimnus ("anxious"), trade expressions of dismay over Comasta's highhandedness, and Tribonius intends to inform Eumenius. He thinks it right that servants suffer for their master, but he is disturbed that Eumenius is also being sinned against. From the barn he has watched Colax bring the prostitutes to the back door. When he and Merimnus start to leave, having been told to procure some fish in the next village and be gone till the morrow, Comasta rushes out to club them for dallying [II, 2]. The cook Daetrus ("carver"), who sees the two trustworthy slaves abused, decides apprehensively to cooperate with Comasta rather than suffer a similar fate, though he knows that a worse lot will be his if Eumenius learns of his disobedience. He is reluctant to assist the unjust steward, whom he dislikes, but he is afraid not to. He also enjoys a feast, and by siding with Comasta he will at least have a good time. Ethically, therefore, he is intermediate between the all-bad Comasta and the all-good Tribonius and Merimnus. As Pantolabus foreshadows Acolastus, Daetrus to some extent presages Asotus. He is not malicious but only weak. He is not vicious, but he likes pleasure; and it seems that life with Eumenius tends to be austere. Colax refers to the old man in I, 3 as stern and unsparing. Macropedius probably intended Daetrus to be viewed as a type of the well-meaning Christian who, despite his good intentions, falls victim to the pressures and temptations of earthly life, suffering remorse for his sinfulness but unable to preserve his innocence. At any rate the diffident cook acquiesces in Cometa's plans [II, 3]. He is the only servant whom the steward has not sent away on some errand, because he alone is faithful to his faithless boss.

Having delivered the girls that Comasta wanted, Colax now wishes anxiously for Asotus [II, 4]. At mention of his name the hero strides in, with a falcon perched on his wrist. Part of the tradition which accreted around the figure of the prodigal son (a part neglected by Gnapheus) was the notion that he was partial to the chase. A possible source for this addition to the bare biblical account, which includes little characterization of any of the personages in the parable, is the following well-known description of a supposedly typical young man, from Horace's *Ars poetica,* lines 161–65:

> The beardless youth, released from his guardian,
> Rejoices in horses and hounds and the sunny Campus—
> Like wax to the moldings of vice and harsh toward admonishers,
> Reluctant to do what is right, and prodigal,
> High-spirited, amorous, and volatile.

Asotus' falcon suggests not only that he hunts but that he is just as unruly himself. Colax explicitly compares him to the bird in being unsettled and untamed, whereupon Asotus sings a song (in iambic dimeters) elaborating the same idea [II, 5]. The first two stanzas are patterned after lines 116–18 of *The Captives,* which run "A prisoner freed is like a savage bird./ If he can ever get a chance to fly,/ Enough! You'll never catch him afterwards." In the third strophe Asotus expresses a hope for the death of his "silly" father (employing the same adjective, *delirus,* that Comasta uses to describe Eumenius in I, 2), so as to acquire his inheritance and be free. This wish,[6] rather shocking even in a song, seems out of character for Macropedius' prodigal, who is sorry that he has not told his father good-by when he does leave home. We may construe his desire as a mere velleity, since he goes on to prove that he is not so unfeeling as this frivolous ditty indicates.

It is nevertheless true that he does not want to see his sire, for he is aghast when Colax teasingly asserts that Eumenius expects him. On learning the truth, he is no less relieved than irked at the parasite's jesting. "Do you think I'm a bird to be played with?" he questions testily. The two make their peace, and though his stomach is starting to growl again, Colax asks Asotus to sing some more. The huntsman does, melodically deploring his lack of money and announcing his intention to petition his father for a full purse. If his request is refused, he lilts, he will claim his inheritance. Throughout the song Colax joins in, singing a response to each of the six-line stanzas warbled by Asotus. At the close of their duet they go inside, and the chorus voices that low opinion of youth which was cited in Section II of the Introduction.

In the opening scene of Act III Cometa ("villager"), the steward from the farm and another good and faithful servant, heads for the home in town, muttering that he believes in dutifulness without reward. Tribonius has reported what is taking place, as he said he would in II, 1, and Eumenius, who is returning, has sent Cometa ahead. Before the latter reaches the house, where the party is in full swing, Colax issues from it [III, 2]. The parasite is scared (to the point of wetting his pants, he confesses) by thoughts of retribution, and ominously a bellicose crow is perched on his left. Suspecting that it portends punishment, he calls in terror for the ringleader, who steps out and chides him contemptuously. A thousand crows, boasts Comasta, would not frighten him. "Come, enjoy the present, for the future is uncertain," he advises, repeating an irreligious idea expressed by Daetrus in II, 2. When they go back inside, Cometa remarks that the parasite is an upright man compared to the shameless townhouse steward. He belabors first one door and then another in an effort to draw Comasta outside again [III, 3], succeeding only to be struck [III, 4]. Though he has the satisfaction of warning that his adversary may soon be dried on a gallows, he is forced to retreat. Comasta is gripped by fleeting anguish at the thought that the meddler from the country might have come as a spy, but he quickly regains his customary bluster. As he re-enters the house, he hears an uproar inside. Perhaps, as usual, there is a fight for the girls, he thinks. It must be stopped, lest the situation worsen.

The melee is not over the strumpets. Although it is not like him to do so, says Cometa, Eumenius has staged a raid, entering through the rear door and catching his trusted villein in flagrant villainy [III, 5]. Accompanied by Philaetius and several slave overseers, he is breaking up the party, and his voice is heard in bitter groans. Margaenium, Planesium, and Asotus are tossed out ignominiously, yet the two harlots are surprisingly unsubdued, immediately launching into a most unladylike quarrel [III, 6]. Clothes and hair go flying before Asotus quiets them. Beset by trepidation over what might lie in store for him at his father's hands, he decides to disappear until Eumenius' anger subsides. As he leaves the stage, he is trailed by Cometa.

After restoring order, Eumenius has a chair brought outside so that we may see him pass judgment on the insurgents [III, 7]. The house, he says, reeks too much of wine. "Oh misery!" he cries, "that this home which hitherto has been a school for virtue should be turned into a tavern and a brothel!" Though a servant reminds him that lunch time has passed and he has not eaten, anger has killed his appetite. When Comasta confesses dispiritedly that his iniquity is too black for pardon, Eumenius, more than ever the despotic authoritarian, bundles him off to be hanged [III, 8], fulfilling Cometa's warning. The overseers plead for mercy in behalf of the condemned malefactor but to no avail. Daetrus is imprisoned pending a worse penalty. Colax, who is a free man, is to be whipped and released. The guilt-ridden parasite feels it only proper that his back should suffer for his stomach's sins. Eumenius, at a loss as to what he should do with Asotus, sends several boys to look for him.

The prodigal returns immediately with Cometa, however, and is accosted by his older brother, with whom only now we become well acquainted [III, 9]. Being a caution to us against obsession with earthly cares, Philaetius punishes himself with ceaseless toil. For this reason he considers the pleasure seeker damned and berates him severely, whereas Eumenius is torn by mixed feelings. Asotus stresses that he is sorry for what he has done, but the apology has no effect on Philaetius, who cannot forgive an easygoing indifference to work. The added pressure, particularly strong at this crucial juncture, when Asotus is particularly sensitive, forces him to a climactic resolve: He will demand his inheritance. Philaetius, told to go to hell, returns to the self-imposed torment of his drudgery—the martyrdom that is his *raison d'être*. Taking Cometa, he stalks off to the market to check prices for grain.

Aware that things have reached a breaking point, Eumenius shows genuine concern for his second-born [III, 10]. He begs Asotus to settle down, to take life more seriously, and to be more obedient and industrious. If the boy will do all this, he implores, no one will rebuke him anymore. Because Asotus, who grimly pronounces "the die is cast," nonetheless refuses to be dissuaded, Eumenius sadly relents, foreboding an unhappy future. The two go inside but remain visible to the audience.

Act III draws to a close with the jubilation (in dimeters) of two of those comic devils from medieval plays mentioned earlier in connection with Pamphagus and Pantolabus. These demons, called Belial and Astaroth, exult over Asotus' decision, since he is sure to be their victims. Astaroth, though, is so stupid that he has to have the situation explained to him. He and Belial become engrossed in what is happening because if they are remiss in toting souls to Hades they will be punished. Intently they plot to snare their prey. With these denizens of the underworld Macropedius effectively interjects an amusing interlude, inasmuch as their buffoonery contrasts nicely with the serious realism of the previous scenes without causing a break in the development of the plot. While they cavort and intrigue, grave Eumenius weighs out his avid son's inheritance in a voiceless pantomime, after which the chorus chants of good and bad servants.

In the initial scene of Act IV Merimnus, whom Comasta sent out earlier for fish with Tribonius, returns, feeling manly enough not to wait until the next day as he was commanded. He finds the antagonist whom he is now prepared to resist hanging harmless from a gallows (probably off-stage), and the reader may well be jarred when he wonders at the unwonted harshness of Eumenius, calling him "the mildest of men." Merimnus arrives just in time to witness Asotus' personal slave carrying his master's luggage from the house on orders to convey it to the brothel. Asotus soon emerges, too, headed for the harbor in the opposite direction and enraptured over the prospect of being free and sufficiently funded to do as he pleases [IV, 2]. He ends a lyrical speech extolling sensual delights by quoting verses seven and eight from the second chapter of the Apocryphal Wisdom of Solomon: "Don't let the prime of life pass by! Let's crown ourselves with roses ere they wither." [7] "Certainly," he adds, "that is my intention." This very day he will sail with his whores to Miletus, the Ionian city fabled in antiquity for lasciviousness. Merimnus, who has overheard this paean to passion, informs Philaetius [IV, 3], who in turn reproaches Eumenius for in effect being a prodigal himself by giving money to one [IV, 4]. The miser has not toiled to pamper a voluptuary in his depravity. Eumenius, who is brokenhearted over Asotus' decision, is also hurt by the hardheartedness of Philaetius, which he holds responsible for Asotus' separation from him. [8] As the father exits in sorrow, it is the elder son who calls him silly. Having gone to the market at the end of III, 9, Philaetius now betakes himself to the country. He, it seems, is as unable as Asotus to remain at home.

The young lover returns from the harbor, still rhapsodic with poetic dreams of fleshly joys [IV, 5]. Meeting his mistresses, he goes off to the brothel with them singing, as Acolastus sings on leaving home in II, 2 of Gnapheus' play. Asotus croons a corruption of lyrics from Erasmus' translation of Euripides' *Iphigenia in*

Aulis (published 1506). In a pedantic touch revealing the hand of a schoolmaster, Macropedius has Tribonius, who chances to hear this distortion of Erasmian verses, sing them verbatim from the *Iphigenia* translation, after even stating that he will follow Erasmus. The inapt display of erudition bothered our playwright no more than the anachronism. Tribonious, just a slave, even feels it appropriate to specify the meter that he uses (glyconic). The insertion of gratuitous book learning is, alas, not uncommon in school drama, and we must brace ourselves to encounter more in other plays by Macropedius. This instance, however, is of all such in his dramatic works the least justified by the context in which it appears.

Returning to the plot of *Asotus,* we find that Eumenius has come forth to inquire what the singing means [IV, 6]. He is told of Asotus' meeting and exit with the prostitutes, and his sadness deepens. He would gladly sacrifice himself to save his son's soul. This is the only time in the play, apart from the prologue and the epilogue, that we find an allusion to Eumenius' symbolic function as God the Father and, consequently, Christ.

In IV, 7 Asotus passes his home again, now on his way to embark. It is at this point that he is unhappy over not bidding farewell to Eumenius, together with the servants and his close friends. Time has become too short; the boat soon sails. If he goes home, he will be constrained to stay, and his brother will reprimand him. The girls catch up with him, after taking a "year" to primp, as women are wont to do according to Clitipho in II, 2 of Terence's *The Self-Tormentor (Heauton Timorumenos),* and with cajolery and caresses they help Asotus overcome his hesitancy to depart.

After a lapse of perhaps an hour, as evening approaches, Eumenius hears that the emancipated son has left [IV, 8]. Philaetius enters again, venting more animosity toward his slothful brother. Eumenius is once more hurt by this fraternal hatred and again grieves over the loss of Asotus. Again Philaetius hurries off to the country, at last permitting the chorus to caution against prostitutes.

This repetitious fourth act is the lowpoint, or even the downfall, of Macropedius' first play. Whereas only a couple of scenes would suffice to present Asotus' lust after a hedonistic existence, his preparations for departure, his regrets at leaving without good-bys, and the father's woe pitted against the brother's contempt, the act is stuffed out with eight scenes comprising over 300 lines. All the coming and going advance the plot but slightly, at a point where retardation is not in order. The author would have done better to use only three acts, combining the present Acts I and II, including both the payment of inheritance and the prodigal's departure in a climactic second act, and using the present fifth act as Act III. He would then have had no need for padding. Horace's dictum in the *Ars poetica* (lines 189–90) to the effect that a play must have neither more nor fewer than five acts was unfortunately not to be gainsaid.

The events in Acts I–IV all fall within a single day. Between Acts IV and V one year elapses, even though in the prologue Macropedius states that Asotus returns "after just a few months" *(post pauculos menses)*. As Act V opens, we first meet Colax again as he passes Eumenius' house and remembers the beating received there. He mentions that the punishment was administered one year earlier. Despite this lapse of time, his wounds have still not healed entirely, and he talks as if the interval has amounted to only a few days.

Just as a schoolboy does not complain of a whipping if his classes are good, Colax observes in the course of his soliloquy, a parasite deems himself fortunate, however flagellated, as long as he can eat. Thanks to Eumenius' unexpected mansuetude, he remarks, he can still fill his belly—unlike pitiable Comasta, who still dangles in the breezes, drenched by the rain. Colax will be more cautious with his services in the future. Hoping for more honest livelihood, he leaves for the market.

Next, Eumenius enters [V, 2]. Like Pelargus early in the last act of *Acolastus*, he is troubled by a vision of his son. He does not elaborate in the manner of Pelargus, though, who imagines Acolastus in rags, filthy and miserable. Because Eumenius would like to meet someone who has seen Asotus, he immediately encounters a merchant from Miletus who remembers the wastrel upon hearing him described. We are told that Asotus is chubby in the face, with dark eyes, ruddy cheeks, well-formed lips, of medium stature, with slender limbs and a scar on his chest. "From a sore he had as an infant," Eumenius explains. The traveler relates that Asotus has squandered his money, is feeding swine, and continuously cries out that his father's servants abound in food while he is perishing from hunger. He will return to his home, confess his wrongs, and beg forgiveness, the foreigner reports. Eumenius hopes for nothing else so much. When he goes back to Miletus the tradesman will tell Asotus this, if the erstwhile profligate has not already left to wend his way home. "Oh do come, come!" Eumenius apostrophizes his absent son. As he goes into his house to pen a letter to send with the merchant, he spots Colax in the distance and grumbles over the parasite's flattery, on which he blames his troubles. He is unjust to do so, however, since neither sycophancy nor seduction seems to be a fault of which this particular professional dinner guest can rightly be accused.

After passing through the market, Colax has gone to the harbor, where he has beheld Asotus disembarking. Like Ergasilus in IV, 1–2 of *The Captives,* he is aflutter to bring the good tidings to the father, ecstatic over the prospects of gustatory reward [V, 3]. So transported is he that his prolixity, always a weakness, gets the better of him. When he catches the old man's attention, he forgets to relay his information because in his irrationality all that he can think of is his still livid wounds and the food which he anticipates [V, 4]. Eumenius is naturally irked, for he strongly dislikes this phagomaniac anyway. It is only when he has almost spoiled his wonderful opportunity and is about to be hauled off by the master's slaves that Colax gains sufficient control of himself to state why he deserves his guerdon. On finally hearing the message, Eumenius makes one of his warmer and more endearing utterances (spoken earlier to the parasite by Asotus and borrowed from *The Captives,* line 866): "You look hungry!" Colax tells the father to hie himself to the harbor and is told in turn to help himself to the kitchen.

Already the haggard castoff of Miletus' demimonde has arrived [V, 5]. Eumenius is astounded at his son's appearance, hardly believing that this ragged vagrant is his own offspring. With sobs he runs to embrace the penitent, welcoming him back with forgiveness, sending Merimnus and Tribonius after new clothes and, seemingly transformed himself, calling for a banquet. When he asks his son who it was that led him astray, Asotus confesses that mainly his own lust drove him to sin, though Comasta gave the initial impetus [V, 6]. What the Milesian merchant recounted in V, 2 is repeated. After Merimnus brings the fresh garments, Eumenius has a musician and a chorus gathered for the celebration [V, 7]. Distraught over the fate of Comasta, Asotus requests the release of Daetrus, who is still languishing in prison, and Eu-

menius demonstrates his own humaneness and his softened heart
by acquiescing. "If only I can win my brother's favor!" Asotus
prays, but Philaetius, as ever the sullen drudge, chafes at what
he considers to be the idiocy of feasting in honor of a lazy spendthrift [V, 8]. He refuses to join the festivities until Eumenius
prods him [V, 9]. Daetrus, liberated, pleads for pardon and is ab-
solved. The ending is a happy one, even though Philaetius' incorrigible moroseness does not augur felicity for long. (Perhaps he
will continue to shuttle between the market and the fields, and
Asotus will be little plagued with the sight of him.) In a twelve-
line epilogue Macropedius reminds us that this play is a dramatization of the Biblical parable and that it contains a message
which, if heeded, will work to the improvement of our morals.

Looking critically at the characters in *Asotus*, we must recognize that Eumenius is faultily handled. That "mildest of men," as
Merimnus calls him, does not earn such an epithet until the
break with his son, and before that point he is sheer cantankerous-
ness. If he was to be a benevolent man really worthy of his name,
who merely demands high standards of his household, Macropedius should have given us evidence of kindness in a less appalling treatment of Comasta and Colax and in a less repellent
opening soliloquy. The Eumenius of the second half of the play
(who sorrows over his sons and readily pardons offenses) would
then contrast less with the brutal and Brutus-like disciplinarian
of the first half. As the play stands, the father seems to undergo a
change, yet this apparent transformation was surely not intended
by the author. Eumenius, after all, represents God.

Otherwise Macropedius deserves favorable notice for his characterization in this first dramatic work. The title figure is more
complex than Acolastus and arouses more sympathy. He is a
good-natured playboy frustrated by his father and his brother, not
an egotistical fool indifferent to other people. While Acolastus
leaves home only for the sake of "self-love," Asotus goes because
he is hot-blooded, the domestic routine is too austere for his love
of life, and his convincingly truculent brother carps perpetually.
The debauch in Eumenius' absence also prepares us for this break,
both by clarifying Asotus' disposition through his conduct and by
effecting a crisis at home which makes the rupture well-nigh
unavoidable.

Of all the characters in this play, Colax, however, not Asotus, is the most successful. Much more than anyone else, Colax talks about himself, and he loves to prate. He is a thoroughly affable and charming chatterbox, winsome in his sociability and friendliness. He is a comic counterpart to Asotus in his erring ways and reform through adversity, though he continues to be ruled more by his stomach than by his head. If Asotus sometimes grows stale because of repetition, Colax is always fresh, ever revealing some new aspect of his vivacious nature. It must be acknowledged, however, that Macropedius deserves less than full credit for the delightfulness of this character. Colax is not our playwright's creation but is essentially a borrowing from *The Captives,* as has been indicated (with "Colax," incidentally, being the title of one of Plautus' lost plays, taken from Menander).

We have seen that Gnapheus uses his parasites in *Acolastus* as the main source for what actual comedy that play contains. The same is true of *Asotus.* Apart from Colax there are only the two devils at the end of Act III and the brawl of the bawds in that act to infuse some hilarity into the work. The demons are extraneous, though, while Colax is a central figure, involved in every act but the feeble fourth. His vicissitudes comprise a subplot, yet they are well integrated into the main action. Colax, in fact, contributes more to the primary plot here than Ergasilus does in *The Captives.* He is also in the truest sense of the word humorous, supplying the kind of comedy that warms our heart while raising our spirits.

Whereas *The Captives* gave Macropedius his model for the figure of Colax, it did not help him with his plot. *The Captives* and *Asotus* are vastly different, even though the old man in Plautus' comedy has two sons, one of whom is abroad as a prisoner of war and returns in the last act. The exigencies of maintaining unity of place in a prodigal-son play suggested to Macropedius instead that he use the first act of another Plautine opus, *The Haunted House (Mostellaria)* as a help in executing roughly the first half of *Asotus* (to the point of Eumenius' return in Act III). Because he would not show his protagonist's dissipation in a foreign country, as did Gnapheus, and because he still needed some demonstration of Asotus' intemperance, Macropedius followed *The Haunted House* in staging a boisterous party at home.

In this comedy Theopropides the father has been absent for three years. His son Philolaches, left to his own devices, has sunk to a state of perpetual physical indulgence, abetted by the slave Tranio (Macropedius' Comasta). As the play begins, a servant from Theopropides' farm, the protatic Grunnio (Macropedius' Cometa), draws Tranio out of the house in town by reviling him, like Cometa in Act III of *Asotus*. Tranio responds pugnaciously, like Comasta, and is similarly reproached for corrupting the master's son. Philolaches has been living in license with his girl friend, the courtesan Philematium, and with his comrade Callidamates, who keeps a woman named Delphium. Besides being generally extravagant, Philolaches has gone deep into debt to purchase the freedom of Philematium. In a long monologue, or monody, he compares himself to a house, nice when it is new but ramshackle with neglect. Formerly an athlete and a paragon of probity, he is now an exemplary disgrace, even to himself. There is little action in this expository act, but the situation which it portrays was enough for Macropedius' purposes.

The fact that he began his career as a dramatist by copying Plautus may help to explain why he chose the prodigal-son parable for his first play. Plautine and Terentian plots often evolve at least partly from the need of a young libertine like Philolaches for money. The biblical story, including a harlot or two, offers a basic resemblance. By using it, Macropedius probably felt that he could most easily graft Christian ethics onto classical comedy, thereby presenting his pupils with a combination of the Latinity and morality that were all important in a Renaissance school. Of the concise tales from sacred literature suitable for comedy, furthermore, none is more inherently dramatic than that of the prodigal.

Asotus is the only play which Macropedius wrote in wholesale imitation of the ancients. It is not the only one influenced by other dramas, however, and some of his works he patterned in whole or in part after others by his own hand. In the following chapter we will deal with an instance of this last practice. The plot of *Petriscus* is a reworking and refining of the action in *The Rebels*. The basic story common to both these plays has affinities with the prodigal-son parable, moreover.

CHAPTER 3

The Erring Schoolboys

"FOOLISHNESS is bound in the heart of a child; but the rod of correction shall drive it far from him." This verse from the Book of Proverbs (22:15) might have served Macropedius as a motto, supported as it is by his two plays about wayward pupils. It is not, however, the seed from which they sprang. The author says in the prologue to *Petriscus* that he took the idea for the story of *The Rebels* from a brief prose playlet by one "Helicon," which he treated "in a far different arrangement and fashion." He adds that the plots of *Petriscus* and *The Rebels* are similar but not identical and that the former cannot be criticized as an adulteration of Helicon's work. Someone, he complains in imitation of Terence in the prologue to *The Lady of Andros (Andria)*, objected to *The Rebels* on such grounds. This latter play thus owes more to Helicon. Prominent differences between Macropedius' two dramas about pupils are the use of tavern scenes and the doubling of main characters in *The Rebels*, reminiscent of the duplication in much Roman comedy. Another change is the fact that Petriscus never parts from his family, however much he steals from them. Helicon's production may therefore have had duel protagonists who were released by their parents and who came to grief in a tavern frequented by gamblers and prostitutes, rather like the two spoiled brothers in the French morality *Enfans [sic] de Maintenant (Children of Now)*, as pointed out by Wilhelm Creizenach.[1] Though the immediate model for *The Rebels* may not have been explicitly intended as a version of the prodigal-son parable, that biblical tale seems to have influenced all of these plays, however indirectly.

I *The Rebels*

The prologue, delivered by the director, is an exhortation to the audience both to pay and to pay attention. This plea is interrupted twice by a fool *(Morio)*, who interjects an "eho!" and an "ehem!" but is silenced each time before he can utter any more. When the speaker threatens buffets to any who talk, snore "fore or aft" *(ante vel retro),* laugh immoderately, or run about, the fool hisses. At the end of the prologue he says that he is going to remain on the stage. He has no more lines in the script but was presumably free to ad-lib commentary on the action, after the fashion of his counterpart in *Enfans de Maintenant* and in some mysteries.

Unlike *Asotus, The Rebels* has a contemporary setting. The teacher Aristippus is even a Brother of the Common Life. At the rear of the proscenium, as we might imagine it, stands the school together with the houses of Cacolalia and the pimp Labrax, as well as a tavern. A ball field mentioned in line 164 can be off-stage, and the trial in Act V seems to be conducted outside. Two devils, Lorcoballus and Marcolappus, who are given lines (in iambic dimeter) at the close of each of the first four acts and in the middle of the last, have a "cave" somewhere on stage, probably at one side. All of the action transpires in the single un-named city represented, yet not in a single day. Unity of time is again forsaken, while unity of place is still maintained, though the setting has broadened to include more territory.

When the play opens we are introduced to wayworn Philotecnium ("child lover") as she hikes into town. She is the doting mother of one of the rebels, Dyscolus ("malcontent"), but she lives elsewhere, apparently in a neighboring village. Her son she seems to be boarding with her cousin Cacolalia ("bad language"), who is the mother of Clopicus ("thievish"). We will find Philotecnium to be generally a timid, anxious woman who wants what is best for Dyscolus but is mistaken in her tender heart as to the nature of that *summum bonum.* She begins her thirty-six-line soliloquy, which comprises I, 1, by lamenting her cares, exactly in the manner of Eumenius in the first scene of *Asotus.* She is getting along in years, having acquired gray temples no less than wrinkles and having eaten not a few Easter eggs, as she picturesquely observes. Her fifteen-year-old boy is also a reminder that she is not a girl anymore. Household worries coupled with the ill-treatment of her husband are hastening old age, she feels. The spouse of whose yoke she complains never appears, and he has evidently relinquished all control of Dyscolus to her. Besides this son they have other children, as the mother reveals, but we never see them either.

Philotecnium goes on in her monologue to protest that everyone who has had charge of Dyscolus has been heinously cruel. So far she has entrusted his education to eight different schoolmasters, all equally savage. Now, she has decided, she would like to try Aristippus,[2] by common consent a learned philosopher and rhetorician. He is reputed also to be pious, an implication that he will make Dyscolus into a dialectician and an orator without whippings. Philotecnium is proud that her boy already has full command of the rudiments of Latin, so that he can make his way "pleasantly, easily, and honestly" in the world, in case she should die. The father apparently cannot be counted on for support. Before she definitely commits Dyscolus to the new pedagogue, though, she wants (like Pelargus in *Acolastus*) to have the advice of her friend, the related but dissimilar Cacolalia.

This harridan now approaches, sure that she knows why her cousin has come—marital troubles [I, 2]. Having heard that Philotecnium's husband beat her the previous evening, she wants to console the sufferer and to relate how she combed her own mate's noddle with a three-legged stool. The two discuss briefly the plight of the female and the instruction of their sons, agreeing to warn the next teacher against corporal punishment. Asked whether she knows the one who is the Brother of the Common Life, Philotecnium says "That old Aristippus with the gloomy brow?" (Thus Macropedius perhaps chuckled at himself.) He has a good reputation, so the women decide to take their boys to him at once.

Coming from the ball field, Clopicus meets Dyscolus, who has overheard the conversation in the foregoing scene and informs him of what lies in store [I, 3]. Clopicus scarcely believes that their mothers could be so foolish as to send them to a tutor who would not cane them. When Aristippus appears at his door, Philotecnium tells him nonetheless that the two newcomers are to be made into philosophers and orators without being harmed [I, 4], just as Mignotte in *Enfans de Maintenant* asks Instruction not to beat her sons. Evasively Aristippus replies that he knows what is best and will handle the lads as though they were his own. Cacolalia threatens reprisals for any use of the rod, prompting the muttered retort that for a boy his mother is an evil spirit.

Scene 5 presents us with two devils exactly like those from the end of Act III in *Asotus.* Only their names are different. Lorcoballus tells Marcolappus, the stupid one, what the women's decision promises them. In the conviction that unruly youths and their indulgent mothers will surely succumb to diligent demons, these two creep into their hole to plan a course of action and to observe what happens next.

A brief chorus sung by Aristippus' scholars and advocating discipline spans several days of plot time between Acts I and II. Like the other choral odes in this play it consists of only two four-line stanzas in iambic dimeters. When the story resumes, Dyscolus and Clopicus have become regular pupils but are enjoying some irregular behavior. With gleeful remissness they have lost or destroyed their lecture notes. From the way in which they converse we gather that the teacher has so far been lenient with them. Certainly he has not been checking them closely. Clopicus says that any other schoolmaster would have flailed them livid as mangy sheep by now. This one must be scared of their mothers.

Encouraged by Aristippus' permissive bearing, the two scamps gamble, at the suggestion of Clopicus. He seems at first more worldly-wise than his friend, and Philotecnium is likelier to have hovered over Dyscolus than Cacolalia is to have sheltered her son. Since the boys are still at school (though outside) as they set about gaming, Clopicus proposes a scheme that will deceive the teacher. Coins are to be inserted at random into a book. The pages will then be turned one by one, in sequences of three. Money on the first page of any series will go to Dyscolus. Supposedly only a coin at the end of a sequence will fall to Clopicus, but he cheats. He says "You'll be first; I'll follow and be third." Dyscolus innocently agrees, not perceiving that his cousin has laid claim with these words to coins on the second pages as well as on the third. When Clopicus tries to enforce his claim, a hassle ensues, and Dyscolus triumphs. The more naive of the pair, he is yet the more manly.

Fisticuffs are too much for Aristippus to condone, and the rowdies are hauled inside to receive the "prize" for their contest [II, 2]. In the third and last scene of this short act the two devils in their cave listen to the wails resounding from the school. Lorcoballus jokingly calls the outcry "singing," and Marcolappus suggests that they join in. "Oh woe, oh woe, oh woe, oh woe,/ Oh,

good master, oh woe, oh woe!" they mock, providing the play with
its principal moment of comedy. The chorus of Aristippus' pupils
approves of punishing misbehavior.

Immediately after the whipping, Dyscolus thinks of using the
incident to secure his and Clopicus' definitive release from school
[III, 1]. The two go home, howling like wounded curs, and tell
Cacolalia that as they were leafing through their books Aristippus
accused them—these intimate buddies—of fighting [III, 2]. On the
basis of this ridiculous charge, as they would have Cacolalia believe, they were thrashed. Wrathful over the assumed outrage,
she sends them into the house and hastens to inform Philotecnium.
Conveniently the latter is again coming to call [III, 3]. Like Pelargus and Eumenius, who see ominous visions of their prodigal
sons, she has had an alarming dream about Dyscolus. Learning
what it betokened at first only distresses her, while Cacolalia
froths with fury. So angry is the maenad that she soon infects her
timorous companion with a modicum of her vengefulness. When
Aristippus and his pupils draw near, however, Philotecnium loses
heart—and almost the contents of her bladder.

Cacolalia singly insults, menaces with her claws, and eventually assaults the astonished schoolmaster, charging that Clopicus
was molested without cause [III, 4]. Well supplied with witnesses
to the contrary, Aristippus is not troubled to justify himself but
loftily predicts that through their mothers' indulgence the brats
will end on a gallows. This dire pronouncement makes Cacolalia
even more rabid. Convinced that the teacher is literally adding
insult to injury, she lunges at him, but he manages to ward her
off, as Philotecnium begs her to desist. The situation, says the gentle mother of Dyscolus, calls for tears rather than blows. Oh, if
only she could have spared her son his pain by suffering herself
the lashes that were inflicted on him! Her only accusation against
the schoolmaster is that of callousness. With a warning to guard
against a calamity which only he can dispel, Aristippus exhorts
the poor woman to stop weeping. She, however, interprets even
this well-intentioned plea as a sign of heartlessness. She sent her
son, she sobs, to be educated, not flagellated. Aristippus counters by stating that he took Dyscolus to be corrected and saved
from a gallows, not to be killed. At these words Cacolalia again
explodes, dealing the offender a vigorous slap. He reacts by ordering his pupils, who have been present during this scandalous

encounter, to drag the women into the school for the same come-uppance as their children received. Such humiliation is too much even for Cacolalia, who joins Philotecnium in begging for mercy. With a contemptuous pun ("Valeant merae tricae!") the victorious pedagogue haughtily takes his leave. Philotecnium is mortified; Cacolalia, still venomous. They immediately agree to withdraw their sons from school permanently and to set them up as tradesmen.

Lorcoballus closes the act by crowing expansively, foretelling what is to follow, and calling for alertness [III, 5]. Marcolappus says that they must prop open their eyes so that not even a mouse will escape or a sparrow fly away. For comic effect the actors playing these roles probably did wedge sticks into the large orbs of their grotesque masks. As was stated in Section II of the Introduction, the chorus at this point terms women more dangerous than fire, ocean, wild animals, or an evil spirit.

When Act IV begins we see that Dyscolus and Clopicus have been outfitted for their new life as merchants. They are clad in tunics and hats and sport swords with plump purses. Presumably a day or two has elapsed, therefore, since their retirement from academe at the close of Act III. Instead of engaging at once in whatever trade their gullible mothers imagine them to have chosen, the two dandies decide to unload some of their plenteous cash for food and drink. Reversing the well-known phrase from line 732 of Terence's *Eunuch* ("Without Ceres and Bacchus Venus languishes"), Dyscolus declares, as if speaking from experience, that they must include some courtesans if their party is to be a success. Clopicus concurs, suavely remarking that they will send a parasite for them, just as though he might have done so many times.

That the poise of these fifteen-year-olds is an uneasy pose becomes apparent when they go to the tavern [IV, 2]. Dyscolus is especially nervous and speaks of the innkeeper as a woman instead of a man. When inquiring about some prostitutes, he embarrassedly hems and haws. The proprietor is startled that two such whippersnappers could go whoring, but he is not about to decline their business. Dyscolus repeats "What is Bacchus without Venus?" in an effort to prove himself a knowledgeable man of the world.

When he published his collected plays in 1552–54, Macropedius added several new scenes to *The Rebels,* one of which, comprising sixteen lines, is inserted after IV, 2. While the inn-keeper goes to a pimp to request the harlots, his two adolescent customers stroll about outside. Clopicus tells his more innocent companion that taverners keep parasites, pimps, and bawds and will do anything for money, but Dyscolus is too lustful to care about lack of scruples. The young rakes go into the tavern as soon as Labrax the procurer (from Plautus' *The Rope*) emerges from his house, redheaded to signal his wickedness.

For some unexplained reason Labrax is unable or unwilling to supply any of his girls [IV, 3]. He will have to receive help from a fellow pimp, he says, and opportunely one named Gaulus ("pail") comes along. The introduction of two panders is not required by the plot. Macropedius may have added Gaulus because Helicon included two pimps, or he may have wanted to balance the two protagonists. Then again he may have been thinking of Gnapheus' Pamphagus and Pantolabus. Like Pamphagus the morning after the banquet in *Acolastus,* Gaulus is hung over from his debauchery of the night before. Unlike Pamphagus, however, he is now completely without money. Naturally he accepts Labrax' offer of exploiting the two callow fools. In return he agrees to give his colleague six gold pieces.

Inside the tavern Dyscolus and Clopicus are served by two girls whose *noms parlants*—Melancia ("blackie") and Dromella ("little runner")—occasion some sport [IV, 4]. Earlier, in IV, 2, Clopicus accidentally calls the jocund looking owner "Bromius" (the surname of Bacchus)out of eagerness for wine, only to dis-cover that "Bromius" is actually the man's name. Here in this scene the appearance and actions of the girls likewise lead Clopicus to guess their appellations in a playing with names reminiscent of Plautus. Dromella has a drink with her clients, and Dyscolus is much taken by her.

In the next scene [IV, 5], Labrax tells Bromius that the pros-titutes will be along in the evening. The pimps then join the boys inside and chat for a moment [IV, 6]. Clopicus asks hesitantly about the strumpets, showing the same uneasiness that marked Dyscolus' initial request in IV, 2. On learning that they will not arrive until later, Clopicus confidently proposes a little dicing to while away the time. The panders are not averse, and the party moves outdoors. As rapidly as Acolastus, these prodigals are bested and stripped. They also resemble the two brothers in *Enfans de Maintenant,* who likewise gamble away money and garments after quitting school. Convinced that he has again been cheated, the stouthearted Dyscolus is incensed. With a "to arms, Clopicus" he draws on his predators, seconded by his friend, but instantly they are routed.

Broke though they are, they are still not broken. Cockily they stake their very lives on recouping their losses through thievery, since an immediate opportunity presents itself. Whereas the prodigal son feeds a peasant's swine after his reduction to penury, these two young wastrels steal a peasant's purse. A drowsy farmer is sprawled close by with his money pouch enticingly displayed [IV, 7]. Nervously urging Dyscolus to keep a sharp lookout, Clopicus snatches the bag. Before they can scurry away, however, their victim awakes. Dyscolus hits him, and the old man shrinks away, preferring to set the chief magistrate on these juvenile but more virile delinquents. Though criminals now in the eyes of the law, they nonchalantly return to the tavern for more fun.

Bromius welcomes them back for their banquet, suspecting that the quick "deal" which they claim to have made was a theft [IV, 8]. If the authorities found out about them, he observes, he himself could be punished for sheltering them. He decides to take the risk, thinking that no one will learn the truth, but two law-enforcement officers who have slipped up on him during this short soliloquy hear what he says [IV, 9]. In an escape attempt Dyscolus bares his blade again, backed by Clopicus, but the boys fence no better with the officers than with the pimps. They are led away in manacles; the peasant recovers his money; and Bromius is promised a summons.

Proudly Lorcoballus takes credit for what has happened [IV, 10]. The arrest is as propitious for the devils as it is ominous for the boys, because Dis, god of the underworld, will be pleased. The diabolic duo must watch carefully, though, when the felons are hung, to be sure of catching their souls. Marcolappus moves Lorcoballus to exclaim over his brutishness by remarking that the rear exits are the ones to be guarded. In its final appearance the chorus of Aristippus' pupils warns against misusing money.

Act V picks up the plot with no omission of time. Philotecnium has come into town again to visit Cacolalia [V, 1]. On this occasion she has no foreboding of misfortune. Instead, in a bit of dramatic irony, she is heartily pleased with the new way of life which she has arranged for Dyscolus. As she congratulates herself on her handling of his affairs, a messenger arrives. Scarcely has he addressed the two women when Philotecnium becomes distressed, thinking him a harbinger of evil. Given a letter from Dyscolus, she nearly faints. On reading it, she is paralyzed with stupefaction. Ruefully she recalls Aristippus' prediction, and the bearer of the notes says that it is precisely he who can help them. They should run to beg his aid.

Philotecnium wonders whether any god can make him propitious, while Cacolalia is ashamed to confront the man whom she maligned and assailed earlier [V, 2]. As he approaches once more with his pupils, she nevertheless joins her cousin in beseeching him to use his authority to rescue their sons. It seems that in Macropedius' day teachers in the Netherlands were commonly accorded legal jurisdiction over their pupils.[3] Aristippus points out that really he no longer has any claim to Dyscolus and Clopicus, since they have withdrawn from school, but he still volunteers to plead for them as sheep that have merely strayed from his herd. No sooner does he take up his rod, the symbol of his office, than Cacolalia descries the defendants being led to trial. Again Philotecnium nearly collapses.

In an effort to purge the city of crime and to free the local peasantry from molestation, the judge sentences Dyscolus and Clopicus to death, more as a warning to others inclined toward lawlessness than as just retribution for their own felony [V, 3]. The defendants have no legal representation in this kangaroo court and are not even given a chance to plead in their own behalf.[4] "Summum jus, summa injuria," they might otherwise quote from their Cicero. Since they utter no word at all, we infer that they are dumbstruck with shock and horror, as well they might be. This nadir of their fortunes marks the climax of our play.

A trumpet sounded as the death knell of the condemned is heard by the two devils, but obtuse Marcolappus does not understand what it means [V, 4]. His ignorance must have aroused mirth in audiences susceptible to the fear of real demons, as sharp as this caricature is dull. Lorcoballus encourages laughter with his own ridicule of the poor dolt and sends him to watch for a departure of the boys' souls through their "belly's door." Marcolappus ends the interlude with an observation which shows that he is not hopelessly imbecillic, after all. How can a spirit go out through a throat squeezed shut by a rope, he queries. He will be the one to bag this booty for Pluto.

The trumpet sounds a second time. In anapestic dimeters Dyscolus mourns his bitter fate, bidding the world adieu, and in the same unusual meter Clopicus apostrophizes his schoolmates, actually addressing pupils in the audience: "Learn obedience by our example" is the gist of what he says [V, 5]. Dyscolus is commending their souls to God when Clopicus spots the teacher hurrying near, escorted by their mothers, and begs that Aristippus be given a hearing. In catalectic trochaic trimeters the schoolmaster informs the court who he is and explains that the two boys are his pupils [V, 6]. His use of the present tense is not really a distortion of the truth, we may assume, because of the changed attitude of both mothers and sons. If the striplings are spared, they will certainly return to the classroom. Peremptorily Aristippus demands that they be released in his custody. Refusal, he adds, would be a derogation of the schoolmaster's privileges. The judge, apparently from his high estimation of Aristippus' office, readily complies, warning the pardoned culprits against a second offense. With the intervention of the noble pedagogue the reversal of the plot comes about. A happy ending is assured as the two devils are summoned to hell in frustration [V, 7]. Lorcoballus, furiously blaming his cohort for their failure, describes the punishment which awaits them for returning empty-handed to a teeth-gnashing Lucifer: Besides fetters and the lash, there will be a potion concocted of fiery pitch laced with an admixture of sulfur.

Dyscolus and Clopicus are so stunned by the swift change of events that they must ask to whom they owe their salvation [V, 8]. Their mothers refer them to Aristippus as the hero who alone deserves credit for their rescue. Having learned their most important lesson outside the fold, the two penitent renegades sheepishly return, to be readmitted with a branding by the rod. This time they are quite willing to be caned, and their mothers benignly concur in the ritual, which seems symbolical of their reversion to the status of pupils and of their resultant submission to the master. The chastisement will be administered inside the school, so Philotecnium and Cacolalia take their leave to go home and make ready a joyful reception. The urchins, reformed by bad experience, will happily bend their necks to the yoke of bourgeois virtues. In the 1553 revision four verses were added at this point. In them the two women tell their sons to make sure that the teacher joins them for dinner, and the boys promise that they will.

In the final scene of the 1535 version, written in catalectic iambic trimeters, as is Scene 8, Philotecnium and Cacolalia confirm that they are no less amended by the near-tragedy than are Dyscolus and Clopicus. Cacolalia in particular seems to have been transformed. Without complaining in the least over the stringency of the judge, whom she might easily call inhumane, and without feeling insulted by the degradation of her son, she proposes that her cousin join her in saying a prayer of thanksgiving and in deploring their mistakes. After stopping by the church they will fix dinner for Aristippus and their friends. In a thirteen-line epilogue mothers in the audience are warned against pampering their sons and boys are admonished not to be rebellious.

In the 1553 revision Macropedius added after V, 9 five superfluous scenes of anticlimactic, undramatic moralization in which the reforms effected are belabored to the point of soporific tedium. These 137 extra lines thoroughly mar the effect of what without them is a passable, though not an impeccable little play. In the first scene Aristippus, now called "Didascalus" ("teacher") as in *Petriscus,* warns Dyscolus and Clopicus against a repetition of their mistakes, and they vow to be well-behaved. They invite him to dinner, and he accepts, sending them home ahead of him to beg their mothers' pardon. In the second scene Philotecnium and Cacolalia assure each other that they will no longer coddle their pets. In the third, Clopicus and Dyscolus ask forgiveness. In the fourth, Didascalus arrives; Clopicus and Dyscolus promise again to be duteous; and the mothers excuse them, also requesting pardon from their benefactor. Naturally he grants it graciously. In the fifth scene, Dyscolus and Clopicus sing a sapphic hymn of praise and gratitude. The 1535 edition of *The Rebels,* which is not vitiated by these appendages, is definitely superior.

Instead of the father who is forced against his will to release his headstrong son, we have in this departure from the Biblical story of the prodigal two mothers who mistakenly encourage their scions in willfulness and voluntarily discharge them into the world. No mention is made of inheritance, though the boys set out with more money than is good for them. The "far country" of Christ's parable is reduced to the local pub, with the result that the menace of the gallows must replace a diet of acorns and husks. Dyscolus and Clopicus could not be brought to their knees merely by the loss of their money. *Asotus,* with its portrayal of dissipation at home instead of abroad already represents a step toward such alteration of the original narrative. Despite changes in plot, the point of that play is still evident: Abandonment to base impulses causes grief. As in *Petriscus,* this moral has been transferred to a setting more familiar to Macropedius' pupils, where it is coupled with the notion that sparing the rod means spoiling the child.

II *Petriscus*

Apart from the information already related concerning Helicon and the composition of *The Rebels,* the prologue offers only an indication of what the play is about with the usual injunction for quiet attentiveness lest the message be missed. "After an hour or two you'll be released," the audience is consoled. At least for those who could follow the Latin, however, the time spent watching *Petriscus* can scarcely have been tiresome.

If *The Rebels* was written for performance at Shrovetide, there is nothing in it to imply as much. *Petriscus,* on the other hand, is set at carnival time and is enriched by some well chosen farce. Like the three plays discussed in the next chapter, it is a Latin Shrovetide comedy, although it differs in having a near-tragic turn in its plot. Whereas there is no unity of time in either *Asotus* or *The Rebels,* the action in *Petriscus* lasts only from early morning to the evening of a single day. The setting is again altogether contemporary—a street in a sixteenth-century Dutch town. At the rear of the stage we are to imagine the house of Petriscus' parents, on one side of which is a brothel with second-story windows. On the other side is a school. There is also a neighbor's house and the judge's tribunal, which seems again to be outside.

The play begins in front of Petriscus' residence early in the morning of Shrove Tuesday. Galenus ("calm"), the protagonist's father, tersely orders his son off to class, refusing to talk to him. In his peremptoriness we already catch a glimpse of his normal relationship with Petriscus (meaning "little stone," perhaps). The fact that we learn nothing of Clopicus' father and almost nothing of Dyscolus' means that part of the rationale for those boys' rebelliousness is omitted. This neglect is not a shortcoming of *Petriscus*, where Galenus' personality helps to explain the title figure's misbehavior. As his name implies, Galenus is customarily passive. He is even calm to the extent of being spineless. For the sake of domestic tranquillity he lets his wife Mysandra ("man hater") rule the house. In the prologue Macropedius puts all the blame for the son's shenanigans on her. "You will see the boy Petriscus (though born of an upright father) consort with flagitious acquaintances because of the mother's indulgence . . ." the speaker declares. This brief remark, however, does not take into account the significance of Galenus' meekness. It is because he abdicates control of his family that his wife can have her way with Petriscus. Galenus does not punish the boy himself but has the schoolmaster Didascalus administer discipline, while he attempts to assert authority vis-à-vis Petriscus only by acting gruff. The scalawag knows that his mother has the final word, so with only a show of deference to his hollow father he goes his merry way, hobnobbing with dropouts and frequently playing hooky. Galenus suspects this truancy, and in the abrupt encounter which opens Act I he informs Petriscus that he is coming to school to invite Didascalus to dinner. When he arrives, he warns, the boy had better not be absent.

After Petriscus exits, Galenus calls to his serf Liturgus ("attendant"), who has been waiting nearby, and questions him concerning some petty thievery committed about the house. More than seven times Liturgus has chanced to see the young master pilfering food and money. He also knows that Petriscus has been keeping bad company. Galenus does not comment on this bit of news but sends the servant straightway to the market to buy food for dinner, at which the teacher is to be present.

On the way to confer with the schoolmaster Galenus complains of how empty and bitter life is, especially for those with children and a querulous wife [I, 2]. Didascalus, who is as peripatetic as Aristippus, now ambles down the street, surrounded by his pupils. As we discover in Act II, he is on the way to the brothel, where Petriscus' two truant friends are ensconced. Didascalus intends to return them to school forcibly, if necessary. Before he reaches his destination, Galenus meets him, asking facetiously why he has taken his "herd" outside the fold. The teacher continues the joke by inquiring why Galenus' own "lamb" has often been absent, submitting excuses signed by the father. On hearing that his son is also a forger, Galenus draws Didascalus aside and requests him to administer a prompt whipping before Petriscus takes flight or gains his mother's aegis with a tear. The implication is clearly that if she intervenes her husband will capitulate. Galenus relates what Liturgus has testified and adds that he would like for Didascalus to find out where Petriscus has stashed his pelf. Thus he devolves distasteful parental duties onto the schoolmaster. As recompense he extends the invitation to dinner.

When the shepherd returns to his flock, they remark that Petriscus is in for a hiding. Not for nothing did his father scowl. Sure enough, they are led back to school. Inside the building but in view of the audience Petriscus is ordered to remove his trousers [I, 3]. He protests his innocence and demands witnesses to prove his guilt, but after he is stripped, held down by four fellow students, and beaten, he witnesses against himself. Under the lash he confesses that he has been a thief, sharing what he has filched with his cronies Cabiscus (apparently meaning "little measure," from Greek *kabos*) and Stypiscus ("little stump"), the two whom Didascalus was about to flush from the brothel. Promising betterment, he is released, only to flee and hurl both anathema and stones from a safe distance. Didascalus lets him go, predicting that he will soon enough entrap himself. Before resuming the expedition against the bordello, the teacher wants a respite.

Petriscus has run home, bawling for his mother to come outside. When she appears, he displays his wounds and bloody clothes, once more professing innocence [I, 4]. Mysandra indignantly exclaims that he was mauled just like a robber. What could he have done to warrant such abuse, she wants to know. It came about because his father accused him of taking some fruit and eggs from the house, Petriscus explains with the understatement of Dyscolus and Clopicus reporting their whipping to Cacolalia. Liturgus, who is the real culprit, brought false charges against him, Petriscus continues. A duplicate of Cacolalia, Mysandra vows deserts for both Liturgus and her husband, as she takes her son inside to dress his wounds. Act I ends without the appearance of the two devils, the inclusion of whom Macropedius eschewed altogether in this rewriting of *The Rebels*. The chorus calls for a tempering of parental love with firmness.[5]

There is no interval between the events of Act I and those of Act II. Philochrysium ("gold lover"), one of the two strumpets in this comedy, emerges from her establishment, musing that her two friends (Cabiscus and Stypicus) fear to fight jointly by day in school with Didascalus more than to struggle singly by night in bed with her [II, 1]. She has ventured outside to reconnoiter. The pedagogue might try to take her customers by surprise, and—lo and behold—here he comes, in fact! Philochrysium scuttles back into her house to sound the alarm.

Didascalus' siege at the brothel with his little band of pupils is uproarious [II, 2]. It was suggested by IV, 7 of Terence's *The Eunuch* but is considerably more dynamic. Macropedius has the two fugitives and their moll fend off their assailants by throwing stones and cascading the contents of chamber pots from second-story windows. Didascalus, spattered with filth, is forced to send for reinforcements in the form of two officers of the law. He pleads with the rapscallions to take their punishment from him rather than from the hangman. Making no headway, he retreats to his academy to await the police, though he only leaves Scylla for Charybdis, because at the school he meets Mysandra and Petriscus.

II, 3, in which this virago fumes that her son was mistreated, is essentially a repetition of III, 4 from *The Rebels*. Mysandra has the role of Cacolalia almost to the extent of physically attacking the teacher. Didascalus, like Aristippus, makes a dire prediction based on the mother's indulgence. More than Aristippus, though, he tries to reason with this termagant, who cannot believe that "such a little tyke" would dare to steal a penny. The scene in *Petriscus* also does not end with the seizure of Mysandra but with the arrival of the magistrates.

They pack her off forthwith and joke briefly with the teacher, who calls them upright [II, 4]. In Greek they as a result call him sharper than Lynceus for perceiving in them what nobody else has ever noticed. Leaving his pupils at school, Didascalus leads the two officers to the whorehouse, where they break down the door and readily seize the two delinquents. The pupils standing in front of the school describe the proceedings, with one of them voicing the hope that Philochrysium will be "kissed asunder by a scourge." The sadistic pleasure of witnessing such a show is denied him, however, for the girl is released unmolested. (As Macropedius informs us in the last strophe of the second chorus to Act III of *Andrisca,* prostitution was legal.) The two subdued truants are led back to school, bound with ropes.

Didascalus conducts Cabiscus inside, to be caned first while the police scoff at Stypiscus outdoors, baiting him like an animal [II, 5]. He snarls back like one. By the time Didascalus returns with Cabiscus, Stypiscus has been disrobed. The teacher taunts him, too, adding further humiliation, it seems, as part of the punishment. While Stypiscus is being flogged, Cabiscus is teased. This essay at correction miscarries, as well it might because of the insulting quality about it. The rebels have only been hurt, not humbled. As a consequence they become even more renitent. Hitherto still nominally pupils of Didascalus, they now expressely sever their ties with the school. In doing so, they cancel Didascalus' claim to exert control over them. Any illegal acts henceforth perpetrated by them will be subject to penalty imposed by the chief magistrate rather than by the schoolmaster. (Petriscus, be it noted, has not taken this crucial—indeed, fatal—step.) As a token of their future behavior, Cabiscus and Stypiscus return to the brothel. Hearing someone's door open nearby, Didascalus ducks into the school with the officers in order to lunch in peace and quiet.

The person stepping outside is Mysandra. On this holiday she is not going to sit at home staring at the walls but has made a date with girl friends to tipple a while at the tavern. Galenus is off in the country and Liturgus is still at the market, so she gives her keys to her son, who is to pass them on to either the father or the servant, depending on which of the two returns first [II, 6]. Petriscus avers that he must hasten back to school, but his mother is too eager for drink to care, thrusting her keys upon him as she hurries away. Scarcely is she gone when "Golly!" he exclaims. Now he can rummage through spices and cosmetics with abandon, purloining whatever his heart desires, including cash. He goes inside and bolts the door, giving the chorus an opportunity to deplore leniency in the raising of young people.

Between the events of Acts II and III a lapse of maybe fifteen minutes occurs, during which Petriscus rifles boudoir, pantry, and office. The time at the inception of the third act is a little past noon. Now the servant finally returns from the market, irked at the inconsiderate butcher who kept him waiting so long for the rabbits, partridges, capon, goose, and shoulder of mutton that he is carrying. Liturgus fears a scolding from Mysandra. The master is gentle and tranquil, he feels, but no one is more unruly than the mistress. The whole town is already chattering about the evil way in which she raged against the teacher for properly correcting her worthless son. At this moment Petriscus emerges from the house, exuberant over his good fortune. His clothes are stuffed with pepper, sugar, and cinnamon, along with about fifteen gold pieces and his schoolbooks. Even if his father notices that this money is missing, he will concoct an alibi, Petriscus assures himself. In fact, he will blame the theft on Liturgus, to whom he now gives the keys, alleging that he must be off to school. His destination is actually the brothel, for a reunion with Cabiscus and Stypiscus, but before he can go there Galenus returns and stops him. Where are his books, the father wants to know [III, 2]. Is Petriscus not headed for school? Galenus demands to see them as evidence that his son's clothes are not hiding something else. Having stolen before, the scamp might be doing so again. In this danger it is Petriscus who is truly the calm one. With cool alacrity he draws forth his readers. As Galenus examines them, his wife enters, having been stood up by her friends but having had some wine while she waited. Despite the early hour, she says that it is time to start fixing dinner, and we have seen that she has a great deal to prepare. When she spies Galenus holding his inspection, the alcohol in her ignites. "Chrysippus," as she speaks of him (using the name of a famous Stoic to suggest that he is playing the stern moralist), is once more bullying her child. Her words here help us to understand that she babies Petriscus at least partly in reaction to Galenus' magisterial manner. Since her husband has not seen her now, she picks up a green stick and hides in the doorway to their house. Petriscus notices her but does not comment on her presence. Upon explaining that he was not going in the direction of the school because he needed to fetch his mother from the market, he is released. Thus he protects her along with himself, and Galenus does not realize that Mysandra has no reason to be shopping, after he sent Liturgus in I, 1 to buy everything needed. Although Petriscus remarks in an aside that he will now join his "commanders"—implying that he is stealing at the behest of Cabiscus and Stypiscus—he cannot yet enter the brothel because his father remains in sight. He has to go off-stage, pretending that he really is looking for his mother.

Grumbling that his son is being spoiled by Mysandra's permissiveness and that a quarrel ensues whenever he objects, Galenus discovers his wife [III, 3]. He notes that her pallor with flushed cheeks is a sign that something is bothering her. Neither asps nor tigers are more pernicious to a peaceful man than an evil woman, he philosophizes, rather like the chorus in Act III of *The Rebels*. She corroborates this aphorism by vituperating him for harming his own offspring. After ordering her to control her emotions a little, he tries to defend the punishing of Petriscus and blames her for their son's mischief. Mysandra rejects as preposterous the idea that a mere fourteen-year-old could be whoring, thieving, and dissipating, as her husband would have her believe. And is she supposed to be responsible for every fault? Whack! She smacks him over the head with her stick. "I'll take this one beating from you, Wife," he gasps, "but I don't know if I'll take a second one." His frustration vents itself in tears, which Mysandra mocks, gibing "Don't cry, wretch!" Disgustedly she tells him to go to the devil and warns that if he comes back he will be dealt worse.

The brouhaha has aroused their neighbor Gnorymus ("friend"), who ventures outside to see what on earth is happening and finds Galenus, blear-eyed, rubbing his face [III, 4]. "My house is full of smoke," the latter pretends in his shame. Smoke? Gnorymus says that he has never been bothered by smoke in the ten years that he has been living here. Galenus invites him to go have a look. This Gnorymus promptly does, only to be bashed over the pate himself by the still armed amazon, who mistakes him for her husband. He reels back to Galenus, groaning good-naturedly that he is not surprised at the smoke with such green wood burning outside the hearth. The two friends agree to go bathe their bloodshot eyes and wash away their pain with wine. Galenus relates how the incident arose and explains that he did not fight back because he prefers peace to disturbance. He should expostulate with his wife after she has calmed down, Gnorymus proposes. A gentle approach is best. With this reasoning, not to say rationalization, Galenus is completely in accord. As the two fellow sufferers go off-stage together, no doubt arm in arm, the chorus ends Act III with the praise of wine mentioned in Section II of the Introduction.

The motif of the eyes stung by "smoke" is well known to readers of the German Shrovetide plays of Hans Sachs (1494–1576), who used it in *Der bös Rauch (Bad Smoke)*. It is a borrowing from the international store of jests accumulated in the Middle Ages and the Renaissance. Macropedius made further use of this material in the three carnival comedies treated in the next chapter and probably also for the pranks of Cabiscus and Stypiscus in Act IV of *Petriscus*.[6] The introduction of such broad humor, well integrated as it is in the first edition of this play, enhances a theme but sparely treated in *The Rebels*. This comic matter in *Petriscus* is moreover of value not only for its own sake but also as a means of furthering character or plot development. The capers of Cabiscus and Stypiscus in their subplot will lead to Petriscus' arrest, as well as their own, at the end of the fourth act. In Act III the story is not advanced at all after Scene 1, but the way in which the "smoke"-motif is employed helps to impress on us dramatically the personalities of Mysandra and her mate. In *The Rebels* it is only Philotecnium who is presented in some detail. A fretful hen of a mother, she spoils Dyscolus in a sincere effort to give him the best life possible and to shield him from being hurt—as she has been harmed by her husband. We are left to imagine, however, why Cacolalia pampers Clopicus, whose welfare is certainly not uppermost in her mind. Mysandra we come to understand as an equally headstrong woman at odds with a husband whom she finds contemptible. Because she does not respect him, she considers his gruffness a menace to their son, and her mothering is an effort at protection.

In IV, 1 Petriscus is free to proceed to the brothel, since Galenus has gone off to the tavern with Gnorymus and Mysandra has retired into their house. Cabiscus and Stypiscus are impressed with his booty and feel spurred to a heist themselves. They wonder whether his theft will go undetected, but Petriscus assures them that his father will not notice the loss, evidencing with his words a low opinion of Galenus. As Cabiscus and Stypiscus set out to scavenge for some loot of their own, they commit Petriscus to the tender care of Philochrysium and her partner Philargyrium ("money lover"), who have been nursing the urchins' derrières.

These lasses welcome the newcomer with flaunted charms, while he digs into his pocket for enough cash to finance three measures of Falernian wine [IV, 2]. Hearing someone come noisily down the street, the little party hastily withdraws.

The din is being made by a happy old peasant, who maybe sings as he shuffles along, because he has just been paid a large sum of money. Before he leaves town he wants to make sure that he has not been rooked, since city people are dishonest, so he stops to count his coins [IV, 3]. This action suggests a ploy to Cabiscus, who is lurking nearby with his crony. Stypiscus is to go over and begin talking to the old man. Having distracted him, he is to snatch one coin and run. As soon as he has lured the codger out of sight, Cabiscus will make off with the purse, which will have been left behind. Stypiscus should then return the coin. If he does, charges will not be pressed against him, and both boys will go scot-free. Stypiscus, less adroit than his comrade, does not perceive that all the risk in this adventure lies with him. He agrees to the plan and appears to bring it off successfully, but he is too greedy to give back the gold piece which he has seized.

The peasant returns, upbraiding himself for his stupidity, only to find that he has now lost everything—the security on which he counted for the remainder of his life [IV, 4]. Hearing his cries of anguish, Petriscus and the two whores come outside to have some fun with him. Upon learning what has happened, Petriscus says in Greek "Cabiscus' wiles, by Zeus!" He fancies himself as clever in thus veiling the culprit's name, but the farmer is sharp enough to catch it. "Who is this Cabiscus?" he queries. "Why are you laughing?" Again in Greek Petriscus quips "The stump *(stypos)* doesn't comprehend." He is wrong, though, for "the stump" grows very suspicious. "What Stypos is that? Do you know about what happened?" the old fellow pointedly inquires, moving Petriscus and the harlots, who feel threatened, to tumble him into the gutter. Smeared with dirt, the man wonders wearily what he should do, since without money he cannot bribe the sheriff to aid him. He decides nonetheless to make an appeal, hoping for luck. Philochrysium, who catches sight of the now fuddled Galenus returning with Gnorymus, warns Petriscus to go inside. The girls will wait for Cabiscus and Stypiscus.

The henpecked milquetoast is still afraid to face his wife, and Gnorymus advises him to wait until dinner time, when—because of guests—Mysandra will ask him to come back [IV, 5]. A bad woman is best treated with contempt, the two friends agree, perhaps confusing contempt with timorousness. Galenus even appears paranoid by hiding in his neighbor's house at the sound of nearby laughter. On the assumption that someone must be scorning him, he prefers to flee rather than to defend himself.

After IV, 5 Macropedius added two scenes in the revision of *Petriscus* published in 1553. In this later edition Cabiscus and Stypiscus are called Meloclopus ("fruit thief") and Argyroclopus ("money thief"), respectively. The two intercalated scenes (6 and 7) present a second, needless caper, engineered by Meloclopus. He and Argyroclopus cheat a fruit vendor named Megera out of produce and cash. This episode is pointless because robbing the peasant is sufficient to effect the downfall of both these pilferers and Petriscus, as we will see in the 1536 version. Macropedius' addenda are almost as regretable here as in *The Rebels*. He was even so careless with his revision of *Petriscus* that in IV, 3, 4, 6, and 7 he used Argyroclopus as Cabiscus instead of Stypiscus, ignoring the contradiction which results in Scenes 10 and 11 (8 and 9 in the 1536 version). As in the case of *The Rebels*, we should be kind enough to the author to refrain from serious consideration of the unworthy 1553 debasement, evaluating *Petriscus* only as it stands in the first edition.

In IV, 6 of this earlier version Cabiscus and Stypiscus return to a warm welcome at the brothel and have fun with their chits, rewarding them with some money. Warned by Cabiscus that he may be in danger for not giving back the gold piece taken from the peasant, Stypiscus struts brashly, vaunting his insouciance. Since sounds are again to be heard in the streets, the four go inside to join Petriscus, just before an informer named Sycasta meets the sheriff and three officers in front of the house [IV, 7]. Hoping for reward and wanting to put a stop to the worrisome mischief of Cabiscus and Stypiscus, Sycasta gives a long account of what he has heard about the pranks of these two, including the latest. Macropedius omitted nearly all of this report in the 1553 version, but the inclusion of it in its entirety is justified. Apart from the fact that what Sycasta narrates is amusing, it shows that Cabiscus and Stypiscus have a history of petty larceny and consequently deserve the punishment which they later receive (by standards of Renaissance justice). Asked where the thieves are hiding, Sycasta conjectures that they are in a dive somewhere, since they are rumored to have been driven from one for a whipping by their teacher. "They're students?" the sheriff asks. Sycasta thinks that they have renounced school, and he is sent to verify this important detail as quickly as possible.

The peasant, exhausted from his search, happens along and meets the sheriff in the street [IV, 8]. After relating his misadventure, he describes Stypiscus—handsome, agile, curly haired, of average height, and dressed in a red tunic with a black cap. The sheriff promises to do all he can to recover the stolen money. Because of Petriscus' chivying in Greek, the farmer suggests that the police check the brothel here, whereupon Stypiscus peeps out to see whether the coast is clear for Petriscus to go home. The officers recognize him from the description and raid the house [IV, 9]. This time the prostitutes will be beaten, while the three boys are to be jailed for trial. The peasant will recover his money. At this juncture in the 1553 edition a scene is added in which Megera accuses Argyroclopus and Meloclopus of having filched her fruit and her money, demanding that they be hanged along with the third cuss, whom she "long ago found is worthless." In both versions the chorus exhorts us to heed and honor the officials who maintain law and order, as we saw in Section II of the Introduction.

By the end of the fourth act Macropedius, having taken a somewhat different course, brings the main plot of *Petriscus* to the same stage at which we found the story in *The Rebels* after Act IV. At this point in both plays the protagonists have been arrested and are confronted by execution on the gallows. The means by which the author achieves this degree of development in *Petriscus* are more significant if not also more dramatic than in *The Rebels*. Instead of a conventional purse snatching, Cabiscus and Stypiscus have used a clever stratagem, and Petriscus has preyed upon the parents who failed to give him a proper upbringing. In Act V the plot will take the same course as in the final act of *The Rebels*, with the reversal again occurring immediately after the climax.

Once the neighborhood has grown quiet, Galenus feels brave enough to venture back outside [V, 1]. He and his friend have been drinking most of the afternoon so are sure to be tipsy. Much as Gnorymus predicted, Mysandra sends Liturgus to fetch her husband with an apology. Galenus condescends to go home in a little while and invites Gnorymus to join them for the dinner. As Liturgus proceeds to look for Petriscus, Mysandra herself comes forth. She really does regret her violence, having just noticed that cinnamon, pepper, and all the sugar have vanished since she gave her keys to her son [V, 2]. Not to allow her mate any advantage, she will keep this discovery to herself, but she wants two gold pieces for new supplies. Though surprised that they are in need of more, Galenus asks only why she has not taken money enough, and Mysandra explains that she is trying to avoid any misunderstanding. Her scruples force Galenus to go to his office. While he is inside, she expresses some anxiety over the absence of Petriscus. Has something happened to him in the Mardi Gras revelry? Liturgus is coming back without having located him. Suddenly Galenus rushes out, shouting "Wife! Wife!" At once he spotted the theft which Petriscus was so confident he would overlook.

Unhesitantly Mysandra tells him that the robber is their serf, to whom she entrusted her keys, as she adds without a blush [V, 3], "He is guilty! He stayed alone in the house!" Clamoring in this fashion, she seeks a scapegoat to save the darling who she must know is the real culprit. Galenus is too drunk and naturally truckling to question the false charges. At his wife's instigation he has some passing police apprehend Liturgus, over the latter's protestations of innocence. He even orders the officials to rough his servant up. The incident creates a further opportunity for both master and mistress to display the ugly weaknesses in their character.

Since Gnorymus has come out again to see what is going on, Galenus sends Mysandra for the spices and tells his neighbor of this new development, feeling very sorry for himself [V, 4]. "I seem to be easily the most wretched person alive," he wails theatrically. The peasant now passes by, on his way home once more but with his money restored. He informs Galenus and Gnorymus that besides the two who robbed him a third boy is being held for stealing cash from his parents. Galenus' first reaction is alarm, yet he assures himself that Liturgus is the youth in question. The peasant contradicts him, declaring that Liturgus has been found innocent. This revelation comes as a staggering blow, since it means that Petriscus has probably been arrested. "Why didn't I stab my wife six hundred times! She alone was the author of this tragedy," Galenus bellows, still exaggerating. It is not in his nature to hold himself even partially responsible.

Mysandra has also heard the tidings and stumbles home weeping, to be denounced by her spouse for mollycoddling [V, 5]. Surprisingly, she accepts the blame, proving honest enough in despair to acknowledge her own failing. As in *The Rebels,* a messenger comes with word from her imprisoned son. Petriscus has penned a letter to his parents and one in Greek to Didascalus. The first is a confession of his wrongs, to which, Petriscus writes, he felt encouraged by his mother's laxness. The second missive is to be carried at once to Didascalus, who is the only hope now that a death sentence is imminent.

Like Philotecnium in V, 2 of *The Rebels,* Mysandra wonders what god will make the teacher sympathetic, but when she and her husband meet him he is favorably disposed [V, 6]. Humbly and tearfully she invokes his help, and Galenus delivers Petriscus' note, written in Greek to stir Didascalus with erudition. "Using your power as teacher, free me quickly from the threat of the gallows, to which I have fallen victim because of my thefts," the imperiled Hellenist pleads. If the schoolmaster will not save him, he is done for. "Come swiftly, I beseech you, and rescue me with your rod, before I die the basest death!" A pupil who is with Didascalus also intercedes in his schoolmate's behalf. The teacher is doubtful that he can prevail against the law transgressed by Petriscus, but he will exert his authority for whatever it might be worth.

The day has waned to nearly evening, and the sheriff has seated himself on the tribunal as Didascalus and the parents arrive for the trial, with Mysandra on the verge of fainting [V, 7]. Petriscus is becoming desperate and is broken with contrition. "Oh little schoolboys, obey your teachers!" he fervently counsels whatever little schoolboys might be within earshot. "Beware of naughty comrades like these," he adds with a gesture toward Cabiscus and Stypiscus. When the sheriff demands to know who it is that has intruded into his court, Didascalus requests the release of Petriscus for punishment by him, in consideration of the parents' tears, the boy's tender age, and a teacher's venerable privilege. Petriscus is his pupil, subject to his ferule, not to a magistrate's laws. The sheriff acquiesces on condition of good conduct in the future, permitting Didascalus to take Petriscus immediately for his whipping, while the parents wait for Liturgus and the money to be returned which was found in their son's possession. As in *The Rebels*, sentence is pronounced against the two less fortunate miscreants without their being defended [V, 8]. With the trumpet blaring, they are led away to be hanged before sunset—a grisly warning to the mischievously inclined. Liturgus is released, and the stolen money is returned.

In front of the school, with his punishment already administered, Petriscus promises to show his gratitude to the teacher, even if his parents do not give evidence of theirs [V, 9]. Ignoring the innuendo couched in these words, Didascalus admonishes the boy to beg forgiveness from his father and mother and ask that Liturgus be freed from bondage. Petriscus complies (like Asotus requesting the release of Daetrus), and Didascalus seconds the petition for manumission. Galenus does not refuse. The dinner party scheduled for this hour is very much in order now. This Shrove Tuesday has become a day for special jubilation in the house between the brothel and the school, since Petriscus has learned which of the two to choose. Gnorymus is called over, and all go in to celebrate. Galenus informs the people in the audience that nothing has been cooked here for them. They will have to eat in their own homes. Before they leave, however, they are told in a twelve-line epilogue that fathers should correct rebellious children and that mothers should not corrupt their young with pampering. Pupils should heed their preceptors, and everyone should give a round of applause.

When he wrote *Petriscus* Macropedius had reached his full stature as a dramatist. From a prior date must be *Aluta*, to which we turn next, not only because it was published earlier but also because it is not so well-made a play. It must be in addition the first Shrovetide comedy that Macropedius composed. Perhaps he then wrote *Andrisca* before using carnival-play motifs in a reworking of the plot of *The Rebels*. *Petriscus* may possibly be his fifth drama, rather than his fourth, even though it was first published two years before *Andrisca*. The sixth is definitely *Bassarus*.

CHAPTER 4

The Farcical Villagers

A LUTA, *Andrisca,* and *Bassarus* are the three works by Macropedius which are most likely to have the widest appeal for
modern readers. Like *The Rebels* and *Petriscus* they are secular
rather than religious plays, and they are character comedies drawn
from sixteenth-century Dutch life. They are not concerned with
schoolboys, however, and they are more boisterous than even
Petriscus. Because of the pervasive ludicrousness, Macropedius
set these plays in the milieu of the village. Only Aluta (possibly
"unwashed") [1] and her husband display the denseness traditionally imputed to the peasant or small-town mentality, but the high
jinks in all three plays are made more plausible by the near-rustic
ambiance. While some of the action is still too drastic for easy
credence, it is supposed to be somewhat farfetched in the interest
of sheer ridiculousness. Behavior is otherwise justified as convincingly as in *Petriscus* and with the same swift facility that, for better or worse, prefers nuance to elaboration. Though *Aluta* still
lacks polish, *Andrisca* and *Bassarus,* like *Petriscus,* show Macropedius at the height of his ability.

I   *Aluta*

The author's shortest play, it is only 617 lines in length. It is
also the most preposterous and the most vulgar of all that he
wrote. This is not to say that it is the least enjoyable. Performed
during a bacchic Mardi Gras, it was probably hilarious. Read
soberly in an armchair, however, it may have less success. For
Macropedius *Aluta* is unusual in still another respect: It does not
maintain unity of place. The time span demanded by the action
is only about five hours, but the play opens in the market of a
town (Utrecht) and closes at Aluta's farmhouse in the neighboring village of Bunschoten near the Zuider Zee. In between we find
the protagonist at a tavern in the city and on the road leading
home. All of these settings may have been indicated simultane-

ously as the play was performed. In that case the action progressed across the stage, since Utrecht must have been at one side and Bunschoten at the other. The imitator of Plautus who would not abandon strict unity of place in his first play came to disregard it in his third (assuming that *The Rebels* was written second).

The only indication that the events in *Aluta* take place during carnival is the first of the two choruses ending Acts I–IV. The usual moralistic odes are preceded in this play by a chant of Shrovetide bacchantes, which does not vary from act to act. The second choruses are, in the normal manner, different after each act. They are not sung by more maenads but rather by matrons from Bunschoten, better suited to deliver the didactic import of these sermons in song. Among the *dramatis personae* is listed "Bacchus, persona muta," although his appearance is nowhere indicated in the text of the play. In performance he must have led the chorus of his devotees.

A link to *The Rebels* is the fool *(Morus)* who again interrupts the speaker of the prologue, but this time he does not say that he will remain on the stage during the action. The prologue itself contains a short rendition of the plot and a long admonition to good conduct and attentiveness during the performance. Despite its cautionary nature this speech tends to induce the proper mood for *Aluta* through the jocose and even coarse language in which it is couched. Besides being told not to smell up the theater, as was mentioned in Section V of the Introduction, the audience is urged to be quiet so that neither the title figure nor her poultry will be frightened away, stopping the performance.

The time is nearly noon as Act I opens at the market of what must be Utrecht. Aluta the peasant woman is sitting alone with her cage of ducks, geese, and chickens, one of which is a rooster. All morning she has been waiting for a buyer, but no one wants her merchandise. She is treated like a block of wood, she complains, for if she speaks to people, they refuse to answer. What is more, she is hungry and thirsty now, impatient to be quit of her wares so that she can eat, having brought no food or drink. She wishes that she were back home with Beata, Greta, Bertula, and Metta. These friends would be good to her, whereas city slickers are a pack of thieves. Like the peasant in *Petriscus* [2] she knows that they would be happy to cheat her, taking her birds and leaving her empty-handed. She, Aluta, Heino's wife, will be on the watch, she announces. With these words, though, she has unwittingly prepared herself to be cozened in the very way she fears. Her hunger and thirst, weakening her resistance, make this simpleminded creature anything but wary.

She has been overheard by a scoundrel named Spermologus ("babbler," as in Acts 17:18 of the Greek New Testament), who exclaims that he has never seen a more senseless woman in his life [I, 2]. He is joined by another rascal, one Harpax ("robber"), who enters carrying a net. This implement is for the eggs which Harpax has been scouring about to steal, but it is as empty as his belly. For three days he has eaten only rotten vegetables gleaned from the streets. Spermologus tells him to furnish the potables, and he himself will provide comestibles enough to swell that flaccid stomach tight as a drum. "Pah!" retorts his crony, no less skeptical of promises than Pantolabus in Act II of *Acolastus*. As though he might have read Gnapheus' play, Harpax adds that the parasitic art (into which Pamphagus initiates Pantolabus) is dead now. In vindication Spermologus points out Aluta, mentioning that she just said who she and her husband are. Harpax understands immediately. "You're going to play like a relative?" he guesses, acquainted with the guile of spongers, even if he does not call it parasitism. Won over, he will assist as the occasion demands.

With his cloak flung over his shoulder as if in imitation of the running slaves and parasites in Roman comedy, Spermologus hurries to Aluta, who fancies him an eager customer [I, 3]. Flattering her as "the famous, noble, and lovely" wife of Heino and addressing her by name, he acts hurt that she does not recognize him. Can she have forgotten her cousin Petronius, who played with her from infancy? This person Spermologus has invented. Aluta does not know any such relative but, lacking much of a memory, she unhesitatingly assumes that she really has forgotten, and circumstances encourage her in her mistake. She is desperate not only for a buyer and for lunch but also for just a little friendliness. Because of "Petronius," who is delighted to have discovered her, she is not alone any more, and he can help her sell the poultry. He says, in fact, that he has a friend who would be interested. Excusing himself, he goes to confer with Harpax, whom he has signaled to get out of sight. Aluta rejoices at her good fortune, since she will perish from hunger and thirst if a purchaser does not come quickly [I, 4]. Neither her short monologue nor the brief conference between the swindlers [I, 5] is vital to the play. With momentary garrulity again faintly suggestive of the classical parasite, Spermologus merely teases his friend and tells him to act as though he is going to buy. Both scenes are helpful, however, in familiarizing us with the three characters.

Leading Harpax along, Spermologus returns to the grateful Aluta and says that his comrade will preempt the whole cageful of birds [I, 6]. The poor woman, a gull herself, is so pleased that she is willing to take less than what she feels is the true value. Now that Harpax must pay, he pretends to have lost his money-belt. Certain that he simply left it at home, Spermologus grandly ordains that he take the poultry on credit. Aluta prefers the money first and is willing to wait, moving Harpax to inquire indignantly whether she mistrusts her cousin. The latter has a compromise solution, however. "Leave the rooster as a pledge," Spermologus proposes, and Harpax generously assents. Asked where the money is to be brought, muddled Aluta says that she will be refreshing herself at the Sign of the Lion. The rogues, taking French leave, promise to meet her there. When they have gone, she muses that Petronius must be very fond of her, to have exerted himself in her behalf. Good thing she kept the rooster as a guarantee, though, she thinks. In the city there is an awful lot of trickery. Before going to the tavern, she must relieve herself in an alley, so she exits. Having secured her poultry, Spermologus suspects from a distance that her cloak (*toga*) can be taken, too— when she is drunk. Thus he prepares us for subsequent developments.

Like the motif of the "smoke" in *Petriscus,* the idea of the rooster being left to its owner as a pledge was not original with Macropedius.[3] The merry and outrageous Till Eulenspiegel pulls the same prank in the thirty-sixth of his mischievous adventures. At the market in Quedlinburg he sees a woman selling a basket of chickens. After momentary dickering with her, he abruptly picks up the hamper and walks away. She pursues, stops him, and demands payment. Claiming to be secretary to the local abbess, he gives the vendor her rooster as security, and she is content. Macropedius embellished this crude tale with enough motivation for Aluta's behavior to make it more acceptable. When Spermologus

and Harpax dupe her, she is at the breaking point, understandably more prone to take a chance than she would be under better
conditions. She has been put off her guard, furthermore, by the
belief that Spermologus is a kinsman, on whom she can rely as a
matter of course. His pose as Petronius is probably another borrowing from joke literature, also made palatable in this farce by
the circumstances prevailing, chief of which is Aluta's dimwitted-
ness.

The pause between the events of Acts I and II is only the
time needed to sing the "Iacche Bacche ohe, ohe," etc. of the bac-
chanals and a brief denunciation of cadgers by the Bunschoten
matrons.[4] Aluta enters from her toilet in the alley, carrying her
rooster and quoting a native proverb to the effect that it is wise to
empty the belly before putting something else in. She pounds on
the door of the Lion until it is opened by the hostess Tolmesia,
whereupon she demands to be admitted with her barnyard escort
and served splendiferously. Because she is of dubious appearance,
Tolmesia asks her whether she has money. "Soon it'll be here,"
Aluta airily replies, but the proprietress remains understandably
hesitant. The behavior of this rooster-bearer is indeed eccentric.
"Ah, money?" she shrugs. "Money is filth! Bring out sweet wine,
charming and Massic! You hear?" "The woman is either insane or
she's tipsy," Tolmesia mutters, though Aluta is only exhilarated,
expecting at any moment to be presented with her remuneration.
As to a famous empress it will be tendered, she flatters herself.
After a morning of deprivation she wants an afternoon of jubilation. The waitress in the pub consents on condition that the rooster
serve as security.

After Aluta has been guzzling a while (necessitating a time
lapse of at least half an hour) Spermologus meets Harpax, who
has sold the fowls and wants to know whether the poulterer cannot be relieved of something else. Spermologus mentions her
cloak. "It's ours as soon as she's drunk," Harpax remarks [II, 2].
That state she has already reached, however, having downed nine
measures of wine. She comes outside, nervous about her money,
and arouses Tolmesia's curiosity [II, 3]. When she describes the
sale of her poultry, saying that she was not acquainted with the
buyer but that Petronius her relative was, Tolmesia asks "What
Petronius is that?" The proprietress suspects an impostor, because
she is not aware of anyone in town with that name. Though her

skepticism proves nothing, Aluta takes it to heart. "Alas, wretched me!" she wails. Upon remembering her rooster, however, she feels better. Would the two men have left this spirited cock if they were not going to pay? Certainly not! "Soon Petronius will come," she assures the hostess. Tolmesia, though, is not so sanguine. Either Aluta pays at once or she forfeits her lord of the dunghill. "Oh watchful guardian of home, thus you flit to another coop?" the inebriate mawkishly declaims. She has no choice but to trek to Bunschoten and complain to Heino, being denied the leniency which she extended to Harpax. "You won't get far before Bacchus puts you to sleep," notes the waitress who hurries the queasy customer into the street to avoid a dirtied doorway. Aluta exits into one of the wings to vomit, yielding the stage to Bacchus and his maenads, followed by the contrasting Bunschoten matrons, who disapprove of taverners.

The excessive drinking during this second, transitional act readies Aluta for her next deception, carried out by Harpax rather than by Spermologus. Act III, in which this further trickery is perpetrated, begins after she has retched her way to the outskirts of town. So much wine on an empty stomach has made her deliriously nauseated. Spermologus and Harpax follow like vultures circling a dying animal. Teetering in her dizzy meanders, Aluta babbles incoherently and cries for help. When she finally collapses, Harpax approaches her with his net [III, 2]. Spermologus acquired the cash for food; he must find the wherewithal for drink. He pretends to be Heino, and she in her stupor is incapable of recognizing him. "I'll help you, dear little Aluta," he coos. "Don't be afraid." "I doubt I'm still the little Aluta of yours that I used to be," she whimpers, thinking of how differently she feels. "Lie down beside me," she pleads. With her consent he first loosens her garments and removes her cloak. When she throws up again, he undresses her. Though aghast at this act of shamelessness, Spermologus is not about to remonstrate. When Harpax rejoins him with an armful of clothes to hock, Spermologus notices that the net was left behind. Before explaining what became of it, Harpax, who wants to abscond as quickly as possible, hastens away with his friend. Perhaps Aluta remains prostrate on the stage during the appearance of the choruses, particularly since the matrons denounce drunkenness in women. She would serve as a case in point.

For readers of the play the explanation of what happened to Harpax' net comes only in the second scene of Act IV. Scene 1 takes us to Aluta's farm, inside the house. It is late afternoon now and Heino, beginning to worry about his wife, sends their young son Paedium ("child") out to look for her. Paedium is afraid of witches, but his father assures him that he will be safe, since it is still daylight. Some porridge will be cooked while he is gone. To himself Heino expresses the fear that Paedium's search will prove fruitless. If someone led his wife to a tavern, he frets, domestic affairs will be suspended for a day, because once she starts drinking she never stops until she has glutted herself.

In Scene 2 Aluta appears outside the house, where Paedium is poking about. Harpax' net is over her head. "Oh! Hey! Where am I? Who am I? What do I see everywhere?" she cries. What demon bewitched her, she wants to know, putting her into a new and reticulate world? Heaven and earth are nothing but a net! Is she Aluta, or is she someone else, she wonders. In thought she is still the wife of Heino, but in appearance she is not. Her clothes are gone, except for a chemise, and the world seems to be falling. "I'll go ask Heino if Aluta's at home," she decides. "If she is, I'm bound to be somebody else. But if she's not, there still might be some hope for me."

Little Paedium, who has beheld his mother in this state of distraction, runs into the house with his hair on end [IV, 3]. Mama has lost her mind! He breathlessly gasps that she wanders around shouting, tossing her head and hands, with her face behexed! "Hush, hush, son. It'll be all right," Heino clucks. "Did witches or evil spirits scare this boy?" he asks himself. "I'll go outside to see what's happened." At this climactic point Aluta is addressing some mute fellow citizens of Bunschoten, asking whether she is at Heino's house [IV, 4]. Unless completely crazy, she is, but everything looks different. Catching sight of her husband, she calls out "Heino! Heino! Where is your wife Aluta? Is she at home?" He informs her positively and tenderly that she is Aluta herself. "But I'm not in my clothes!" she protests. Heino is dumbfounded. What is he to do? Someone has cast a spell on his poor wife. Paedium must run to the church and get Mystotus the priest, who can exorcise any demon that has possessed her. "Fly!" he implores his son. Meanwhile he will put Aluta to bed, leaving her otherwise just as she is until Mystotus arrives. When the stage has cleared, the choruses make their final entrance, and the matrons sing of the burden imposed on a good man by a foolish wife.

The loss-of-identity theme was known to Macropedius in at least two forms. One of these is the *Amphitryon* of Plautus, in I, 1 of which Mercury persuades the slave Sosia that he is not himself.[5] The English interlude *Jack Juggler* (1562) is a sixteenth-century comedy utilizing this source. Macropedius, however, made use of folklore. The woman who decides that she must be a different person occurs in the thirty-fourth and fifthy-ninth of the Grimms' *Fairy Tales,* to cite but the best-known instances.[6] In the former story the peasant Hans places a fowler's net hung with little bells over his lazy wife Else, asleep in the field. Awaking at night, she is no longer certain who she is. She returns home wondering what happened to her and finds the door locked. When she knocks on the window, asking Hans whether Else is inside, he says yes, so she goes away perplexed, never to be seen again. In the fifty-ninth tale, the peasant woman Catherlieschen goes out to cut fruit but is so drowsy that she snips her clothes in two and falls asleep. When she wakes up after dark and discovers herself half naked, she questions who she is. Running home and rapping on the window, she asks whether Catherlieschen is inside. "Yes, yes," says her husband, "she's probably asleep." Figuring, then, that she must be someone else, the simpleton leaves. What sleep and night effect in this folk treatment of the theme, slumber and drunkenness bring about in *Aluta,* preparing the protagonist to accept altered appearance as altered reality. We the readers are readied for the particularly improbable behavior of Act IV by the preceding comic episodes, which build toward this high point of absurdity. Act V will lower us to normalcy after a lesser degree of farce—Aluta's exorcism.

Paedium's fear of evil has led Heino to think of witchcraft as the likeliest explanation for his wife's weird antics. As Act V opens, she is still babbling about fraud and Petronius, so Mystotus, when he arrives, has reason to agree with the husband's diagnosis. He comes in surplice and stole, gesturing and murmuring in suitably hierophantic fashion. After Heino explains that his wife went out sane in the morning and came back afflicted, the two go inside to where she lies grimacing in bed [V, 2]. Mystotus has the net removed and asks to be alone with the possessed.

Heino, reverently acknowledging that it is not seemly for rustics to witness sacred mysteries, takes Paedium outdoors.

As Mystotus orders the demon in the name of the Father, the Son, and the Holy Ghost to leave this servant of the Lord [V, 3], Aluta cries "Oh Bromius, oh Iacchus, you're here" (these being other names for Bacchus, whose spirits have begun again to spook about inside her). Not understanding her condition yet, Mystotus says "I exorcise you, Bromius; I adjure you, Iacchus, by the Son of God either to depart or . . . ," whereupon Aluta spews out more of her wine. With this effect of his ritual the priest realizes what is wrong with her. He hurries out to Heino and reassures him, promising that by tomorrow she will be out of danger [V, 4]. The plot ends at this point, though Mystotus continues to speak. Turning from Heino to the audience, he needlessly explain's Aluta's ailment and reveals—what he must have learned by supernatural means—that Spermologus and Harpax have been arrested and will be exhibited in the stocks the next day. Though having thereby shattered the dramatic illusion, he then addresses Heino once more, proposing that the two of them have a nip themselves. In a ten-line epilogue the hope is expressed that viewers have been moved to better their Latin and their morals and will guard against temulence, theft, and fraud.

Aluta is Macropedius at his lustiest—almost blasphemously ribald. One finds exorcism as a comic motif elsewhere in late medieval and Renaissance comedy (e.g., in Shakespeare's *Twelfth Night*, *Kälberbrüten* by Hans Sachs, the Dutch *Nu noch,* and Lorenzino de' Medici's *Aridosia*) so is not surprised to see it here, but vomiting in the name of the Lord comes unexpectedly from a staid Brother of the Common Life. Let us not question his piety, however, but only his artistry. Even in what he intended to be distinctly low comedy he gave thought to motivation, yet *Aluta* is rather too brief. The title figure, simple as she is bound to remain, could nonetheless be made more memorable through more disclosure of herself and more balanced through the attribution of some positive qualities to offset her woeful shortcomings. The gap between II, 1 and II, 2, while she is tossing down wine in the tavern, offers a ready occasion for at least making us better acquainted with her. Not only would a lacuna be filled, but she would be particularly loquacious at that time.

Mystotus' remarks to the spectators in his final speech con-

stitute a real flaw. The very apprehension of Harpax and Spermologus is improbable, particularly with no complaint brought
against them. The author might simply have forgone the poetic
justice of their arrest, but if he deemed retribution requisite he
should have contrived a way of announcing their capture more
within the framework of the plot.

In his preface addressed "to the Reader" he confesses to an
awareness of hiatuses and inchoateness. He wanted to make re-
visions, he says, but came to see that writing a new work would
be easier than correcting this old one. He contented himself with
adding a few words here and there, excusing the defects remaining by saying (as though with a yawn) that the play is only for
boys, anyway. If it was because he could not bring himself to
refine *Aluta* that he gave us *Andrisca* and *Bassarus,* we can rejoice in his disdain.

II *Andrisca*

Perhaps composed between *Aluta* and *Petriscus,* this comedy
at any rate contains similarities to each. On the one hand, the
setting is again Bunschoten, and the chorus of the bacchantes
in *Aluta* is reused verbatim between acts, along with varying
choral odes sung by a group of boys. The maenads are now simply boisterous Mardi Gras celebrants, however, and their chant is
treated as part of the action, with Bacchus omitted. Andrisca at
the end of Act I and her neighbor Porna at the close of Act II join
these female revellers themselves. On the other hand, Georgus
("farmer"), the already henpecked husband of Andrisca ("manly")
even though the pair have been married only seven months,
bears at first glance a resemblance to the browbeaten Galenus.
Like Mysandra, the title figure is a shrew, but her spouse proves
virile enough to tame her.

A second plot, interwoven with the marital problems of Georgus, concerns those of his friend next door, Byrsocopus ("tanner"),
who is very much like Galenus, though his wife Porna ("whore")
is unfaithful. While he is busy at his shop, she dallies with the
local priest, Hieronymus ("of holy name"). Both conflicts are
resolved concomitantly, and both couples unite to end *Andrisca*
with a festive dinner, like *Petriscus, The Rebels, Asotus,* and
later *Hecastus.*

The prologue is given over to the praise of drama as a pedagogical tool that was mentioned in the Introduction. School plays help with scansion yet are close to prose, and they assist the grammarian, the rhetorician, and the dialectician, we are told. They inculcate grace and morals while furthering elocution. Spectators are not only entertained but also edified. Again the image of the mirror of life is used to describe comedy. In this reflection of society we are supposed to be able to see and contemplate what is to be avoided and what done. Away with prudish censors! Nothing is chaste to the unchaste; to the chaste nothing is unchaste. The Muses, we are informed, have bestowed nothing better, more delightful, more glorious, and richer than comedy. Shifting from the genre as a whole to *Andrisca* in particular, the speaker states that it is set in Bunschoten for the greater amusement of the people of Utrecht. With a call for quiet and heedfulness, the prologue ends.

As in *Petriscus* Macropedius observes the unities of both time and place. The scene throughout is the street before the homes of Georgus and Byrsocopus, which stand side by side. Next to them is the village tavern. Byrsocopus' tannery lies off-stage, like the land that Georgus and his serf cultivate. The play opens on the morning of Shrove Tuesday, as do *Aluta, Petriscus,* and *Bassarus,* with the men going about their work as usual.

Georgus, setting out to check on his servant in the fields, orders Andrisca to put away the dishes and to have lunch ready when he returns. She had better see to it that what he wants is done, he cautions, and she is not to be lured out by revelry, fond as she is of parties. When he finally turns to leave after a second admonition, Andrisca impatiently stalks back into the house. Georgus' dictatorial manner (reminiscent of Galenus at the outset of *Petriscus*) suggests that he is trying desperately to assert himself over his headstrong wife, with control of her slipping from his grasp. If he seems to succeed in imposing his will on her—for she agrees to his commands—the reason is only that she wants to be rid of him so that she can skip to the tavern. "Why does he keep blathering here in front of the door," she mutters under her breath in the course of his harangue.

Byrsocopus, leaving for work himself, overhears the last of his neighbor's injunctions plus an added complaint about a domineering wife being the worse possible bane to domesticity. "That's certainly true, as I see in my own home," the tanner commiser-

ates. "Who's talking here?" asks Georgus, looking around surprised. Discovering Byrsocopus, he is overjoyed at sympathetic
ears into which he can pour his troubles. Andrisca is from an
excellent family, he begins, with great wealth and a keen mind.
She is more difficult and shameless, though, than he can bear. As
soon as he sets foot outside the house she is off drinking somewhere or, he fears, engaged in something worse. Brysocopus is
reminded of his own cross. "You know that priest at the Chapel
of the Chaste Virgin?" he inquires. "As well as you," replies
Georgus, describing the man as barrel chested, potbellied, red
faced, and curly haired. "That's the one," sighs Brysocopus. Anything but chaste himself, the reprobate has been conducting an
outrageous affair with Porna. Several times the husband has
chased the lover away. Georgus cautions against violence, for a
priest is supposedly exempt from civil law and hitting one could
bring divines around like swarms of wasps and hornets. Giving a
shove would probably not be thought sinful, however, he conjectures. In anguish Byrsocopus wonders how Porna's insolence
can be borne, and he pales at the thought of administering a
whipping, as suggested by his friend. "Who would dare?" he
whispers in awe. Georgus assures him that discipline is needed.
If Andrisca does not toe the line from now on, she too will be
punished, he declares.

At this instant she starts to leave for the tavern, expecting her
husband to be long gone. Anticipating a storm at the sight of
her, for lightning flashes in her eyes, Byrsocopus hurries off. She
is indeed no less irked than surprised to come upon Georgus [I,
2]. "Are you still here, good-for-nothing?" she thunders. While he
has been loafing, she has completed her chores. Since he is not
earning his keep he does not deserve to eat before supper, she
chides, cleverly excusing herself from the nuisance of fixing lunch.
She tries to push him away, dismissing him like a child, but he
tells her to let him be and to heed his warnings, or the two of
them will fight for the pants in the family. Contenting himself
temporarily with this further caveat, he departs. Smugly Andrisca remarks that farmers and dolts are to be treated like her
husband, who as a result of her forcefulness will not be back till
evening. If he does come sooner, he can serve himself. Is this
not Mardi Gras? Who is going to sit at home on such an occasion
and not have fun, she queries, reminding us of Mysandra in

Petriscus II, 6. Porna, who now sticks her head out the door, she will invite along, though well aware that her neighbor is looking for the priest.

Despite Andrisca's eagerness and the fact that a lavish feast has been prepared, Porna declines, using the excuse that she has already promised to meet other friends [I, 3]. Bluntly Andrisca exposes this pretense by saying that she knows of Hieronymus. Probably hurt at being snubbed, she reproves Porna for infidelity, but she is in turn branded a wino *(meribibula)*. In a huff she marches back home to lock up, permitting Hieronymus, who has been hiding nearby with a flagon and a chicken, to join his paramour. Since Andrisca soon reemerges and the chorus of jubilant women is heard approaching, Porna and the priest hastily withdraw. In the six-line fourth scene of Act I Andrisca steps from her house in time to hear the neighboring door slammed shut. Guessing what that means, she scoffs. The merrymakers, who by now are dancing onto the stage, she accompanies in rejoicing, and subsequently all of them probably enter the pub together. The chorus of boys intones praise for agriculture, defending peasants from ridicule in the last strophe of its ode.[7]

When the second act opens, one hour has passed. It is almost noon. The neighborhood has grown quiet once more, so that Hieronymus and Porna can step out for a breath of fresh air. She has a scheme for enabling the priest to escape if her husband should return unexpectedly. She and the maid Paedisca ("young girl") will come out singing and holding up a wet sheet, behind which Hieronymus can run away unseen. Hearing Georgus coming back now, they resume their indoor sports.

The farmer says that he would not be returning so early if his servant were not famished [II, 2]. Because of Andrisca's acerbity he has no desire to be at home. Seeing the place shut up, he bets that she has disobeyed him, and to confirm his suspicions she emerges from the tavern, looking about for carousers. In doing so she espies her husband. Angrily she strides to confront him, while he braces to receive her with forbearance, ineffectual though it has proved so far.

Accustomed to take the offensive with her peace-loving spouse, Andrisca wastes no time in railing at him as an idle sloth forever hungry [II, 3]. He will have to make do with bread and cheese, since she refuses in a righteous pose to cook any lunch for a bum.

Georgus becomes aroused, demanding to know why she is disobedient. By what insanity is she possessed, he asks, that she is eternally dissipating and squandering his money? She spends as if he plucked it off poplars in the woods. Any children of theirs will be paupers! She counters by reminding him superciliously that she has her own property and a great deal of it. He is well-off because of her dowry. Consequently, what right does he have to gripe? "Shut up, clod! You worthless blockhead!" she shouts. She will reduce him to such meekness, she screams, that she will kill him with it! Though the time for mere words has passed, Georgus is again satisfied with only the specter of reprisals. On this occasion he does swear, however, that they will have it out once and for all if she sets foot in that saloon any more. Andrisca sneeringly assures him that she will never yield an inch and that she is too manly to let the "filthy, dirty yokel" lay a finger on her. After ending her tirade by ordering him to hell, she storms into the house. Referring to the audience as citizens of Bunschoten, Georgus says that they have been witnesses to his wife's outrageous conduct. It seems that even though he has formally committed himself to action he is still afraid of being unfair if he chastises her. He wants to make it clear, even to himself, that he is in the right.

Since the time is nearly noon, Brysocopus is coming home. Before returning to the fields with his bread and cheese,[8] Georgus decides to wait for a moment in order to see whether his neighbor has better luck obtaining some lunch. On the assumption that he has left, Andrisca saucily retraces her steps to the tavern. She probably has her arms full of food, because Georgus will announce in IV, 4 that she has cleaned out the pantry. As will be confirmed in IV, 1, he does not see her, evidently because he is looking in the opposite direction. His house must stand between the pub and Brysocopus' home.

Soaking wet and shivering, the tanner arrives to find himself locked out [II, 4]. "Is the priest inside again?" he wonders. When he yells to be admitted, he is told to wait while a sheet is folded, whereupon Paedisca and her mistress come prancing out, holding aloft an expanse of cloth and chanting a mocking duet: "While a wet piece of linen I fold/ With my servant out here in the cold,/ My husband the two of us gyp;/ Hieronymus gives him the slip." Seeming to perceive nothing, the cuckold says only "Aren't you through yet?" From his hiding place Georgus mutters "She's through, by God," for he sees the priest slink away. Having watched enough, he goes to his farm. Making use of the fact that Byrsocopus is already wet, Porna has a pitcher brought and tells him to go fill it. Despite his chill he complies, giving the maid a chance to put the house in order. Basking in her triumph, Porna flatters herself that she could make her stupid spouse believe that cats lay goose eggs. To his face, however, she is all compliance and devotion, calling him "sweetheart," having the fire stoked, and ordering a meal served. If the food is disappointing, she promises solicitously, she will do better at dinner. Wilier than Andrisca, she seeks to gratify her husband rather than to grate on him. Since he wants to believe the best of her, she helps him to. The sooner he is contented, the sooner he will leave, and the sooner Hieronymus can return. While he lunches, Porna goes out briefly to join the chorus of orgiastic women, who have reappeared in the street. Like Andrisca previously, she shares in their joyful cheers to Bacchus, after which the chorus of boys condemns intemperance in general and sexual indulgence in particular.

On this occasion also the roisterers seem to enter the inn after their chant, because as Act III begins Porna is there. She and Andrisca, who will not permit "the priests' whore" to remain and who even slaps her, are squalling at each other like bristling cats. Porna has no reason to linger, however, because Brysocopus has had time to finish his meal, and she wants him out of the house. Heated from her squabble, she is prepared to use Andrisca's strong-arm tactics if necessary to expel him. Just at this point he appears, looking for her.

He is most unhappy that she left him to eat alone, and he grouses about neglect plus a sorry snack [III, 2]. Furthermore, he adds, the house smells of wine. An honest man does not do things behind her husband's back, he minces, not daring to be direct in accusing her. Just as he cannot yet break out of his habitual diffidence, Porna falls back on her customary duplicity, lying to him profusely. She intended to join him, she apologizes, and as for the odor, he must have sniffed apples munched by the children. Wine has never passed through their portals against his wishes, she solemnly avers. The dissatisfying lunch will be compensated for at dinner. With this show of consideration Byrsocopus is pacified and departs, leaving his wife to ask complacently

"When a man can be cajoled, why quarrel?" Thus she formulates her cynical policy of husband manipulation. Through pliancy she makes it difficult for her meek mate to accuse her.

Seeing the interloper exit up the street, Hieronymus steals back [III, 3]. He is worried that Byrsocopus suspected what was afoot, but his imperturbable mistress assures him that the one inkling which their stooge entertained she disposed of effortlessly. As she goes inside once more, the priest delays, needing to urinate, but to the relief of women in the audience he is prevented from doing so by the squeaking of the tavern door. As it opens to emit the proprietor and Andrisca, who are discussing Georgus' threat, the oft-frustrated cleric leaps into Porna's house.

The innkeeper is amazed that Andrisca can be so unruffled as to sit in his bar eating, drinking, joking, and making fun of everyone when she is menaced by a beating for doing so [III, 4]. Of course she herself does not fear Georgus in the least. In the seven months of their married life he has never uttered a sharp word, despite her ceaseless excess, she claims. She is exaggerating, as we know, but not greatly. The innkeeper does not share her childish hybris and says with an ingratiating laugh that there will surely be a fight for the pants. "Stop your foolishness, and let's go drink," Andrisca curtly retorts. Concerned not to lose what is probably his best customer, he offers to watch for Georgus in order to sound him out regarding his intentions. By means of this espionage she can know better what to expect. The chorus of carousing women gathers again to repeat its bacchic refrain, but Andrisca is oblivious to it. For the duration of these huzzahs and the added chorus of the boys, protesting against adultery, both she and her confidant retire to their cups.

The carnival clamor has died away as Act IV opens and the innkeeper returns to honor his pledge. He does not have to wait, for Georgus, who seems determined to reach a settlement today, comes right away to check on his wife. He definitely does not know that she is once more in the tavern, although she sashayed there at the end of II, 3 while he was concealed to observe his neighbors. Descrying the innkeeper now, he frowns. The fellow must be waiting for her, he thinks; or, as is more likely, he is guarding her. Naturally a cultivator of conviviality, the taverner saunters over and tries to strike up a conversation, but he encounters only rudeness. To confuse Georgus, he invites him for some lunch, saying that it is too late to find any at home. Though he would be flabbergasted if his invitation were accepted, he counts rightly on sufficient dislike of himself to preclude that embarrassment. Georgus makes no secret of his antipathy by accusing the fellow of luring Andrisca to extravagance—a charge warmly repudiated. When Georgus goes away, the innkeeper remarks that Andrisca is in for trouble. Her husband is incensed, and farmers are strong, he notes, adding that he himself would never dare to challenge this man.

Like the tanner in Act II, Georgus finds his house shut tight [IV, 2]. Flattering himself that his wife would not still ignore his prohibitions, he unlocks the door and goes inside. Maybe he will discover her in a nook, cowed by his blame and contemplating her misdeeds, he dreams. While he is out of sight, Porna and Hieronymus take the air and summon Paedisca, because plans have to be laid in case of another surprise by Byrsocopus [IV, 3]. If he should intrude again unexpectedly he will be sent to fetch more water. Porna is sure that however wet and cold he is he will not refuse, giving Hieronymus a chance to escape. Agreed on this scheme, the three go back in. While time is left, Porna wants to enjoy the priest some more. It might be said of Renaissance lovers in general that the men are never lame and the women, always game. In this case, however, the lady seems the more demanding.

No sooner do Porna, Hieronymus, and Paedisca recede than Georgus reappears [IV, 4]. He has hunted all over his house but found neither Andrisca nor the makings for supper. She has taken all the victuals to the tavern, he says, and that is where he also goes. Seeing him wroth, the owner backs inside and closes the door. "Come out here," Georgus barks. "Where is the wife?" "My wife is at home. Why do you ask?" the innkeeper evasively replies. When Georgus makes quite clear whose wife he means, the taverner mendaciously declares "Yours isn't here." Georgus wants to see for himself but is barred with the excuse that in his excitement he would upset everyone. He is urged to go away and quiet down. When he asks again where Andrisca is, the voice through the door growls "What's that to me? Watch over your wife yourself! Go home!" This leads Georgus to think that even though the barkeep is a worthless chap he is nevertheless wiser and more levelheaded. Taking his advice, Georgus will be calm and wait for Andrisca, readying two staves while he does. With his last doubts dispelled, he procrastinates no longer in preparing for their duel. Even so, on seeing his neighbor come home, he realizes that this friend is in a worse fix than he.

Byrsocopus is despondent. He assumes that "the wife with her confederates" will be eating up his food and that they will send him like an idiot to draw more water [IV, 5]. He does not know for certain that Porna was playing games with him when he came for lunch, but he suspects more than she gives him credit for, eating out his heart in impotent inertia. "Am I not wretched," he groans, with the self-pity of Galenus in *Petriscus*. Georgus greets him and relates what Andrisca has been doing. Perhaps to encourage his friend he explains that he is definitely going to fight her for the pants. Byrsocopus approves but views his own situation as gloomier. To impress on him just how gloomy it really is, Georgus tells him all that he observed during the sheet-folding and water-drawing dupery, hoping that the full truth will shock him out of lethargy. "Right now the priest is in the house with your wife," Georgus adds as a further jolt. (He must have seen them together in IV, 3.) His technique works, for Brysocopus is electrified to hear his suspicions confirmed so blatantly. Georgus accordingly takes him inside, out of earshot, for some man-to-man advice. When they disappear, the dionysian women enter and for the last time howl their "Iacche Bacche," after which the chorus of boys sings of male superiority, as "documented" by the story of Adam and Eve.

Macropedius has done a good job of differentiating the two husbands, particularly since their situations are similar. Like uxorius Galenus, both tend toward passivity in dealing with their wives, but Georgus is different in being merely so scrupulous as to seem indecisive. His delay in taking action is only a measure of his concern for equity, and it is characteristic that he proposes a duel, in which Andrisca, who smacks of the legendary Brunhild, can conceivably prevail. Georgus never relinquishes his rightful claim to mastery, but he hesitates to enforce it. He eschews violence as a gentleman, even though the effect on Andrisca is that of cowardice and effeminacy. She is not a woman to respect soft speech when no big stick enforces it, particularly when it comes from a farmer, for like most townspeople of her century she seems contemptuous of peasants as a class. We wonder why she married Georgus. In contrast to him, Byrsocopus is not strong-minded enough to act on his own initiative. The tanner is confronted by an ecclesiastic who in all likelihood can count on powerful support, yet Porna alone has him completely under her thumb. He must be aroused by his friend before he will put an end to the indignities which he has gutlessly endured, overreacting then in the release of his pent-up resentment.

At the outset of Act V the innkeeper has informed Andrisca of her husband's anger, and she has accepted the prospect of combat. In fact, she welcomes it. We find her in front of the tavern, with the proprietor warning her against the match. She turns a deaf ear, saying that she was born with the spirit of a male, which has been fortified by successful battles and by wine consumed during the day. Her courage is largely Dutch indeed, and her adviser cautions against presumption. At play men will let themselves be beaten, he says in regard to her previous victories, whereas contending in earnest is altogether different. "The fists of men are very heavy," he warns. Be they of bronze or lead, Andrisca insists that she will oppose them with her featherweight dukes. She is not to be dissuaded. Wary of alienating her, the innkeeper takes a different tack and urges her, since she will fight, to fight with vigor. His encouragement swells to flattery. If she wins, she will have gained not only dominion over her husband but immortal fame as well, he gushes. This fulsome support Andrisca appreciates. In preparation for the fray she wants more wine, so the host guides her back to the bottles.

The sparks from Georgus' mettle have fallen upon ready tinder in the tanner's indignation, for in V, 2 Byrsocopus comes from his shop aflame, dragging a horse's hide and carrying a whip. On Georgus' advice he intends to fetch the water which he expects Porna to request and to dump it over her. After she has taken off her dripping clothes he will beat her raw, rub her with salt, and sew her up in the salted hide to mellow. Even if she does not ask for water he will draw some, in order to let the priest depart, with whom he is not presently concerned. Calmly he knocks at his door, as though nothing were unusual.

The house is locked, and for a moment no one opens, indicating that Hieronymus is within [V, 3]. Byrsocopus has to shout several times before Porna appears. Seeing him wet and dirty again, she affects sympathy, orders the fire stoked as before, and asks him to bring more water from the river. No sooner is he gone than she bids her "joy" adieu, but only for a couple of hours. She will put Byrsocopus to bed shortly after supper, she promises Hieronymus, and the two of them will be free to resume where they left off! To the maid she insists that everything be in order and nothing allowed to displease her husband. Already he is trudging back, muttering darkly.

Georgus comes from his house to watch what transpires [V, 4]. Beholding his friend submissively toting water, he expresses pity, not realizing that this show of docility is only a prelude to the rebelliousness which he has awakened. Byrsocopus notices Georgus eyeing him, and his awareness of being observed seems to make him more resolute, as does the thought that one show of unforgettable force will end his tribulations. The house is still not in order as he arrives, so Porna gives him a second pitcher to fill. At this effrontery the tanner excoriates her. "Am I supposed to feed your sloth, your folly, your lust, you sacerdotal prostitute?" he roars, throwing the water all over her. "If you need more, go yourself; you're also wet," he taunts triumphantly. Stunned, Porna cries to the audience as citizens of Bunschoten that she is being mistreated. Her husband replies that she has not suffered the hundredth part of what she deserves, whereupon she reviles him in return, threatening to cut his throat or to poison him in revenge for being doused. When she rushes into the house to change her clothes, Georgus, chuckling gleefully, remarks that if this show continues as well as it has begun none could prove better. Byrsocopus waits outside, giving Porna an opportunity to undress.

In Section IV of the Introduction to this study reference was made to the stretching of time here in *Andrisca*. The tanner stands quietly while Georgus' servant Ponus ("toil") comes famished from the fields to ask for food, sees his master fashioning cudgels, thinks that he himself will be drubbed, is told that they are for a "bitch" *(canis)* that made off with the groceries, and is sent to buy more fare for dinner [V, 5 and 6]. The few seconds that Porna needs to fling off her soggy garments have been lengthened to a couple of minutes. The explanation for Brysocopus' suspended animation is not carelessness or naïveté by the author but rather his studied intention to heighten suspense by braking the action at a crucial juncture. The resultant distortion he rightly accounted of no moment, and it was probably not noticed by his viewers.

Whip in hand and horse's hide over his shoulder, Byrsocopus now enters his house [V, 7]. Georgus draws closer, in order to hear what goes on, but Porna wails so loudly that he might remain at his own doorstep. Mercilessly she is tanned. When she calls for help, Paedisca runs outdoors to arouse the audience as men of Bunschoten, and Georgus becomes a little concerned himself. "The master is murdering his wife with a scourge," sobs the maid. His belatedly aroused virility has made Byrsocopus downright virulent. Georgus hushes Paedisca and sends her back so as not to damage her people's reputation. He guarantees that Porna will not be killed. Already her voice is failing, and the whip yields to salt and hide. "What land, what sea, or what barbarians have ever tormented anyone in such a way as this?" she rightfully protests. Georgus, though, thinks highly of it and tells the audience that treating a misbehaving wife "so sweetly" engenders domestic peace and prosperity.

Byrsocopus has the sewed-up sinner brought outside as an example of how balky women should be broken [V, 8]. Though the worst of his procedure is over, yet a little remains. If he failed to catch what Porna and the maid were singing as they folded the sheet at noon, he understands in retrospect. To get even with Paedisca, along with his spouse, he makes the girl dance and second him in crooning the following ditty: "My wife was in love with a priest./ And wouldn't bear me in the least./ Now whipped and with salt rubbed in,/ She's stitched in a horse's skin." Other gibes draw a plea for compassion from inside the nag. Georgus tells Porna to promise obedience and he will have her released. With no hesitation she complies, explicitly abjuring further adultery, but Byrsocopus is unbending. He orders her lugged indoors and left till the morrow. "You see?" burbles Georgus, "You see how effective punishment is?" "Very effective indeed," his protégé complacently agrees. Now it is Georgus' own turn to subdue a fractious wife.

As though knowing that she is expected, Andrisca exits from the tavern, escorted by the owner, who is giving her last-minute pointers [V, 9]. Like Byrsocopus he will be an onlooker. Georgus displays a pair of trousers to the audience and proclaims them the victor's prize. Andrisca is startled to see the staves, for she has expected to box. Her objection provokes a peroration by her husband in which he sets forth the reasons for the duel, explaining that he has not desired contention but considers a showdown his last resort. Whoever carries off the breeches will forever rule the house, he closes, cut short by Andrisca's impatience. She gets her choice of clubs, and after the formal exchange of a kiss the contest begins. With a vicious swing Andrisca deals a staggering blow, prompting Byrsocopus to shout that Georgus is done for if struck on the head. This is true, and her cudgel gives Andrisca a much better chance to win than her bare hands would. In his *Courage the Adventuress (Lebensbeschreibung der Erzbetrügerin und Landstörzerin Courasche,* 1670) Hans Jakob Christoffel von Grimmelshausen (1622?–76), the German novelist of the Thirty Years' War, portrays just such an incident as Byrsocopus warns against. Challenged by her third husband to a similar engagement with sticks the morning after their wedding night, Courage triumphs by knocking her fatuous groom unconscious. Andrisca is not so fortunate, however, for her initial, vinous gusto soon flags; and Georgus, having conserved energy, easily proves superior. He indulges in revenge no less than Byrsocopus, flailing his wife like the grain on his threshing floor. When he stops—perhaps from exhaustion more than pity—the humbled scold surrenders both pants and authority. The tanner and the innkeeper intercede for her, and Georgus agrees to pardon if she pledges to obey. At last imbued with the respect which all along she surely wanted but which her husband seemed not to warrant, she promises eager submissiveness. With a second, heartier embrace their truce is sealed. Byrsocopus will free Porna at once, and Georgus invites them to the dinner which he sent his servant Ponus to procure. The innkeeper is also welcome, provided he be honest. Byrsocopus goes home, the taverner returns momentarily to his establishment, and Andrisca withdraws to set the table.

Apparently two hours are supposed to have passed during the course of the last six scenes, because at this point Hieronymus creeps back. As in II, 4, Georgus hides, perhaps in his doorway, to watch what happens. Bringing another flagon of wine, the priest calls mutedly for Porna, and Paedisca admits him as if nothing has changed [V, 10]. For a few seconds near silence reigns, with Georgus muttering that Ponus must be feasting on the grocery money, to be gone so long. Then a tumult erupts. Byrsocopus bellows to Paedisca to pull and rip, stripping Porna's man of the cloth. Indifferent now to the sin of striking an ecclesiastic, he veritably pummels Hieronymus, who totters into sight with the admission that he is being dealt with as he deserves. Literally unfrocked, he flees in his underwear.

In the final scene [V, 11] Byrsocopus rejoins Georgus, bringing the abandoned flask and word that Porna, who has been crying for shame, will be along at dusk. Ponus comes back with the food; the innkeeper strolls over; and all go in with Andrisca for the party. Like Galenus at the conclusion of *Petriscus*, Georgus announces that the actors have nothing for the audience to eat. Spectators must dine at home. In a nine-line epilogue we are told that a compliant, honest, and sober wife should be cherished. The "weaker vessel" should be treated with kid gloves. If she is shameless, wanton, or given to drink, however, she must be brought into conformity with her husband's "upright conduct." Nothing is more harmful to children and ménage than a bad woman.

While *Andrisca* is Macropedius' most misogynous play, combining both of the commonest female types in late medieval satirical literature, it is also his most dramatic, insofar as it contains the most vigorous action. (*Hecastus* will prove to be the most suspenseful.) Though an intertwining of two threads, *Andrisca* is effectively wrought and essentially unflawed, like *Petriscus* and *Bassarus*. With allowances for comic exaggeration, behavior rings true throughout, including the transformation of the wives under duress. As long as their husbands lead, they will be content to follow, aware that they can no longer flout the men with impunity. Each of the four main characters is unique within the play, and equal attention is given to each. For this reason, however, the title is inappropriate. As we have seen, Andrisca is not even the key figure. That is Georgus, who transforms the whole quartet, beginning with himself.

In the contemporary vernacular farce *Plaijerwater* a woman acting sick sends her concerned and obtuse husband Werenbracht on an extended wild-goose chase for *plaijer* ("hoax") water, which she says is the only thing to relieve her illness. While she is entertaining a priest after his departure, Werenbracht is smuggled back into the house by a poulterer, who carries him in a basket. The priest sings ridicule of him, thinking him absent, and the poultryman summons him in song from his hiding place. *Plaijer* water rains on the lovers in the form of blows. If Macropedius used this play or a variant which also lacked the sheet-folding motif, Chapter 123 of the fourteenth-century *Gesta Romanorum* can have supplied him with the addition.

Being sewed in a horse's skin occurs in another sixteenth-century Dutch comedy, *Moorkensvel (Moorken's Hide)*, where a merely bossy woman is the butt. Knowing that the Latin word for "hide" *(scortum)* also means "whore," Macropedius switched her punishment to Porna, both because of the pun and because an adulteress deserves the brutality more. The hide suggested in addition that Porna's husband be a tanner. Folk literature easily furnished the conjugal duel as a substitute in the Andrisca-Georgus plot. It occurs, like the "smoke" motif, in Hans Sachs' *Bad Smoke,* for instance, as well as in Dutch comedy. A battle with a man is also more appropriate for a virago.

Although *Andrisca* is indeed filled with action, it does not have one moment of especially concentrated tension which can be called *the* climax. Each of the two plots has instead its own culmination, the castigation of the wife. *Bassarus* is more curious from the point of view of structure, for it is an agglomeration of several different, though congenial plots, the main one of which is not the most dynamic. In this play, though, as in nearly all by Macropedius, story and structure are secondary to character. The delicacy and humorousness of its characterization make *Bassarus* the most charming work which the Utrecht dramaturge wrote.

III   *Bassarus*

In 1496 the German jurist and Hebraist Johann Reuchlin composed two comedies which, we are told in the preface to the 1535 edition of *The Rebels* and *Aluta,* induced Macropedius to try his own hand at writing for the stage. The earlier play by Reuchlin, entitled *Sergius, or Head of the Head (Sergius vel capitis caput,* first published ca. 1504), is a static, unarticulated dialogue in three short acts satirizing primarily a hated Augustinian who wielded such influence at the court of Duke Eberhard VI of Württemberg as to be "the head of the head." From him Reuchlin was forced in 1496 to take refuge at Heidelberg, where he vented his rancor in this grotesque portrayal of an encounter between a wit named Buttubatta and a group of parasites. Buttubatta is prevailed upon to display a filthy, fetid skull which supposedly belonged to one Sergius, an apostate monk in the service of Mohammed. Although we will meet a minstrel in *Lazarus the Beggar* who is called a Buttubatta, *Sergius* cannot have inspired Macropedius so much as Reuchlin's more felicitous second play, a 470-line farce generally dubbed *Henno* in preference to the actual title, *Scaenica progymnasmata* (first published 1498). On the theme of this work—deceiving those who are themselves deceivers—Macropedius constructed *Bassarus,* though out of different plot material [9] and with superior skill.

Henno is divided into five acts of two scenes each, with a chorus separating one act from the next. It opens with the peasant woman Elsa complaining over the prodigality of her husband Henno, who has good reason to comment, like the title figure in the French farce *Pathelin* (ca. 1465), that despite their labor they have nothing. In self-defense, no doubt, Elsa has become a skinflint. Even now Henno wants to have a new coat made from material bought on credit, he informs her. For his confidant and servant Dromo he has a different tale, however. Eight gold pieces which Elsa buried in the barnyard he has discovered and kept. With these he can pay for the cloth, and he sends Dromo straightway to the moneylender and draper Danista ("usurer"). He makes the mistake, though, of saying "Be sure not to give the money to anyone else," for Dromo, another Eulenspiegel, takes him literally.

Meanwhile Elsa makes one of her frequent visits to her hidden hoard. Like Euclio in Plautus' *Pot of Gold (Aulularia),* she lives for her treasure. Appalled at finding it stolen, she calls her neighbor Greta for advice. In town is an astrologer, says the friend, skilled in the ways of the "astrolip" (i.e., astrolabe).[10] For a gulden he will reveal the thief.

Alcabicius, as the charlatan is called, divines with satisfactory hocus-pocus that the robber is an elderly rustic in a red hat and a deerskin vest. "Sounds like my husband," Elsa remarks. He likes to drink. "It must be him," she says. He goes often to the public baths. "It's him." He whores terrifically. "That's not him," she decides. "When we're in bed he hardly kisses me." In short, Alcabicius concludes, the culprit is someone from Elsa's farm. The "laws of astronomy" forbid the seer to disclose any more.

As the two women leave, they chance upon Henno arguing with his menial. Danista, it seems, is retaining both the cloth and the cash, requesting that Henno call on him in two days. The truth is, however, that Dromo still has the eight gold pieces and has sold the material to a visitor from out of town. The money made on this sale he has likewise pocketed. Henno is too dull to suspect him, but when they visit Danista at the appointed time, the merchant takes the go-between to court.

Dromo hires a shyster named Petrucius, who proposes a subterfuge used by his French colleague Pathelin: No matter what he is asked during the trial, the defendant should utter only "blay" ("ble"). On complying, Dromo is acquitted. As a supposed deaf-mute he is unable to testify, and the plaintiff has no witness to call. When Petrucius demands payment, his client continues to bleat, tricking the lawyer with the lawyer's own tricks.[11] In the final scene Dromo explains to Henno, Elsa, and Greta all that has transpired and sues for the hand of the daughter Abra, since he has been declared innocent. The parents consent, and Elsa is even willing for him to keep her savings as a partial dowry.

She is at fault in her miserliness; Henno, in his theft; Danista, in his usury (though no instance of it is seen); and Petrucius, in his legal practices, yet not because of his courtroom ruse, as we would naturally suppose. No criticism is made on that score. He is held to be culpable only in stipulating as his fee a percentage of the money at stake. All of Dromo's victims nevertheless deserve to be cheated, so that his highhandedness is slightly extenuated. In like manner the dishonest draper in *Pathelin* is hoodwinked by the pettifogging title figure, who in turn is duped by Dromo's equivalent, the roguish shepherd. Reuchlin's portrayal of character is much cruder than in *Pathelin* and weakest in his two principal personages, Henno and the servant. The man Friday is a blackguard unworthy of his happy end, and the master, who takes everything at face value, scarcely has more brains than Buttubatta's hollow skull. This shortcoming is emphasized by the fact that the best scene is the women's session with Alcabicius, in which neither Henno nor Dromo appears (and which is superfluous). By contrast Macropedius matches the unknown author of *Pathelin* in demonstrating what a real dramatist can do with the same idea.

In the dedicatory preface to *Bassarus*, addressed simply to "his Albert," he alleges that he is offering this comedy as a gift and that it is not to be printed. The reason, he avers, is "because some people might take umbrage at the inclusion of a priest who, otherwise upright, tends to hoard his substance a little more than is proper." This is an understatement, for the ecclesiastic in question is not only avaricious, though cupidity is presented as his worst fault. More scandalous is the fact that he frequently entertains a wench named Corasium ("little girl"), telling the world that she is his niece. The author probably preferred not to call attention to this point in view of the criticism which he was already receiving as a satirist. In the prologue he relates that no play has been given in a year, partly because of hostility stirred up by the belief that he has been twitting all ecclesiastics and mayors *(seculares praesides)*—apparently a reference to the figures of the pastor and the mayor in *Bassarus*.

Another reason for the suspension of performances, we are told, has been opposition to school theater in general. Most of the prologue is accordingly devoted to another defense of the genre. "I by no means deny that tender and unsettled minds can be corrupted by filthy language or gestures, such as should not be seen or heard on the stage," the speaker concedes. "Yet more grace and probity can frequently be discerned in those who freely and successfully take part in dramas, I dare say, than in the people who, because of stupidity or ignorance, are unfit for effective action (like asses that dance to the lyre) or who retreat into corners out of laziness, idling indolently while others eagerly perform or laughing at an actor's slip of the tongue." Macropedius did not consider his own comedies harmful, though he subsequently yielded to objections in ceasing to rework farcical material in the manner of Reuchlin. Fortunately he was not intimidated to the point of suppressing *Bassarus*. We can be sure that he wanted it printed, for otherwise he would not have sent a copy to his friend Albert, who rightly understood that the request not to publish it was only a ploy to forestall further censure.

The setting is a sixteenth-century village street in the Netherlands. Bassarus' house, Hieronymus' house, and a tavern are to be imagined side by side and ranged, let us say, from left to right as the audience would see them. Just off-stage to the right is the local church, flanked by a cemetery which is visible and in which are a charnel house and a gallows. From the last, two corpses are hanging. Out of sight beyond the church are to be pictured the homes of the mayor Euergetes ("benefactor," possibly from Luke 22:25 of the Greek New Testament) and his parasite Creoborus ("meat devourer"). The time is afternoon of Shrove Tuesday, in early March. In keeping with the occasion, the chorus between acts is grotesquely masked.

The choral odes to *Bassarus* are distinctive. Not only do all four have the same form and the same number of strophes (three), but the first three also respectively denounce gluttony, greed, and ambition as silly, while each stanza of the fourth praises the opposite of one of these vices as wise. A translation of the fourth chorus will help to clarify the matter:

> To eat in moderation
> Is wise, is wise, is wise.
> To flee from sordid Venus
> Is wise, is wise, is wise, is wise.
>
> To spurn both silver and gold
> Is wise, is wise, is wise.
> To search for genuine wealth
> Is wise, is wise, is wise, is wise.
>
> To scorn esteem and fame
> Is wise, is wise, is wise.
> To adopt humility
> Is wise, is wise, is wise, is wise.[12]

In no other play by Macropedius are the choruses so artfully arranged, though the repetition in the refrains here may cloy.

Because of Mardi Gras, Bassarus ("fox"), the village sexton, wants to invite friends to dinner. As the play begins he dispatches his wife Bassara to the market for capons, ducks, a goose, and a shoulder of mutton. She asks whether the pastor will attend and is assured that he will be the guest of honor. "If luck is with us, we'll milk him nicely," Bassarus chuckles. "As we've already done from time to time," his wife responds approvingly. She expresses the fear, however, that Hieronymus' gout will keep him at home. Bassarus tells her to go, noticing that a thunderstorm is brewing. "What thunder are you dreaming of in the month of March, my good man?" Bassara scoffs, only to be shown black clouds glowering in the south. No sooner does she set out than a clock chimes three, the hour to ring for vespers. Bassarus changes his mind and stops her, for at church he might learn something useful from the pastor. Only now the thought of stealing enough food from his guests to avoid buying any seems first to occur to him. As she enters the house, Bassara reports that the priest has sent his housekeeper Graidium ("old hag") to the market.

In the same moment Creoborus approaches alone. Alluding to Aeschylus in *Seven against Thebes* (224–25), he grumbles that according to poets Obedience was the wife of Jove the Redeemer and their daughter was Success but that all Joves (i.e., patrons) are ruinous now and married to Harpies, with Misfortune as their offspring [I, 2]. He always obliges the rich, this descendant of Colax maintains, but his reward is forever misery. His loquacious musings are interrupted by Bassarus, who inquires why he is not waiting on his Jove. Bitterly the sponger complains that when he congratulated Euergetes for hanging two thieves today he was told to go to the devil. "If I had snitched on some guilty rich men that he could have strung up in his smoke chamber,[13] I'd be like Ganymede," he fumes. "As it is, like some harbinger of evil I've been banished from the pantry." In the manner of Sycasta in *Petriscus* he serves as an informer, a matter which adds to his contemptibleness. The mayor in turn is objectionable as a judge, since he profits from the prosecution of the wealthy—evidently through the acceptance of bribes.

Bassarus suggests that Euergetes may have prepared a special meal inadequate for his wife, himself, and a glutton. Creoborus relates that the maid was indeed fixing a fat goose stuffed with eels but that he for his own part would be content with beef and pork—in addition to sow's udder, sausage, and tripe. All that he has at home is a little bag of walnuts, bought to give friends on Mardi Gras, he swears. This information confirms Bassarus in the plan to rob his guests of the wherewithal to regale them. He promises a splendid goose for dinner in return for the key to the mayor's residence, which the parasite has had for some time. Because it is together with the key to his own house, Creoborus hands over both. After being told to join Euergetes at church, he leaves, and in the same moment Graidium returns with her groceries.

Before proceeding inside, she calls the pastor out in order to show him in daylight what handsome poultry she has bought—for a small price, as she is careful to make clear [I, 3]. When she goes in to prepare it, Bassarus comes over with an invitation to dinner. Hieronymus thanks him politely but firmly declines, alleging that his gout worsens in the evening. It is to no avail that Bassarus, pleading for company, offers to haul the sufferer in a wagon. Forced to give up, he mutters that the priest is a thorough hypocrite who deserves to be plundered of his dainties. Hieronymus grumpily orders Graidium to help him to church, too impatient in his ill temper to lock the door, despite his housekeeper's reminder that because of such carelessness a freshly slaughtered pig was filched from the house two days ago. "Never mind that," he snaps. "I can't dawdle!" The sexton has finished ringing, and they see him off-stage, talking to the mayor. "Make sure he doesn't know what goodies we have," Hieronymus cautions, unaware that the slyboots already knows and is plotting to seize them.

Bassarus does not stay for the vesper service but returns [I, 4], gloating that the mayor has also thought of robbing the pastor of food to be served him. This agreement of (albeit crafty) minds tends to argue the justice of the caper, lessening any guilt. Bassarus further vindicates himself by asserting "Then it'll be plain to everyone how false the wily dog's excuse was for refusing to come to my party." Hieronymus will be forced to accept the invitation when he finds his own dinner stolen. Knowing that the priest leaves his door unlocked, Bassarus tries it at once and finds it open. "Why not break in?" he shrugs.

While he is at his mischief his wife steps out, observing apprehensively that a storm really is threatening. Even so, she dare not go shopping unbidden. She seems a far cry from Mysandra and Andrisca, though Bassarus calls her a "cacolalia" and complains of her yapping. She is pert, but she is no shrew. Instead, like Elsa at the beginning of *Henno*, she sighs over a married woman's servitude. Soon Bassarus scurries furtively from the scene of his crime, hiding Graidium's poultry under his cloak. Darting past his quizzical mate, he tells her to hush and to a wait a moment while he disappears into their house. "Has he made off with the pastor's whole pantry the way he took his pork before?" she wonders. "You hit the nail on the head!" he exclaims, coming back with his booty in a basket. He instructs her to hurry to the market and to return as though having shopped. During her absence he will watch the premises and decide what to do about Euergetes.

Between Acts I and II a quarter of an hour passes. Daylight has begun to fade as Bassarus comes outside again with his two young sons, Harpax (like the knave in *Aluta*) and Phorus ("thief"), who are wearing monstrous masks for the celebration of Mardi Gras. He gives Harpax the key to the mayor's house and proposes a method for ransacking the kitchen. At dinner time (seven o'clock) Euergetes' wife will leave with her maid to look for her husband, who will not have come home because of the dinner invitation extended at church in I, 3. She will assume that he is here, Bassarus predicts. As soon as she and the girl have set out, Harpax should slip in. Phorus having meanwhile pilfered Creoborus' walnuts, the two brothers are to meet at the charnel and come home together. "If you handle this properly, the way I hope," says their father, "there won't be anything funnier or more talked about. You'll be helped by the dark and the thunder and lightning." Hearing the church doors creak to emit the pastor now that the vesper service is over, Bassarus retreats inside and the boys go to the entrance of the pub [14] to wait for dusk.

Hieronymus hobbles into sight, leaning on Graidium [II, 2]. "Get over here on my right!" he barks. "How many times do I have to tell you?" When she replies that it is his left foot which hurts worse, he grumbles about old women always having some excuse for contradicting whatever a man says. "Don't you understand that the better you prop me on the right the more you stabilize the left?" he scolds. "Walk gently!" After a pause, during which he ponders the delicious feast scheduled for the evening, he asks Graidium sweetly how she is going to prepare the food. Offended by his previous arrogance, she tells him curtly to let her handle the cuisine or to hire somebody else. "Don't be angry, honey," he wheedles. "Blame my sharp words on the ailment." Easily appeased in her devotion to him, she explains that she will roast the capon and nine birds, while the two chickens she will parboil and cook in wine seasoned with saffron, pepper, cinnamon, and sugar. "That's a banquet for Venus, dear Graidium," the lecherous curmudgeon drools, associating the goddess with Corasium, on whose account he rejected Bassarus' invitation. Having reached his house, he sends Graidium to his "niece" with word to come at dusk. While she is gone he will wait by the door.

The sexton comes out to see whether his wife is on her way back [II, 3]. "Females," he observes, probably speaking for Macropedius, "are all a worthless, vain, stubborn, and impudent lot!" Eyeing Hieronymus next door as Bassara arrives, he tells her sotto voce to show what she has presumably bought. In declamatory tones aimed at the pastor he raves about the capon, and pulling out the chickens, goose, and other poultry, asks Bassara why she has purchased so much. "What are the friends you invited supposed to eat?" she asks, cooperating in his knavery as readily as Guillemette assists her equally vulpine husband Pathelin. Bassarus announces for his neighbor's benefit that he expects no one to come in the bad weather. "The pastor doesn't want to," he emphasizes. "Doesn't want to?" Bassara cries with histrionic disappointment. "I had so hoped he would!" To himself Hieronymus mutters that indeed he would, had Graidium not brought the same items. "Go cook everything for tomorrow," Bassarus concludes, dismissing his wife. He himself lingers to overhear the report from Corasium. Tripping back to beat the rain, Graidium relates that the maiden is in demand but will oblige Hieronymus tonight because of his kindness, his regard, and his gifts. "Let's go in," the goat bleats contentedly. "My affairs are all shipshape." "Watch out you don't sail into Charybdis," the sexton warns in an aside, likewise withdrawing as Graidium helps Hieronymus through their doorway.

About ten minutes of plot time elapse before Act III opens. The rain has begun to pour with a strong wind, and the air is becoming murky. Bassarus steps out, exclaiming over the gloom, which gives the impression of Judgment Day, he says. Though in a sense he is making this a day of judgment by exposing deception, his mood is anything but religious, for he remarks "It's the first of March—the month, they think, in which the world began. I'd say we're about to end in it, too. Let's eat and drink, regardless!" Suddenly in the cloud burst Euergetes and his valet appear, sprinting from the direction of the church and followed by Creoborus. "Forgetting his dignity," says Bassarus of the mayor, "he isn't ashamed to slacken the reins like the rabble. The rains won't slacken for him, though." Arrived at the sexton's stoop, Euergetes makes no secret of the fact that the "turbulence of the elements" has forced him to come rather against his will, even though he accepted the invitation in I, 3. "How lucky for me that you can't deny us your company—even if you'd like to," Bassarus wryly comments. The mayor asks about Hieronymus' food and is pleased to hear that it was successfully bagged. Seeing Creoborus stand in the downpour, Bassarus inquires why he does not join them. "He offends me with his impudence," Euergetes sniffs. The egalitarian

host nevertheless calls the grateful parasite into the house, sending the mayor and the servant Dromo after him. Because Hieronymus' door is opening, Bassarus himself remains to eavesdrop,
sitting down on his steps. The rain is already abating, but the fog
grows thicker, night is falling, and lightning flashes from time to
time. Phorus and Harpax probably leave the tavern at this point
and go off-stage on their appointed missions, though exactly when
they set out can only be a guess, for no indication is given in the
text.

The pastor puffs into sight, in a dudgeon over the discovery of
his loss and the ruination of his evening [III, 2]. Graidium notes
that the thief who stole their dinner must be well acquainted
with their house, because she hid things cleverly. "Yes, you did
everything cleverly," her master snarls, "but if you had just
locked the door you wouldn't have brought me in my misery to
this ultimate sorrow!" He takes no more responsibility than Galenus in *Petriscus,* even though Graidium reminds him that his
haste and carelessness were to blame. Like both Galenus and
Byrsocopus he pities himself. "What good will quarreling do?"
he sighs. "I'm the one who suffers. Vexed by gout and rent by
village envy, I own little, owe much, and can't keep the mite I
have, thanks to the gall of thieves. What's left to me but a rope to
hang myself? To cap it all, the girl is due. It wouldn't be proper
to send her away, and she'll call me a terrible skinflint. Yet if I
keep her, gourmet that she is, I don't have anything to serve but
uncured sausages. She'll never believe what's happened." So loyal
is Graidium that she willingly panders to his vice. To make him
happy, she offers to arrange for them to eat with Bassarus, after
all. Hieronymus doubts that they would be welcome now, but she
is confident, remembering all the poultry which the sexton displayed in II, 3. (She was off-stage at the time, but she can still
have seen it.) In desperation the pastor tells her to try her luck.
As she leaves, he goes inside, with Corasium flitting through the
twilight and into the house behind the spinster's back.

Bassarus greets Graidium and asks what brings her out in this
weather [III, 3]. She says that she has come because of a great
misfortune. Acting startled, he inquires what has happened, elicit-
ing a tale of two little birds bought for a light repast and gob-
bled by cats during the vesper service. At such a fib Bassarus
is really startled. "There's more," Graidium adds. "A nice young

lady is coming over to visit the pastor in his infirmity, and we don't have a thing to offer her." Magnanimously Bassarus implores them to share his abundance, muttering under his breath at the hag's mendacity when she departs. He asks her, furthermore, to bring two sausages from the pig that was slaughtered, and she claims that all were stolen. Many were, as we later learn (V, 4), but Hieronymus mentions above (III, 2) that sausages are the only meat left in his house.

Between Scenes 3 and 4 of the third act Heino the coppersmith comes onto the stage with a couple of pots and lies down under the gallows in the cemetery. The sexton, still standing at his door, does not see him because it has grown completely dark. To himself Bassarus complains of womankind's incorrigible penuriousness [III, 4], a notion new in Macropedius' plays. Aluta, Andrisca, and Porna are even the opposite of moneygrubbing. Along with Bassara and Graidium, however, we will subsequently find tightfisted females in *Hecastus* and *Lazarus the Beggar*. The idea that women are naturally grasping was adopted from Reuchlin's *Henno*, where in I, 1 the title figure speaks of his wife's hoarding—further evidence that *Bassarus* was written under the immediate influence of the *Scaenica progymnasmata*. As the sacristan ends his misogynous tirade, directed especially at his wife and Graidium, a thunderclap resounds, jolting both him and the tinker, who cries out in alarm. "Anyone's a fool who doesn't get himself home, yet somebody shouted over there by the gallows," Bassarus remarks. He is about to go inside when he sees the pastor limping out on a cane and leading his girlfriend, with the housekeeper lighting the way. Gesturing toward the rickety Romeo, Bassarus sneers "Listen to how sweetly he chatters with his chatty old bag and his baggage!"

"Come, niece," Hieronymus coos [III, 5]. "Come to my left, Corasium dear. I'm taking you to a scrumptious banquet." She is not impressed, for she assumes that he is simply avoiding the cost of feeding her himself. "I hate your paltriness and your meals begged from other folks," she rasps. Nervously trying to soothe her, he alleges, more accurately than he suspects, that he gave their impecunious host meat and a number of delicacies for the dinner. He calls on Graidium for confirmation and, to furbish his image, demands compliments which Bassarus supposedly paid him. The housekeeper manages to think up a couple, but he shrieks for more. When she remembers to say that the sexton welcomes them, Corasium consents to go without demur. "What cunning!" exclaims Bassarus, who has overheard this exchange. "Who wouldn't respond to such trickery with tricks? A hard knot calls for a hard wedge," he moralizes in righteous self-exculpation. As though venturing outdoors just at this moment, he greets the arrivals and ushers them in. The gouty cripple gasps that he is so exhausted from his hike that he can scarcely yawn. After the guests have entered the house, Bassarus stays outside for a moment to vent his satisfaction. "Now I have both of the misers," he gloats. "I'm squeezing one. If I can wring out each of them, how jolly!" At this instant he hears a nut cracked at the cemetery, signaling the successful robbing of Creoborus. Reassured on that score, he goes in to tend his party.

In III, 6 Phorus prepares us for one of the subordinate plots which fill Act IV by announcing that he will munch nuts in the charnel house while waiting for his brother. In III, 7 the coppersmith sets up the other subplot by rising to inform us that according to an old saying lightning never strikes a privy or a gallows. During one flash he glimpses the corpses swinging over his head but assures himself that he is safe. "Go on dangling, you two," he addresses them. "I'll just sleep here till somebody happens along and wakes me up." Thereupon he flops back down and probably ends Act III with a snore.

There is no time lapse as Bassarus opens his door to begin the fourth act. He and the mayor stand in the entrance, looking out at the coruscation and the gusty wind. At every flicker Euergetes cringes. "Jupiter is hopping mad, by George!" he exclaims. "I'd hardly dare set foot outside, even with a light, and that fellow brags of going all the way to the gallows!" "That fellow" is Creoborus, whom the mayor summons with a string of unflattering epithets, like "chief of sloths" and "prince of braggarts." The parasite is not an idle boaster, however, for he is ready to make good his claim. Both he and Euergetes have offered to donate something to the dinner, but the sexton and the mayor have agreed to absolve him from his contribution for the sake of a little carnival sport. If he will mark both posts of the gallows with chalk in the dark and the blustery weather, Euergetes will make his donation for him. Should he fail, Bassarus will absorb the loss. After reminding the sexton to ring the church bells (a matter clarified in IV, 3) the adventurer prays "May Saint Satiety preserve me" and gropes his way into the night, to disappear at the rear of the stage. As he does so, Bassarus sees a light gleaming near the mayor's house.

Soon Euergetes' wife Merimna ("care") comes searching about, with her maid Droma holding a lantern [IV, 2]. As the sexton predicted in II, 1, she is looking for her husband. This scene is accordingly part of the main plot, in contrast to nearly all the rest of Act IV. By the sound of their voices Euergetes guides Merimna to him. Despite her light, she has difficulty finding the proper place, as though to emphasize the fierceness of the gale and the blackness of the night. Her husband asks her why she did not merely send the maid. "Now somebody will break the door down and clean us out," he forebodes. Droma's timorousness soon explains why Merimna came along. When the master orders the girl back to fetch their goose and mutton, she balks in terror. "Sir! I wouldn't dream of going alone!" she protests. "Really, sir! Even if you kill me, I wouldn't dream of it!" Though Merimna offers to accompany her again, Euergetes calls Dromo outside instead, and his wife goes in to the party. In earshot of Bassarus he first tells both servants to bring the food, two flagons of wine, and a mantle, subsequently drawing his valet aside, to where he thinks the sacristan cannot hear him, and issuing different instructions: Dromo should get only the cloak and say that the victuals were snitched by thieves. The wind, however, carries the deceitful words to Bassarus, who angrily mutters "It'll serve him right to fall in his own ditch—as I hope he will." When the servants leave, a blast of thunder sends the mayor springing into the house, just before the pastor exits from it, bearing Bassarus a torch.

"Why aren't you tolling the bells in this state of utmost peril?" Hieronymus demands [IV, 3]. Asked what clanging bronze will do against lightning and thunder, he cries "Infidel! You doubt that sacred bells can prevail against a storm? Do you think, varlet, that they were consecrated in vain?" How can Bassarus dawdle, he wants to know, in view of this confounding of ether, air, water, and earth, a portent of catastrophe. The sexton replies that since it is nearly dinner time he is waiting to see whether one or two more guests appear. Reminded coolly of his duty, he hands back the torch with a sigh and launches into the raging night. Though motivated primarily by superstition (which Creoborus shares, as was indicated in IV, 1), the priest also has another reason for sending Bassarus away. He calls Graidium outside, where he can now talk to her in private, and complains that with so many people present he may be tricked into contributing some wine [IV, 4]. "If I'd known the mayor was going to be here, I'd never have left home," he says, reaffirming his unsociable niggardliness. While the host is absent he wants to abscond, trusting that something to eat will turn up and preferring to risk the loss of Corasium rather than of anything he owns. His housekeeper acquiesces, but Bassarus foils their scheme by dashing back in mock fright, shouting "Rescue me!" "Did a witch or screech owls bite you?" Hieronymus queries in consternation. Pointing and gasping for breath, Bassarus stammers "In the cemetery! . . . In the charnel house! . . . A devil's crouching!" The credulous priest gasps "With fangs, maybe." Soon he steadies himself, deciding that the prankster must only be pulling their leg, as usual. When Bassarus insists that a demon is crunching bones, Hieronymus jeers with an "oh pooh," convinced that the sexton's tale is just an excuse for not doing his job. "If I weren't hampered by gout, I wouldn't press you in this business," he says, whereupon Bassarus offers to carry him to the church. Hieronymus passes the torch to Graidium and climbs onto the sacristan's shoulders. As Euergetes comes out to see what is happening, Bassarus trots into the dark, the clergyman astride his neck.

When they reach the cemetery, Hieronymus hears shingles thudding on the ground, blown off by the wind, and imagines them to be bones [IV, 5]. At the charnel he is terrified by the cracking of nuts. On catching sight of Phorus' mask in the lightning, he pleads with his mount to turn back, but Bassarus tells him to hush, that his sacraments will protect him. After they have passed the graveyard, Phorus, who has followed them, suddenly inquires "Do you have him? Is he fat?" "Fat or thin," Bassarus replies, setting the anguished rider down, "take him." Phorus screeches "boo," and panic becomes worse than podagra for the whimpering old man, who starts to hop. The mayor, gazing into the dark, anxiously asks the audience what is going on, as Bassarus runs up, with Hieronymus hard on his heels. "Forgetting his gout, even he is sprinting. How he flies!" Euergetes utters in amazement at the priest. Flinging open the door, all tumble into the house, including the speechless Graidium with her torch.

At the end of the fairy tale about Catherlieschen, cited in connection with *Aluta,* the same motif is used. As she is stealing turnips from the local parsonage, a passerby mistakes the slattern for the devil and fetches the pastor for an exorcism. Because of a lame foot, the cleric rides piggyback to the scene but is so scared at the sight of Catherlieschen that he runs away. Lesser known versions are closer to Macropedius' more elaborate treatment, which adds night, spooky locality, and sound effects. (See note nine to this chapter.)

Creoborus, who has been out of sight at the rear of the stage near the cemetery, comes forward for the enactment of another anecdote, explaining in a monologue that he was relieving himself behind the dike [IV, 6]. When he discerns the gallows looming up, hung as it is with dead men, his knees begin to wobble, and he remembers a popular tale of hanged thieves coming down to frighten the living. Getting a grip on himself, he slashes the first post with his chalk. "There's one for the mayor," he says, starting for the other, when lightning flickers and he sees the corpse of a certain Heino stirred by the wind. "What's this? Are you still alive, Heino?" he cries in alarm, waking up Heino the coppersmith, whom he has not noticed. "Who would have killed me?" the tinker queries,[15] putting the scaramouch to flight. Realizing what has happened, the coppersmith bangs on his pots to make Creoborus think Heino the robber is after him, dragging both gallows and chains. He follows the parasite to Bassarus' house and raps for admittance [IV, 7]. Warily the sexton peeps out, letting merriment resound, so that Heino learns of the party. On explaining who he is and what has taken place, he is invited to join the fun and to amuse the other guests with his story.

New hubbub is heard in the night as the boys, still masked, head home with their spoils. Harpax totes two large sacks, and Phorus has his small pouch of nuts. The storm is abating. After pounding on the door, they hand in their haul to their father but remain outside to gamble with Hieronymus and Euergetes, whom Bassarus fetches [IV, 8]. Creoborus comes as an onlooker. What transpires is the portrayal of a widespread carnival custom, according to which silent mummers issued challenges to games of hazard that were considered obligatory for their chosen opponents.[16] Merely growling, Harpax and Phorus squat and place two stivers on the ground. The mayor matches the wager, and each side takes turn rolling the dice. There are four throws in all, and all are won by the boys. The process is repeated with the pastor, who also loses, showing that Providence favors the youths, whose cause is just. Revealing their identity, they say that the winnings will be a contribution to the meal. Bassarus announces that dinner is ready now, so everyone goes inside except Creoborus. At the last minute Bassarus asks him to get his walnuts, perhaps wanting him gone so that the rest can sate themselves in peace. The glutton consents but with the intention of claiming, on his return, that his house has also been ransacked. As a result, he does not even go home between Acts IV and V but simply wanders about.

Although most of the fourth act could be deleted without harm to the main plot, the material added there does not destroy the unity of the play. Instead, it enlivens the work and contributes a strong element of superstitiousness to the personalities of both Creoborus and Hieronymus. The gambling scene affords Harpax and Phorus more exposure and intensifies the carnival atmosphere. By delaying the disclosure of Bassarus' trickery, Act IV as a whole tends to create suspense regarding the effect of this revelation on the other characters.

At the opening of the last act half an hour has elapsed, the storm has passed, and Euergetes' servants are coming back. Because Droma is wailing, Creoborus lurks quietly to hear what is wrong and learns that she is distraught over the missing food. When Dromo tries to console her with the reminder that they are supposed to say that it has been stolen anyway, she sobs that it is tomorrow which worries her. As soon as the master discovers that everything really was pilfered, she will be blamed. "Sufficient for the morrow be the evil thereof," her companion philosophizes, slightly misquoting Matthew 6:34. Indignant at Euergetes' duplicity, Creoborus mutters "Just look at the pettiness and cunning! Like me he wanted to claim that his things were robbed!" He accosts the domestics, slyly offering them a hand with the load which they are supposed to have. Tearfully Droma tells him that they are not burdened with food and wine but with sorrow and affliction, for scalawags have taken their dinner. Creoborus maintains, more correctly than he realizes, that he is in the same predicament.

Bassarus' door opens at this point to emit the mayor and the host, who have finished eating [V, 2]. Euergetes notes that the wind has died and the sky is clearing. He wonders what is keeping his servants, prompting them to step from the dark with the story of what has occurred. After a tongue-lashing mercifully cut short by Bassarus, the maid is sent inside with Dromo, and Creoborus approaches. When he also professes to have been robbed, the mayor is genuinely irate and unwilling to let him eat but relents on hearing what happened at the gallows. As Merimna comes out, the parasite rushes in, like Colax at the close of *Asotus* I, 3, and with an echo of Plautus' *Captives* 903–5. Bassarus follows, leaving Euergetes and his wife alone.

She says that it is time to excuse themselves and to express appreciation for the hospitality [V, 3]. Informed that all their food is still at home untouched and that they will return the kindness double, she is shocked at her husband's dishonesty. "If Bassarus finds out," she warns, "we'll be disgraced forever—you, me, and the servants!" The mayor's stinginess is certainly not to be blamed on her, contrary to Bassarus' opinion of women. To save face with her, Euergetes promises to give the sexton six stivers. He sends Merimna back into the house as he calls out Bassarus and the pastor, however, so that he can donate only two stivers, along with proffering thanks. Hieronymus follows suit and invites the sacristan and the mayor, plus wives, for lunch the next day, showing that he can be generous. Unlike Euergetes he knows that he must buy more food. Perhaps he wants to celebrate the curing of his gout, which has been driven away, he says, by the scare that he received. The mayor in turn asks the pastor and Bassarus with Bassara to join him for a cold supper tomorrow. The sexton thanks both men for their invitations and their money and announces that he would like to speak a few words to the whole party. In order for us to hear him, too, the mayor summons everyone outside. Obediently Graidium, Merimna, Dromo and Droma, Corasium, Bassara, Creoborus, Heino, and the two boys troop from the house, some nibbling nuts.

Dispensing with preliminaries, Bassarus launches into a confession [V, 4]. "The food, Pastor, which you fixed today for the secret delight of your niece and yourself (not without being two-faced about it) I stole at the mayor's prompting," he declares, excusing himself rather more than he ought. "Ouch!" cries Hieronymus, and Graidium laughs. "The food, Mayor, which you think you still have at home and which you pretended was stolen I have put before you tonight," Bassarus resumes. "Ouch!" cries Euergetes, and Graidium laughs again. "As for you, fine Creoborus," Bassarus continues, "the nuts which you lied about and which you believe are still in your house you're cracking and eating right now!" The old crone cackles once more, and Creoborus says "Serves me right, since I gave you the key to my house and to the mayor's." "To mine?" Euergetes explodes. "You are certainly a first-rate scoundrel! Will you clear out?" Once again Bassarus must intervene in the parasite's behalf. To Hieronymus and Euergetes he reports that the money which they reluctantly gave he is happily returning for dessert, and he adds "At dawn tomorrow, Pastor, I'll also return the pig I rightly pinched from you, so you can salt it." "You took it?" blurts Hieronymus. "Was that a fair thing to do, Bassarus?" "Quite," his nemesis replies. "You claimed that the pork and the sausages were stolen right after the slaughter, so you wouldn't have to share the wursts with people in the neighborhood, as we always do. Consequently, wasn't I just in taking all the meat from you and serving the uncured sausages roasted to these deserving folks?" [17] "Very just," Graidium interposes. Hieronymus protests that Bassarus suggested that bit of craftiness to him. "I did," the sexton acknowledges, "but it wasn't me who made you so stingy. That was Graidium. So aren't you rightly punished?" (Macropedius probably felt that if the housekeeper were responsible for the most conspicuous fault of her master the latter would be less shocking as a priest.) Hieronymus shamefacedly accepts the loss of the sausages provided he recover the pig. Assured that he will have it safe and sound, he inquires how it was robbed, but the host reserves that story for later. The party is not yet over, so everyone re-enters the house. "You who have watched what was happened have nothing more to hear," Bassarus informs the audience. "Give us your applause." Therewith Macropedius' most delightful work comes to an end—minus any epilogue.

If we compare the sexton to Reuchlin's Dromo, we see that each preys on the dishonest about him, but Bassarus does not do so for his own aggrandizement. He intends his pranks to be funny and beneficial without adverse consequences. Mardi Gras is also an appropriate occasion for them. In contrast to Dromo, Bassarus does not forfeit our sympathy, since his escapades are not ethically abhorrent. He is not an unprincipled rascal but merely a mischievous wag, the justifiableness of whose jokes in a corrupt society Macropedius took pains to make apparent.

Hieronymus replaces Henno as the master and chief adversary, being also the guiltiest with his selfishness, lust, superstition, and hypocrisy. The stark contrast between what he is and what he is supposed to be makes him inherently comic. His physical infirmity, which heightens his ludicrousness, might be interpreted as symbolic of his moral decadence, and with the cure of his gout his avarice, if not his other faults, seems to be overcome. For all his foibles this queer chameleon of a man is Macropedius' most endearing figure, multifarious and amusing. The fact that we can respond positively to him, no less than to Bassarus, insures his success as a humorous character. As a memorable lampoon of the clergy he is a match for Machiavelli's Fra Timoteo in *Mandragola* (composed ca. 1518), though that much lauded precursor of Molière's Tartuffe is a mercenary opportunist, outrageous rather than weak, for he takes advantage of others. Hieronymus transcends his pettiness in Act V, but we find no evidence that Timoteo is ever more than Machiavellian.

Andrisca and *Bassarus* are two comedies of the early northern Renaissance comparable to the best of contemporary Italian *commedia erudita,* the very acme of which is *Mandragola.* Though pieced together from the stuff of crude farce, they are quickened with infectious zest and ennobled by ample and convincing characterization. In neither of these two Shrovetide plays by Macropedius is there a figure so improbable as Machiavelli's Messer Nicia or Madonna Lucrezia. For tightness and intricacy of fast-paced action the ribald Tuscan comedy is superior, but in order to succeed its plot requires both a stupidity in the dupe of a husband every bit as appalling as Henno's or Aluta's and doubtful behavior on the part of the signora, contradicting everything said about her. Rather than to shallow intrigue, Macropedius gave priority to psychology, which furnished a humor of greater depth.

His low opinion of human nature in *Bassarus* could have wrung an appreciative smile from the author of *The Prince.* In this irreligious though artfully homiletic work the Dutchman is as cynical as that later portrayer of another fox, Ben Jonson. Like Reuchlin, he makes good use of his theme's potential for negative social commentary, and just as astrologers and shysters are singled out for special ridicule in *Henno*, so are reprobate priests particularly pilloried in *Bassarus*. The ethics called for in the latter work are nevertheless not so much Christian as generally humanitarian. Hieronymus' stinginess is forthrightly criticized, whereas his lack of chastity is passed over without comment. It is on antisocial avarice that Macropedius focused his indignation throughout *Bassarus,* even while incidentally exposing other corruption, like the mayor's venality. By consistently aiming at miserliness he gave his play a unity which *Henno* lacks, being an indiscriminate shotgun blast at a host of unethical practices. Led by *Bassarus* to expect further satirical comedy, we will be surprised to find that what follows in our survey has, almost steadily, more a medieval than a modern flavor.

CHAPTER 5

The Epicures

AFTER *Bassarus* Macropedius never wrote another secular play. In 1539 he published *Hecastus,* which is transitional insofar as it begins on a worldly plane and ascends to a religious one. It is a development of the Everyman theme, dramatizing the salvation of sinful humanity. Because the title figure is saved primarily by faith and expires confident that his soul will win admittance to paradise, the author was stigmatized as heretical by some of his fellow Catholics. In the preface added to the revised edition of this work, penned in 1550 and released in 1552, he disavows any heterodoxy, stating that the errors of which he has been accused are redemption by contrition and faith alone and "that everyone is held to believe in his sure salvation." "That," he adds, "I never dreamed of nor ever wanted to teach." Hecastus' justification is not effected in a manner at odds with Catholic dogma, despite the emphasis on faith. Macropedius asserts that his drama portrays the redemption of someone who dies too suddenly to make satisfaction for his sins.

In *Lazarus the Beggar,* first printed 1541 and presumably not long after the journey to Rome, he carefully avoided controversial doctrine. Both plays present the death of a wealthy prodigal. In the one case the roué is admitted to heaven after much ado; in the other, he is hustled posthaste to hell. Like the three insubordinate schoolboys of Chapter 3, Hecastus is converted by impending death. Laemargus, as the rich man is called in *Lazarus,* is given no opportunity for conversion. His function is simply to contrast with the beggar, his antithesis in both terrestrial and celestial fortune. In *Hecastus* Macropedius preaches redemption principally through faith; in its successor, through unswerving devotion to the Lord, as demonstrated by the godly pauper. Despite Lazarus, though, the more prominent figure in each work is the affluent worldling. Laemargus upstages the character whom he is supposed to serve as a foil.

I *Hecastus*

Sometime in the late fifteenth century a Dutchman and an Englishman wrote the morality plays called respectively *Elckerlijc* and *Everyman*. One of the two is a translation of the other, but so far no one has succeeded in proving conclusively which deserves priority. The authors are also unknown, though *Elckerlijc* is the work of a certain Peter of Diest, perhaps identifiable with a Carthusian named Petrus Dorlandus of Diest (1454–1507). Since the two plays are essentially identical, for our purposes they may be treated together. We are concerned with *Elckerlijc* as a forerunner of *Hecastus*.

The titles indicate that the leading character in *Elckerlijc-Everyman* personifies all humanity. Disgusted with his hedonism, God sends Death to summon the voluptuary to judgment. Casting about for help in his hour of direst need, the moribund sinner finds himself forsaken by everyone and everything that he has hitherto relied on. Friends, relatives, and possessions leave him in the lurch. The allegorical figure Good Deeds is too weak from neglect to assist him until her sister Knowledge (i.e., Awareness of Sin), together with Confession, fortifies her by having the ward do penance for his faults. After flagellating himself, he is clothed in contrition and joined by four other allegorical figures, Beauty, Strength, Discretion, and Five Senses. At the sight of his grave, however, these attributes of mortality depart, leaving Knowledge to console him as he dies, while Good Deeds will defend him before God. From a priest the penitent has received the host and extreme unction.

In 1536 the Cologne printer Jaspar von Gennep published a Latin reworking of *Elckerlijc* entitled *Homulus*. The author was a schoolteacher named Christianus Ischyrius (or Sterck). Like Elckerlijc-Everyman, Homulus is abandoned by comrades, kin, and wealth, to be saved by Good Deeds (Virtue), after she is restored to health by penance through the agency of Knowledge and Confession. Beauty, Strength, Discretion, and Five Senses again take leave on beholding the grave. Ischyrius made his version a little less abstract than the vernacular model. In *Elckerlijc-Everyman* the playboy's friends are represented by one figure, Fellowship. His relatives are portrayed by two, Cousin and Kindred. In *Homulus* Fellowship becomes six individuals, while Cousin and Kindred are multiplied into ten. Whereas Elckerlijc-

Everyman merely cries out to Mary to intercede for him with her Son, in *Homulus* both she and Jesus appear in a raised booth as the title figure prays to her and she pleads in his behalf. Before Christ's throne he also castigates himself. When he visits the priest for confession and the sacrament, two loutish devils are added in an interlude of slapstick rather too burlesque for the otherwise elevated tone of this earnestly religious parable. Since he was revising a medieval play for Renaissance readers, Ischyrius divided it into the classic five acts, introduced by a prologue in asclepiads which summarizes the plot. *Elckerlijc-Everyman* has no act or scene divisions. Act I of *Homulus* ends as Death goes away; Act II, as the friends fail; and Act III, as the kinfolk desert. Act IV concludes as Wealth refuses to escort her merely temporary owner into the beyond.

Macropedius continued the trend toward increased realism and vividness, but his changes are more drastic than those ventured by Ischyrius. *Hecastus* is considerably different from its predecessors, not only by virtue of the substitution of Faith for Knowledge. Macropedius transformed the entire scheme of the original allegory. His first act introduces the protagonist in a graphic scene from his daily life. He is also given an immediate family, for besides relatives he has a wife, two sons, and some daughters. The last fail to appear, however, except possibly in the chorus, which is composed of three boys and three girls from Hecastus' household. The second act brings not Death but a messenger from God named Nomodidascalus ("teacher of law"), whose interview with Hecastus is first delayed and then protracted in suspenseful plot retardation. Nomodidascalus also contributes to the drama by permitting the appearance of Death herself to be delayed in dread anticipation after he has heralded her. Only in the third act does Macropedius follow *Homulus*. There Hecastus is deserted by companions, family, servants, and wealth. In Act IV Death makes her climactic entrance, followed by Virtue, and in Act V Faith engineers the redemption of the former sybarite. The allegorical figures Beauty, Strength, Discretion, and Five Senses are deleted; Mary is barely mentioned; and there is no self-castigation. The two raucous demons of *Homulus* are replaced by a more subdued Satan, and the criticism of corrupt priests voiced by Knowledge in both *Elckerlijc-Everyman* and *Homulus* is omitted, perhaps as a result of the public's reaction to *Bassarus*.

In a short prefatory note the author asks readers not to be surprised at the plenitude of roles in *Hecastus* (twenty-five), because he wants to give as many pupils as possible an opportunity to participate. He is using more characters than necessary, he confesses, yet the number is not excessive. Instead of introducing six friends and ten relatives like Ischyrius, Macropedius includes only three of each, plus the immediate family and six servants. He admits only three allegorical figures, Virtue, Faith, and Death.

The prologue is spoken by Hecastus' steward, who informs the audience that the play to follow is chaste and respectable. There will be no "lover of virgins," no pimp, and no shameless prostitute to offend pious eyes. In fact, the unprejudiced spectator will find nothing offensive, the steward promises. In passing he mentions that "Hecastus" is equivalent to "Unusquilibet" in Latin, which is to say that it is from the Greek for "everyone." The audience is to see in the protagonist's fate a reminder of their own impending death. In the middle of this twenty-line prologue sixty-four verses are intercalated in the 1552 edition, repeating the same defense against charges of heresy that is found in the new preface. At the close of the lengthened introduction a chorus of four sapphic stanzas, urging us to repent before it is too late, is also added in the revised version.

The play opens in the afternoon of a summer day. The stage contains only the houses of the lead and his neighbor Daemones (from Plautus' *The Rope*), along with Satan's cave, as used by Lorcoballus and Marcolappus in *The Rebels*. Hecastus comes outside and, ironically, counts his abundant blessings. Since he has the means to enjoy the world, he should do so, he tells himself, ignoring the fools who warn of Judgment Day, for everyone is master, not steward, of his possessions and entitled to dispose of them at will. He calls his wife outdoors, to arrange for an impromptu dinner party before joining Daemones for jokes, dice, and drinks.

Epicuria ("assistance"), who is loathe to expose her delicate bloom to the heat, also balks at the expense of another banquet if she cannot use all that remains from yesterday's feasting [I, 2]. Since he is inviting the leading men of town with their wives, Hecastus wants everything fresh, however. Epicuria asks whether food for three guests will be enough, goading her lavish husband to exclaim over the avariciousness of the female sex. He is bringing nine or ten. She reminds him of what the priests frequently preach, namely that on doomsday we will have to give account of everything squandered. Again Hecastus sneers at the idea of judgment in the hereafter, considering it a sacerdotal ploy for milking money from the gullible. He also repeats the notion that he has discretion over his own property. What the priests say pertains only to parricides, robbers, "circumcised dogs," and infidels. "Baptism and Christ will save us," he declares, "or if any wrong remains we'll atone for it afterwards with tears." Besides, he adds, they give alms to paupers, orphans, and pilgrims; they go to church regularly; and they have nothing to do with heresy. Anyway, Judgment Day is eons away, and they ought to make the most of life while they can—an idea developed in the chorus to this act. Hecastus is a typical Christian, Macropedius is implying. When reminded of religion, he fancies himself one of the faithful, but he serves Christ only with his lips, never with his heart. "Go, my rose!" he tells his wife. He is spending the rest of the afternoon next door, he informs her, and does not want to be disturbed. If anyone should ask for him, she must not let on where he is. Taking a servant named Panocnus, he goes into Daemones' house, while Epicuria remains, plotting a compromise solution for his prodigality and her parsimony. She will have the cook (Daetrus, as in *Asotus*) buy just enough new food to fill out and disguise the leftovers.

Given two guldens and told to shop for ten people, Daetrus protests that twice that sum would hardly be sufficient [I, 3]. He proposes Epicuria's own scheme of mixing the old with the new, willing to take any blame which results. Of course he meets with approval. After his mistress has returned to the house, Daetrus echoes Bassarus' opinion that stinginess cannot be eradicated from women. For this reason he has suggested the plan which he knew Epicuria had in mind. Seeing Daemones' door open, he hurries off to the market.

Hecastus and his friend come out to gamble, with the loser having to drain a tankard of wine [I, 4]. Panocnus is sent home to insure that all is prepared for a gala evening and that no one comes to bother the master. A chorus is even to be gathered to welcome the guests with song, though it actually never materializes. The two leisured sports cast their dice, resulting in Hecastus' defeat. Just as his loss in this game of chance indicates that fate is against him, so he is immediately struck by a stabbing pain in his right side. He asks to go in out of the breeze, for the wine that he is drinking does not relieve his discomfort, and the first act closes as Daemones helps him into the house. In iambic dimeters the chorus sings a lilting anacreontic based on the *carpe diem* theme of Wisdom of Solomon 2:3–9.

Though he also is meant to be representative, Hecastus is initially made more concrete than the abstractions quickly accosted by Death in the prior Everyman allegories. Like them he typifies monied gentry, but his irreligious *joie de vivre* is amply detailed in both word and deed. Macropedius replaces God's expository denunciation of sinful man at the outset of *Elckerlijc-Everyman* and *Homulus* by a more dramatic presentation of this sinfulness in the person of his protagonist. Instead of being told that Hecastus is only a nominal Christian, we see him both declaim and act out his essential paganism, which excuses vice with a pretense of religiosity. Epicuria's anxious stinginess not only characterizes her but also draws forth the swaggering extravagance and hybris of her imperious lord.

Perhaps half an hour of plot time passes between acts before Hecastus' steward, whose name is Apeleutherus ("freedman"), appears with a twenty-five-line monologue on the cares of being the overseer of a staff of serfs [II, 1]. He nostalgically recalls his own period of servitude as relatively blissful, thereby warning the ambitious that people of humble station enjoy more security and peace. To see what is detaining Daetrus, he goes off-stage. Panocnus and his fellow underling Philoponus ("lover of toil"), who are also waiting for the cook, come outside to chat [II, 2]. Philoponus feels that the uncommonly worthless dinner being prepared is an ominous sign. Thunder often follows Phoebus' heat, and laughter ends in grief, Panocnus presciently observes. Their common sentiment, arousing anxious expectation in the audience, is that Hecastus has reached the summit of excess, from which he may vertiginously topple. Philoponus reminds his comrade of their duty to make ready for the banquet, whereupon Apeleutherus returns with Daetrus and scolds the pair for loitering, as Panocnus has anticipated. The cook orders them into the house with him, and they are about to follow when Philoponus descries a regal looking stranger approaching. He is stately, dignified, and authoritative, frightening Panocnus (whose name means "cringing from everything"). The imposing caller seems to be a legate from the Holy Roman Emperor (Charles V) or other great ruler, Panocnus exclaims in awe.

He is none other than Nomodidascalus, delegated by God to summon Hecastus, or "Hisecastus," as he says.[1] Philoponus tells him that he has found the right place but that the master is away [II, 3]. Nomodidascalus therefore asks to speak with the lady of the house. While Panocnus fetches her, honest Philoponus reveals that Hecastus is drinking and gaming with a companion. The heavenly emissary has stern words for so frivolous a waste of precious time when death may interrupt at any moment. After a delay occasioned by her culinary concerns, Epicuria appears with a maid, and Philoponus leaves them. In accordance with her husband's orders, she feigns ignorance of his whereabouts, incurring reproach from the visitor [II, 4]. His severity so dismays her that she yields and sends her maid after a valet, who in turn is to go for Hecastus. Nomodidascalus reprimands her further for being preoccupied with eating and drinking when her husband may be dead by evening. Epicuria is naturally incredulous, for neither she nor her spouse has passed the age of thirty-five, she says. The maid returns with Panocnus, who is dispatched next door after some recalcitrance occasioned by the master's injunction to be left alone [II, 5]. Epicuria has the maid carry on with arrangements for the banquet, while she herself stays to talk with Nomodidascalus, hoping to learn his message. What he tells her is in effect *memento mori* [II, 6]. She is too much given to bodily and material interests. She asks why she and her husband ought to be mindful of death when they are still young and healthy. Referring to the parable told in Matthew 20:1–16, she questions whether they cannot hurry into the vineyard at the eleventh hour. The answer which she receives is that one can die unexpectedly and that God may be so angered by a life of sin that He refuses admittance. Redemption is a gift, not a reward, Nomodidascalus adds, weakening his argument. He has also stated earlier that true repentance can never come too late. His logic is not exactly divine, but it is lost on Epicuria anyway. Though momentarily frightened, she quickly slips back into her habitual confidence that enjoyment of fortune's bounty cannot be wrong. Her husband now exits from Daemones' house, so she returns to her domestic affairs, viewed by Nomodidascalus as a lost soul. From a young assistant who has accompanied him, he requests the code of celestial law and the summons.

Hecastus is curious about the important caller and asks Panocnus whether the man is dressed in purple and gold [II, 7]. He is not, the servant answers, but he exudes such authority, maturity, and probity in speech, looks, and demeanor that by comparison he makes Hecastus look like a peasant. On seeing him, the ailing aristocrat is also impressed. He is informed that Nomodidascalus has been sent by "the King of kings and Supreme Ruler of earth" to summon him to court for an accounting of all deeds and transactions. To prove his authenticity, the legate shows the ethereal citation. Like Panocnus, Hecastus thinks that Charles V is meant. What right does the emperor have to demand an accounting from a free citizen, he wants to know. Nomodidascalus refers him to the official writ. "By Jupiter!" Hecastus exclaims. The letters are unrecognizably exotic, awesome as if traced by the finger of God. Perhaps his younger son, who has been studying the classics, can read them. While Panocnus fetches Philomathes ("lover of learning"), Hecastus vents his anxiety, from which he is suffering no less than from his worsening indisposition.

As soon as he sees his father, dejected and pressing his side, the young bookworm, fresh from devouring Hippocrates, makes a hasty inspection of tongue and pulse [II, 8]. "Pleurisy," he diagnoses. It can be rapidly fatal, but he will also consume Galen. His patient is more concerned at the moment about the visitor and the document inscribed with perplexing characters. Philomathes is eager for a look at it, to show the gentleman a sample of local erudition. Whatever pertains to philosophy or law and is not couched in a barbarous tongue he can interpret, he boasts. When Nomodidascalus gives him the paper, however, he is stumped [II, 9]. Hecastus becomes infuriated at this evidence that his money spent on education has been wasted. "Either read that or be damned, you good-for-nothing," he snarls, cuffing his son. As shamefaced Philomathes slinks away without another word, Nomodidascalus rebukes the philistine father for catering to merely temporal considerations. He proceeds to explain that he is on God's errand, not the emperor's, and that Hecastus must defend himself against the charge of abusing divine gifts. Like both Death and Goods in *Elckerlijc-Everyman*, Nomodidascalus denies that anyone is free to do as he pleases with what he has.

Wealth is loaned, not given. It was at the thought of just such a reckoning that Hecastus scoffed in his opening monologue and in I, 2. Now confronted with the immediate threat of judgment, he is no longer jaunty but witless with fear. Since he knows of no one who can decipher the summons for him, he trusts the bailiff from above to translate it. It consists of two fragments from Biblical verses, written in Hebrew, supposedly the language of God. The first is the "Mane, Thecel, Phares" of Daniel 5:25. The second is from Isaiah 38:1—"Set your house in order, for you shall die and not live." Hecastus protests that he is but thirty years old, a quinquennium less than indicated by his wife in II, 4. Youthful though he be, he will not see the morrow, Nomodidascalus assures him and departs. The forlorn secularist laments his prospects and leads us to the third act by wishing for a friend to accompany him and to entreat in his behalf [II, 10].

Since he starts Act III with another monologue, he may remain on stage during the interval, taking part in the singing of the chorus, a medley in iambic dimeters from Ecclesiasticus,[2] the Psalms, and Revelations. His soliloquy in III, 1 repeats the gist of the preceding one. After it Daemones appears with two other comrades, and Hecastus asks them for support [III, 2]. The neighbor vows full cooperation until he learns that death is involved, whereupon he reneges, followed by the pair who are with him. Reprehended for this perfidy, he recommends an appeal to the relatives, who are to be seen issuing from the house, led by one Syngenes ("kinsman"). Blood, however, proves no more binding than amity. Though promising assistance, the relatives also break their word when they hear what is entailed [III, 3]. Syngenes advises Hecastus to take along his most loyal servants, his sons, and his money. The kinfolk will oversee household affairs and even accompany the voyager to the city gate when he sets out.

After friends and relatives have all gone inside, Philomathes and Philocrates ("lover of strength") come forth, professing to be tearful[3] over their father's imminent demise [III, 4]. Whatever is in their power they swear to do for him, but when he says that they should die with him, they refuse. Philomathes proposes that he take servants and riches, because the former can provide defense and the latter, bribes. "Alas!" Hecastus wails as the sons go away. With his own flesh and blood deserting him, what can he expect from bondmen? At least them he can command, and he orders Philoponus to haul out his wealth [III, 5]. There is no point in soliciting the aid of maids, mistresses, and mate, he fears.

Niggardly Epicuria stomps out to protest the removal of the family treasure [III, 6]. Probably with arms akimbo, she wants to know whether her husband is sick in mind as well as in body. He informs her that he is to die, and he asks her to join him. "I wouldn't dare go with you," she cries, wilted merely at the mention of death, but she concedes gold, silver, and servants as a surrogate. Her maids object vociferously as regards themselves, so she limits her concession to money and the male domestics. As she withdraws, Philoponus and Panocnus lug the money chest out [III, 7]. Inside is not merely wealth but the god of it—Plutus, the title figure of Aristophanes' most popular comedy in the Renaissance. The blind old divinity remains closed up, but he is heard to complain over being disturbed. When informed that he is going to be transported for the benefit of his master beyond the grave, he protests, refusing to help dead men. He will consort with someone else, instead. Undaunted by this insubordination, Hecastus has his servants heave the trunk back into the house and hunt some poles by which to carry it. Meanwhile he closes Act III with a short monologue in which he states that his pain is increasing and his end is near. Unless he can convey Plutus with him, he will have to face the Judge alone. Before embarking on man's longest and saddest journey, he wants to see that affairs are in order and to change his clothes, so he retires, leaving an empty stage for the chorus.

While it chants of death,[4] the servants find the poles, and as Act IV commences they gingerly carry Plutus' crate from the house in a scene which passed via Hans Sachs' 1549 German version of this play into Hugo von Hofmannsthal's modernization of *Everyman*, 1911. Hecastus orders the menials to go on ahead, for he must bid final adieu to family and acquaintances. Panocnus and Philoponus obediently march off-stage, to scamper back a few moments later without their baggage [IV, 2]. Death is coming! The friends vanish, raced by the family and the serfs. Forsaken at this climactic moment, Hecastus stands alone, himself immobilized by the futility of flight. In a terrifying mask Death leaps before him, brandishing her spike. Why has he been dallying, she demands to know. Without trying to bribe her like Everyman-Elckerlijc and Homulus, he meekly begs for still more time, a reprieve until tomorrow. She grants that he may have another hour, after which, deaf to further entreaty, she will drag him to trial and to hell. For the nonce she glides away, leaving him to ruminate again on his dismal prospects, partly with a paraphrase of Lamentations 1:12—"All you that pass by behold and see if there be any sorrow like mine!"

At this crucial juncture his Virtue slowly enters, dirty and emaciated. When he was a young boy Hecastus honored her, but since puberty he has been indifferent, notwithstanding the charity and church attendance of which he boasted in I, 2. In memory of the happier days she returns, greeted with embarrassment by her charge, who tells of his plight and implores her backing [IV, 3]. Even if she were vigorous she could not profit him alone, she says, but at least she is no turncoat. She advises him to be moved into the house and to have a priest summoned. For her part, she will try to persuade her sister Faith to visit him. If Faith consents and if he receives her, his case will not be hopeless. As Virtue exits, Hecastus marvels over her graciousness, a far cry from the rebuff of his hoped-for earthly champions. To Philoponus and Panocnus, who have crept back, he calls for a lift into bed and a cup of cool water, chiding them for their disgraceful rout [IV, 4]. He also wants his sons brought, who can fetch a pastor for his soul if they are unable to do anything for his body. Panocnus reports that they are strolling with the friends in the garden in an effort to recover their senses. Carefully the two servants raise their dying master and carry him from sight. In trochaic dimeters, alternately acatalectic and catalectic, the chorus observes that a just man expires contentedly.

Fifteen or twenty minutes elapse between the last two acts. Philomathes checks his father's urine during that interval and reports to his brother outside in V, 1 that its dark color indicates impending death. Philocrates accordingly sends Panocnus to the next street for Hieronymus the priest (not at all like the previous Hieronymuses) and on to order a casket, while he and Philomathes wrangle over the inheritance. Philocrates is the firstborn, but his brother vows to sue for an equal division of the legacy. Their quarrel is interrupted as Hieronymus arrives and enters the house, for they must follow to insure that he does not wheedle overly much for aliens and the poor.

Virtue returns with Faith, informing her of Hecastus' upright youth and pitiable decline [V, 2]. She begs her sister, "who is accustomed to save the impious," to intercede for her protégé, undeserving though he is. Faith replies first that without Virtue her work is in vain or even dead (James 2:26) and second that she cannot assist a person whom the Father has not visited with His grace. Someone should talk to Hecastus about Christ's remission of sins. Perhaps then God will admit her to him. Virtue says that she has considered this point and that on her advice a priest has already been called. To forestall Satan, who is now approaching, the two sisters hurry inside.

The Adversary has a sheet of paper and a quill for writing out his case against Hecastus, in order not to weaken it by a slipup in court [V, 3]. Seating himself in front of the house, he tells the audience not to be impertinent or he will make note of their cachinnations. "First of all," he says in regard to the prospective defendant, "he's proud and arrogant—he's proud and arrogant—and arrogant." The repetition results from thinking aloud of what is to be indited and then setting it down. Satan continues in this manner for a moment before deciding to work silently lest someone betray him. As the focus shifts in V, 4 to Hecastus' bedroom, God's Prosecutor remains outside, pensively scratching on his parchment.

Perhaps from the outset of Act V as the play was staged, the dying man was visible, in which case his confession was pantomimed during the course of the previous two scenes. If not, as is more likely, the door or curtain was opened after V, 3, revealing him in his bed. At the beginning of the new scene the confession has ended, and Hecastus is to receive the eucharist and extreme unction, provided he is strong in faith. At first he is not. When asked whether he believes that Jesus is truly God, born of a virgin to save mankind, he replies "So they say. So I remember to have read." After another such answer the priest enjoins him to speak for himself. Asked next whether he accepts what is written of Christ as Son of God, crucified, buried, and raised on the third day, Hecastus responds like a humanist, doubting the Bible no less than Sallust, Livy, or Caesar. Omnipotent God can do all things, he adds. Both Faith and Virtue are present during this exchange, and now the former begins to draw close to him. The priest stops her, however, because Hecastus has not progressed far enough. Only when the sinner gives sincere evidence of repentance does

Hieronymus admit Faith, signifying that Hecastus is becoming a true believer. The catechist then proceeds with an interrogation over various tenets of the Apostles' Creed. Hecastus feels that the enormity of his transgressions precludes remission, until he is assured that trust in Christ as Redeemer can justify him. His fear of Satan and Death is diminished by the promise that Faith and Virtue will shield him. At the close of this protracted yet decisive scene (169 lines in the 1539 edition; 176 in the revision), Hieronymus abruptly leaves, though his work is not completed. The allegorical sisters remain.

Outside, Death returns [V, 5], to be upbraided by Satan for taking "a year" to get ready, like the prostitutes in IV, 7 of *Asotus*. The priest who just left may have rescued his prey, the devil angrily points out, and he accuses his "sister" of ingratitude. She reciprocates by asserting that everything which he has to feed upon he owes her. If he is dissatisfied with the number of the damned, his complaint should be with "the lion which sprang from the tribe of Juda" (i.e., Christ—Revelations 5:5). Thanks to Him, she who previously attacked both bodies and souls is now granted only the former. Abashedly Satan calls for a truce and an immediate assault on the victim at hand. While Death sharpens her spike, he attempts to enter the house.

With a cross Faith keeps him at the door and in another wordy dialogue convinces him that he no longer has a claim on her ward [V, 6]. At first Satan insists that according to the Bible Hecastus belongs to him, being proud, ostentatious, sybaritic, cruel, selfish, and irreligious. He has never done anything good but a great deal that is bad. Virtue amends this indictment to take into account his youth and present reform. The devil asks Hecastus whether he would deny any of the charges, but Faith answers instead, arguing at some length that he is saved by his belief in Christ. In frustration Satan rends with his teeth the paper on which his case is penned and bellows a wish to mangle Faith in like manner. Because as he slinks away he spies Hieronymus returning with the boy Acolytus, he creeps into his cave to see how Death fares. Philomathes, who comes from the house with an inky urine specimen, anxious lest the priest delay too long, hurries Hieronymus inside [V, 7]. In the 1552 edition Macropedius added after this scene the fifty-eight line colloquy between Philomathes and Acolytus that was described in Section II of the Introduction.

Having whetted her spike long enough, Death dramatically pounds on the door for admittance [V, 8]. Faith opens but does not at once let her in. While Hieronymus gives Hecastus the eucharist and extreme unction, the two hostile females conduct an extended logomachy over the power of Death. Faith begins by calling the intruder tyrannical and by asseverating that her despotism will totally collapse. Elaborating on a matter broached by Death herself in V, 5, she explains that her opponent has already lost her sway over the souls of Christ's followers and that their bodies will be restorted at the end of time. Whoever sides with Faith does not fear Death's sting, and Faith is the protector of Hecastus. Making no headway in this altercation, Death retreats for reinforcement from Satan, forgetting that she is an agent of God, who has called the mortal to trial.

While she is away, the priest tells Hecastus not to be afraid but to trust that he will ascend to heaven [V, 9]. Hecastus professes joy and assurance but begs Faith and Virtue not to forsake him. They promise to remain steadfast, as Death returns with Satan. Repeating what Faith dictates to him, Hecastus speaks scornfully of the marauder and confidently of eternal life [V, 10]. By now his cheeks are fallen, his complexion is wan, and he gasps for breath, almost too weak to talk. Though Death is once more disconcerted by Faith's contempt, she deals Hecastus the *coup de grâce*, freeing his soul to take wing, escorted by angels and the two guardians. Satan and Death take to their heels.

Outside, to friends and relatives gathered beside a casket of willow wood, Philoponus announces his master's demise [V, 11]. As the visitors wax dutifully lachrymose, the immediate family joins them and the servant returns to the house. Though all weep and wail satisfactorily in the first edition, Macropedius added a fifty-three-line scene in the 1552 revision in which one of Epicuria's maids is particularly emotional, rhetorically lamenting the transitoriness of life in the passing of Hecastus. Hieronymus emerges from the house and reprimands the mourners [V, 12], saying that they should rejoice because on the last day the deceased whom they are bemoaning will arise among the faithful. At these words the hypocrites are suddenly transformed to sincere Christians in a dubious *coup de théâtre*. Though there was talk before of a splendid funeral, Philomathes renounces ostentation, seconded by the entire group, and no one hints at an ulterior motive. The turnabout is meant to be taken seriously. Philocrates calls out the steward and Daetrus, to learn whether dinner is ready. The meat can be pulled off the spits at once, so the elder son—now man of the house—invites his guests inside, to partake moderately of the banquet conceived in intemperance. The steward tells the audience to applaud and go home, since the corpse will not be buried for two days. Like *Bassarus, Hecastus* has no epilogue.

In this 688-line final act the priest in Macropedius took precedence over the dramatist. He did not carry through to the end his skillful handling of the subject matter in Acts I–IV, for there is so much discussion of doctrine here that the tempo is improperly slowed to a crawl. Since after Act IV it is apparent that the protagonist will be saved, his redemption and death should be brought about with no more delay than a brief confrontation between the opposing forces of good and evil, involving a minimum of theology. Hecastus is also unable to dominate a lengthy last act, lying in bed with his life ebbing. As it is, he is superseded by Faith. The improbable conversion of friends and family at the last moment, moreover, makes for no grand finale but shows Macropedius' religious enthusiasm also to have overridden his feeling for psychology. Despite its flaws, however, *Hecastus* is still original and moving enough to be honored as a major Continental drama of the sixteenth century.

II *Lazarus the Beggar*

As *Petriscus* is based on *The Rebels,* so *Lazarus the Beggar* has *Hecastus* as its foundation. Of course, the source of the plot is the parable told in Luke 16:19–31, but Macropedius' treatment of this story smacks greatly of his Everyman allegory. The names Daemones and Daetrus recur for the friend next door and the cook, while Laemargus ("gluttonous") and his wife Tryphera ("delicate") are Hecastus and Epicuria under different names. The steward reappears, along with two bondservants, who are called Thraso (from Terence's *Eunuch*) and Cynopa ("shameless one"). In the preface, where Macropedius tells of his trip to Rome, he relates that when it was initially performed *Lazarus* had no expository act. In the prologue he confesses that the protasis is borrowed from *Hecastus* (though actually only part of it is). Shortage of time forced this expediency upon him, be explains, but even when he set out to dramatize the parable of the rich man he probably had the play about wealthy Hecastus in mind, since it is the immediate predecessor of *Lazarus* in order of composition.

Much of the prologue is devoted to Macropedius' views on the presentation of Christ in a drama, as summarized in Section III of the Introduction. The Lazarus to be portrayed, we are told, is not the one whom Jesus raised from the dead but rather is the beggar in the parable, so that the Son of God does not have to appear. Perhaps in reaction to criticism of *Hecastus,* Macropedius requests that any doctrinal error discovered in this play be brought to his attention. He will not stubbornly defend it. The prologue ends with the usual call for silence.

As with *Hecastus,* the setting consists of only the houses belonging to the prodigal and to Daemones, though the final scene shows Laemargus in hell and Lazarus in the bosom of Abraham. Two devils again appear, but no mention is made of a cave for them. In II, 4 we are informed that the drama takes place in Palestine, despite all the Greek names, so the city in which Laemargus resides is probably ancient Jerusalem. The action lasts from morning until mid-afternoon of a single day.

Laemargus begins with a monologue, like Hecastus, but he does not count his blessings and scorn the notion of Judgment Day. Instead, he gripes about Tryphera's stinginess, ending his complaint by quoting an adage from line 42 of Reuchlin's *Henno:* "A miser needs a spendthrift." Before calling his wife outdoors, like Hecastus, he sends Thraso to invite his five brothers to a midday meal and has Cynopa tell Daemones to expect him soon for breakfast. When informed of the intended luncheon [1, 2], Tryphera does not remind her husband of priests' warnings against extravagance, in the manner of Epicuria; instead she pleads for frugality so that something can be left to their children (who are seen only in the chorus of Act III). Laemargus parries with a lengthy catalogue of their possessions, which indeed seem proof against future want. "And who should we save all that for?" he asks. Priests? Beggars, whom Typhera says she detests? Or even the children, when no one knows how they will turn out? Speaking more truly than he suspects, he says that they should eat, drink, and be merry, for it is proverbial that soon they will die. He succeeds better than Hecastus in dispelling his wife's obsession, for she concedes that they ought to gather rosebuds while they may and she tells him to bring plenty of appetite for her cuisine. As he goes in to change clothes, she calls the cook and the steward outside. Like Epicuria she sends Daetrus shopping "with two or three gold pieces," but in biblical Palestine that amount was evidently enough for ten people. The cook does not object, and there is no talk of mixing in leftovers or scrimping in any way [I, 3]. Laemargus' lecture has so reformed Tryphera that the steward is taken aback. He and Daetrus leave for the market, after the mistress has returned to the house. Cynopa is to accompany the master.

Before further borrowing from *Hecastus* in I, 8, four entirely new scenes are added. In I, 4 Cynopa helps Laemargus dress in sight of both the audience and two beggars, who are named Bronchus ("windpipe") and Typhlus ("blind"). The latter really is blind, and his companion tells him that since Laemargus is primping for a brunch they might get a handout. In this time of need the rich are their only hope, Bronchus remarks. He will watch where Laemargus goes, so that they can beg there. As Daemones waits outside, Lazarus crawls up to him, covered with ulcers and faint with hunger [I, 5]. For three days all that he has ingested is dirty water. He asks Daemones for a crumb but is driven away. When Laemargus, followed by Cynopa, joins his friend and the three go inside, Bronchus leads Typhlus to Daemones' house, despite the rejection of Lazarus [I, 6]. Though he is lame, Bronchus wants to hurry in order to be first at the door. He fears that Lazarus, who is creeping back, might beat them. The more altruistic Typhlus reprimands him, convinced that Lazarus as a true son of Abraham deserves more and is not out to compete. Bronchus is deaf to remonstrance, however, and orders his blind comrade to stand behind him. The ulcerous rival can be third. Most of the seventy-four-line seventh scene is given over to a trading of pious pronunciamentos by Lazarus and Typhlus on the subject of stoic forbearance, anticipating *Hypomone*. It begins with comments on their prospects for a donation, which Lazarus thinks are dim, and ends with criticism by Bronchus for discussion of spiritual matters when food is needed. Laemargus is opening the door.

The trio cry out to him as he emerges to send Cynopa home [I, 8]. Like Hecastus dispatching Panocnus to insure that dinner is prepared and that no one comes to disturb him, Laemargus instructs his servant to make certain that all is ready on time, including musicians and a chorus, though his real motive is to dispense with this potential informer now that he is about to throw money around in gambling and possibly whoring. He does not want Tryphera to know of his mischief. As Cynopa leaves, Lazarus commences to beg again, causing Laemargus to reproach his friend for tolerating the "putrid herd" at his stoop. Daemones accordingly calls for servants to scatter the pests, and the latter promptly retreat. Spunky Bronchus hopes that the roués are nauseated by their gluttony. Before entering his master's house, Cynopa comments that both he and the mendicants are being expelled because the party is about to become a debauch. At a safe distance Lazarus exhorts his two "brothers," as he says, not to utter harsh words but rather to join him in a hymn to God. Their singing, in glyconics and based on Psalm 85 of the Vulgate, constitutes the chorus to Act I.

After a time lapse approximately the length of the chorus (ninety-six lines), Cynopa and Thraso begin Act II by waiting for Daetrus in front of Laemargus' house, just as Panocnus and Philoponus stand conversing as they await the cook in *Hecastus* II, 2. They grumble about Tryphera's asperity and miserliness, being allowed only black bread and cheese for breakfast. It is the nature of the affluent to be penny-wise and pound-foolish, Thraso observes. Whatever the masters do, servants must sustain and abstain, he continues, quoting the motto of Epictetus. Mostly in the words of Philoponus he says that they should prepare for the banquet as ordered. Cynopa sees Daetrus returning with groceries (though minus the steward, who left with him in I, 3) and predicts, like Panocnus, that they will be accused of laziness. Echoing verbatim the steward in *Hecastus*, Daetrus carps at the two for dawdling. On the point of following him into the house, they notice Bronchus and Typhlus returning, just as the serfs in *Hecastus* II, 2 see Nomodidascalus approach. Cynopa jokingly calls the beggars parasites, but Thraso is contemptuously blunt: Lame, blind, and scabrous dogs he terms them, thinking of Lazarus, as well.

On finding the door slammed in their face, Bronchus is sullen and angry, while Typhlus remains cheerful and expectant [II, 2]. Because he is little concerned with bodily needs he can even jest, saying that maybe an ablative (taker) lives in this house instead of a dative (giver). Bronchus agrees, for he has not received anything here in several years of begging, despite the owner's wealth. He hopes the selfish gourmand will gobble himself into his grave, but Typhlus admonishes him with the thought that the rich are their mainstay. Why have they come to this neighborhood, Typhlus asks, if neither Laemargus nor Daemones is likely to feed them? Sometimes, Bronchus explains, scraps are left over from the dogs. Seeing two newcomers approach, he urges his sightless friend to huddle with him at Laemargus' door. Though nothing happens in this scene, it contributes characterization of the villain and, incidentally, of the two beggars, as well.

Lazarus, who is slowly making his way toward them, is overtaken by the strangers whom Bronchus has sighted [II, 3]. One of the duo is a man named Molobrus ("greedy beggar"), and the other is his boy. Both are cynically profane. Lazarus' devoutness having been matched with the comparable piety of Typhlus in I, 7, it is now contrasted with the impiety of these new arrivals. When the leper tells them that the rich man toward whose house they are headed is not accustomed to make generous handouts and that he himself would be content with crumbs fallen from the table, Molobrus is incredulous. He assumes that so lugubrious a tale is contrived as a dodge to steer them away. Both he and the boy accuse Lazarus of guile when he wishes them more success than he has enjoyed. In frustration over the miscarriage of his certainly naïve benevolence, Lazarus cries out to God for deliverance from this vale of tears. "Nevertheless, not my will but Yours be done," he concludes, like Christ praying in Gethsemane. Finding some shade, he collapses in it.

Molobrus greets the two beggars waiting at Laemargus' door, and Bronchus asks him what country he left for Palestine, since he is different in features and dress [II, 4]. He is a prodigal son from Sparta who has been reduced to minstrelsy and begging, Molobrus reveals, offering a share of his anticipated earnings in return for help in hiring out his services. Bronchus is interested, but Typhlus considers such a mode of life dishonorable and tries to discourage his more worldly-minded friend. He tells Molobrus to seek work and not to deprive the handicapped of what few alms are to be gleaned. The entertainer makes his proposition to Bronchus alone but is still refused, since for all his mundaneness the cripple is too loyal to forsake Typhlus. Following Psalm 39:5 in the Vulgate, the blind man calls him blessed for trusting in God rather than in vain delusions. Molobrus vows that he will have himself admitted to Laemargus' house while Bronchus and Typhlus are routed. Bidding his boy to sing and dance, he starts to strum his lyre. The chorus of Act II, in iambic dimeters, is their version of Ecclesiastes 2:4–10, which serves as a commentary on Laemargus. As in the chorus to Act I, Bronchus and Typhlus sing a two-line refrain after each stanza.

Perhaps having heard the music, Tryphera begins Act III by opening the door and shouting at the filthy group to go away and stop polluting her air. Bronchus and Typhlus beg in vain for mercy, as Lazarus inches up. The haughty lady calls for Thraso and Cynopa to come, informing the beggars that there will be no food except what the dogs reject. Lazarus wishes for no more. Molobrus briefly tells Tryphera of his past and his talents, whereupon she welcomes him as a godsend, to play and to aid with the chorus during the luncheon. Her choice is perhaps meant to characterize her (and her husband) by reflecting her sense of values. She takes into her house trash with whom the pious refuse to consort. The godless, we infer, rate people who are merely useful over those who are morally superior. Since the two servants have not heard Tryphera's summons, for her voice is weak, she sends a maid after them.

They have been feeding the dogs, and Cynopa carries out a basket of leftovers [III, 2]. Tryphera tells Thraso to conduct the minstrels inside for food and wine and to return with a cudgel. To amuse his mistress, Cynopa tosses scraps to the "two-legged canines," and Bronchus scrambles for them, snatching bits from Typhlus, to Tryphera's delight. Only Lazarus makes no effort to eat, being either too weak or too disdainful. After Cynopa warns the beggars to go away if they want to avoid a beating, Tryphera sends him next door to let Laemargus know that the banquet is ready. She herself retires to hurry Thraso.

As Lazarus berates the impenitent Bronchus for his greed, Thraso emerges with a stick and clubs all three of the pariahs [III, 3]. Typhlus groans over being granted nothing at this house but welts, while Lazarus calls upon God to witness his misery and to forgive his sins. After begging his persecutor for a moment of reprieve, he explains that because of his sores he must move slowly. He adds that he has not eaten for three days and implores permission to remain at Laemargus' door for crumbs, since he will perish if not nourished now. Thraso becomes faintly sympathetic but is unwilling to oblige him because the master is soon due back and would be outraged at his smell. Lazarus must withdraw a little. "Ugh!" Thraso grunts as he half drags the leper along. "He stinks worse than a corpse!" Seeing Cynopa leave Daemones' home as a sign that the guests will soon be arriving, Thraso hastens inside, wondering what soap will wash off such a stench.

The fourth scene consists entirely of a slightly altered Psalm 12 from the Vulgate sung by Lazarus as a prayer for deliverance. It is in six four-line strophes with another two-line refrain after each by Typhlus and Bronchus. The meter is iambic dimeter. At the start of the hymn Cynopa enters Laemargus' house, and he exits from it at the close, frightening Bronchus and Typhlus away. The time is now noon, as the master comes with Daemones, while four of his brothers approach from off-stage [III, 5]. Cynopa summons the chorus, which is formed by the servants and children of the house and is led by Tryphera. Though not mentioned, Molobrus must also be present. Cynopa resumes his chores, leaving the guests to be greeted with the choral ode to this act, a differently worded version of the chorus to Act I of *Hecastus* with the meter changed from iambic dimeters to glyconics.

At the fading of the last note Act IV begins, while everyone is still outdoors. Tryphera extends salutations to her husband, Daemones, and the four brothers, detaining one of them, named "Aphron" ("witless") [5] as the rest of the party go inside. She inquires about the fifth brother, who is called "Merimnus" ("anxious") like one of the slaves in *Asotus*. He is in the fields, Aphron replies, "worriedly gathering silver and gold for me." Merimnus does not make money for himself, Aphron explains, because like the other three brothers he has no children. Aphron, whose expectations show the futility of pursuing earthly treasures, will eventually acquire all the family's fortunes but Laemargus'. Twice during this scene Lazarus, who crawls closer to the house, calls attention to himself, but not even Tryphera pays heed.

After she has withdrawn with her in-law, the beggar mourns (like Aluta) that he is ignored just as though he were not human [IV, 2]. Cynopa comes out to look for Merimnus and advises Lazarus to disappear, refusing him food. Seeing that the missing

guest is now approaching, Cynopa returns to the feast to announce
the late comer and to serve the second course. Addressed by Lazarus as he enters the house [IV, 3], Merimnus merely sniffs, saying "What is this corpse at the door?" Through the open entrance
the banqueters are in full sight of the starveling, who watches
wistfully as Merimnus falls voraciously upon his plenteous fare.
The host strikes up a drinking song in iambic dimeters and drains
a tankard of wine, a *tour de force* of excess that is reiterated all
around the table. When the revelry temporarily subsides, Lazarus
clamors for a few crumbs [IV, 4]. God rewards charity, he en-
treats, and death will claim him if he is not fed, for he feels his
life ebbing.

This time he is heard. Furious that the obnoxious intruder has
been allowed to reach his doorstep, Laemargus insists with his
brothers' approval that nothing be given Lazarus [IV, 5]. Sternly
Tryphera reminds Thraso of her commands, and he confesses that
he felt sorry enough for the leper to move him to a less frequented side of the house. For his compassion Laemargus berates
him, issuing a final order to get rid of the nuisance for good.
Though we are not told why, Thraso fails to obey at once. He
delays long enough for the carousers to circulate a tankard again,
to the raucous accompaniment of another drinking song (also
in iambic dimeters). This prolonged repetition, since each guest
must guzzle the flagon dry, would probably be tedious in performance, though it stresses the contrast between the lusty
sensualists within and the lonely soul without. The earthly lot of
true Christians, the allegory hints, is to be ostracized by others.
After the tankard finishes its circuit, Thraso emerges and closes
the door [IV, 6]. He snickers to see dogs licking the outcast's
ulcerous shanks, as in Luke 16:21, but his heartlessness yields to
indignation when he discovers the leper all but dead. His master's
selfishness makes him happy to be a slave without property rather
than an uncharitable rich man, and he cries that he is as terrified
as though a deity were present.

After shouting excitedly to be let back inside, he makes known
Lazarus' condition [IV, 7]. Laemargus condescends to leave the
wretch, lest they incur reproach, but he is not sufficiently stirred
to have assistance rendered. His concern is not for a fellow mortal
but merely for his own reputation. To forget about death and
suffering, he spurs his guests to eat and drink, asking them in addi-

tion to praise what they most admire of all that he possesses. Wife, home, servants, furnishings, children, fields, and herds are extolled. "Oh fortune!" he gushes, "How can I laud you worthily?" Everything is going as he desires, except that like the rich fool in Luke 12:13–21 [6] he lacks barns enough to store his bumper harvest. He will have to tear the old granaries down and replace them with larger ones, he decides. As he reaches the peak of his ebullient complacency, an angel enters, seen only by him. It is presumably the "deity" sensed by Thraso at the end of IV, 6. This day Laemargus is to die, the counterpart to Nomodidascalus announces. The other people present hear the voice, as if emitted from a whirlwind, but without comprehending what it says. In alarm they ask the host what has suddenly befallen him, that he is pale and trembling, and he tells of the divine message. Soon demons will break in and snatch his soul to hell, he conjectures distressfully. While Tryphera wails, the brothers put him into a bed and close the door. He has perhaps only overeaten, Daemones sanguinely remarks.

Outside, Belial and Astaroth, whom we met in *Asotus* III, 11, arrive with tridents and a sack [IV, 8]. Again they speak in iambic dimeters, and Astaroth does not know why they have come or what the purpose of the bag is. It is for a "nice little wandering soul," Belial explains, using the death bed verse of Emperor Hadrian ("Animula vagula blandula"). Seeing Lazarus sprawled on the ground, Astaroth asks whether it is his spirit that is earmarked for their clutches. Angels come to console the beggar and to keep the devils away from him, paraphrasing in song (iambic dimeters) the first two verses of Isaiah 57: "The righteous perishes, and no man lays it to heart . . . ," etc. Lazarus is aroused at the sight of the fiends and declares that he is not theirs but is destined for Abraham's bosom. Because the angels second him, the demons burst into the house for the rich man's debacle, scattering the people inside like a flock of birds. The first chorus to Act IV, based on verses one to six of Psalm 30 in the Vulgate, is sung in sapphic stanzas by Lazarus, with a refrain by the angels. A shorter second chorus rendered in iambic dimeters by the angels offers Lazarus reassurance. Like the other choruses in this especially musical play, these are an extension of the action, and at the end the title figure quietly dies. As is subsequently revealed, the devils seize Laemargus' soul at approximately the same moment, behind the closed door of his dwelling.

Act V begins with no time lapse. Bronchus and Typhlus return, surmising that the party is over by now, so that some remains might be available. By not going too close, they hope to avoid being beaten. As soon as he sees Lazarus, Bronchus is sure that the leper has passed away. He regrets having grabbed up all the scraps in III, 2, thereby incurring partial responsibility for Lazarus' starvation. Typhlus wants to remove the body for burial and has Bronchus help lift it onto his shoulders, as they hear a tumult in the house. With the cripple leading the way, he carries the dead man off the stage.

No sooner do they vanish than the steward flings open the door and lunges outside with Tryphera and Daemones [V, 2]. Immediately after Belial and Astaroth took Laemargus' soul, his body began to reek, and the stench is already becoming intolerable. The steward insists to Tryphera that the corpse be hauled away and disposed of at once, without ceremony, for God has clearly rejected her husband. The reluctant widow is persuaded by Daemones, who adds that God may otherwise punish them, since they have lived no better lives. The "foreign Buttubatta" (Molobrus) can be paid to cart off the body under a cover and to bury it in unhallowed earth, the steward advises, observing that delay may cause rioting in protest, for the whole city is bound to hear of what has happened. Tryphera empowers him to do whatever is best, and the three go back into the mephitic house, holding their nose. Lazarus was as putrid as a corpse in life, but Laemargus as a corpse is more putrid in death. He who complained of the leper's odor has become doubly offensive himself, thus stigmatized by God.

Thraso flees the smell with the alibi that he is waiting for Cynopa, who was sent out (evidently during the course of IV, 6) to buy more wine [V, 3]. He wonders whether Lazarus has already given up the ghost and says that he would rather be dead with the beggar than alive with the glutton. Wanting to broadcast the fate of his late master as a warning against carnality and selfishness, he cries out the news as though in grief. Cynopa returns during this vociferation and assumes that his fellow servant is drunk. On becoming convinced that Laemargus really has died, Cynopa asks to hear the full story, and Thraso narrates the events of IV, 7. After frightening witnesses away, the devils apparently

dug Laemargus' soul from his chest with their tridents, because
he was found lifeless and mangled. (Hence the commotion mentioned in V, 1.) Thraso also relates the plans for disposal of the
odious carcass and sarcastically tells Cynopa to wait a moment
more in order to see the splendid funeral pomp.

Behind the disreputable Molobrus and his boy as pallbearers,
everyone debouches from the house [V, 4]. The brothers, who fled
at the end of IV, 8, have returned. Scarcely is the procession outdoors when Belial and Astaroth dart in to appropriate the body.
Though gone in an instant, they cause such consternation that no
one sees the corpse spirited away. Molobrus perceives by the
lightness of the bier that it has been taken, but he keeps the discovery to himself, in order to earn his fee. When the cortège
leaves the stage, Thraso and Cynopa stay behind, wisecracking
again [V, 5]. The person who denied Lazarus a spot in the street
has been expelled from his own domicile, Thraso quips. The
steward comes back momentarily to have the two flunkies watch
the premises while he is absent. Accordingly Thraso and Cynopa
go in to enjoy the wine and the remaining food, leaving the stage
vacant for the final scene [V, 6], which renders the dialogue between Laemargus in hell and Abraham in heaven from Luke
16:23–31.

How this confrontation was portrayed can only be guessed,
but certainly Abraham with Lazarus in his lap was elevated.[7] In
all likelihood Laemargus simply stood on the neutral proscenium.
He begs in vain for a drop of water from the tip of Lazarus' finger
and is reminded that for his life of pleasure he must atone with
pain. Besides, Abraham observes, no one can cross the void between them. Laemargus requests that Lazarus be sent to warn
his brothers. If they do not heed Moses and the prophets, Abraham replies, they will pay no mind to an emissary from the dead.
Laemargus must burn till Judgment Day, while Lazarus reclines
in ease. An eight-line epilogue spoken by the steward closes the
play, just as Apeleutherus ends *Hecastus*. The audience is told that
it has no reason to linger, for neither the epicure nor any of his
family will return today. If the actors have been found acceptable,
they should be applauded.

In contrast to *Hecastus*, this play does not drag during its final
moments. Act V is held to a suitable length and is enlivened by
the sudden, unexpected incursion of the devils. Psychology, more-

over, is not strained for the sake of a happy end. Thanks to its probability no less than to its contrast, the unmitigated tragedy here is definitely a plus, arousing fear if not also pity. We are not supposed to sympathize with Laemargus, in fact, but only to view him as an object lesson. The conclusion of *Lazarus* is technically better than that of *Hecastus*, but the work as a whole is less original, less dramatic, and lacks particularly interesting major characters. The rich egotist is necessarily shallow, and the all too passive title figure suffers from the insipidity of his saintliness.

The minor personages are well handled, however. For the first and only time in our author's dramas the devils in *Lazarus* are more than comic supernumeraries but have an integral part in the action. Bronchus and Typhlus are sharply distinguished, with the cripple remaining generally considerate despite his human inclination to think first of himself. He and Thraso, who abandons callousness for concern, are the least simplistic characters in the play and Thraso is the only one clearly changed by what takes place, except that Laemargus is belatedly remorseful in hell.

Even after death the voluptuary maintains preeminence in this piece, just as he dominates the Biblical parable, though Macropedius' title suggests that he is supposed to have secondary importance. Indicative of his *de facto* primacy is Lazarus' utter silence during the final scene, exactly as in Luke. Contrary to his apparent intentions, Macropedius found egotistical Laemargus more fertile as a frightening deterent than the eponymous pauper as an inspiring model. In his next drama, *Joseph*, the protagonist is again overshadowed by his antagonist. Potiphar's wife is the most memorable figure there, being the most complex character that Macropedius created.

CHAPTER 6

The Models of Virtue

IN 1536 Cornelius Crocus (Croock, ca. 1500–1550), a schoolmaster in The Hague, published his influential *Joseph*. He states in his lengthy preface that he was motivated by a desire to impress on his pupils the moral excellence of the young man who wisely resisted seduction. To achieve unity of plot and unity of place, he utilized only the temptation by Potiphar's wife, the imprisonment for two years, and the release with prospects of recompense (Genesis 39:7–41:14). The result is a tightly knit drama of virtue tested and rewarded. The subject matter would not permit unity of time any more than the parable of the prodigal son does, and like Macropedius with *Asotus* Crocus excuses the inclusion of a lengthy interval between Acts IV and V by referring to Plautus' *Captives*. He also cites Terence's *The Self-Tormentor,* where a night intervenes between Acts II and III.

Macropedius followed his colleague at The Hague in selecting the same closely related episodes for his own *Joseph,* published 1544. He did not keep identical act divisions, however, and he did not adopt Crocus' small cast or imitate his long monologues with action merely reported after transpiring off-stage. He added the interpretation of Pharaoh's dreams, the elevation to second in command, and the marriage with Asenath, daughter of the priest Potipherah (Genesis 41:15–45), whom he identified with Potiphar. His version is nearly two-and-one-half times as long as Crocus'; his cast is three times as large; and his major characters are more developed. He embroidered on Crocus' play, but he kept the same moral slant. He tells us in both the prologue and the epilogue that his Joseph is to be viewed as a "champion of chastity" *(castitatis vindex).* Potiphar's amoral wife, whom Macropedius calls "Aegla" instead of Crocus' "Sephirah," assumes preeminence, but like the rich man in *Lazarus* she serves as a warning against sin.

The Pupil Jesus, printed 1556, is a similar, though weaker, attempt at creating a paragon of decorum for boys to emulate. Macropedius' concern in his final play was not with sexual abstinence but rather with humble and studious devoutness. The maudlin tone of this work, together with the fact that Jesus is twelve years old and sometimes seems younger, indicates that it was aimed at a preadolescent audience. This point might be taken as an extenuating circumstance, for *The Pupil Jesus* does its author little credit, even if we consider the advanced age at which he composed it. There is no Aegla—not even a Laemargus —to fortify this anemic play.

I *Joseph*

In the preface Macropedius makes three interesting remarks. The first is that *Joseph* was written at least as early as 1543. The second comment, concerning his lack of free time, was cited in Section V of the Introduction. The third expresses pride in his works. He asks Jacobus Delfius, to whom *Joseph* was dedicated, to have it printed if Delfius likes it. If not, Macropedius goes on to say, he himself wants a copy for further emendation, because it is natural for a mother to save her offspring from extinction, however poorly they turn out. Everyone thinks his own progeny are beautiful. The monkey nourishes and loves its young, be they ever so ugly, and the bear licks its cubs into shape, according to Pliny's *topos.* Thus Macropedius was prepared to undertake more revision if necessary but was pleased with *Joseph* as it stands. In his other prefaces he tends to belittle his plays, with the disparagement of *Aluta* being strongest.

He has presented only part of the title figure's life, Macropedius informs us in the prologue, because the whole story would not be commensurate with the demands of drama. He refers to *Joseph* as being comical or rather tragicomical, but he means only that it has a happy end, since it is without humor except for bits of sarcasm. It is the first play into which Macropedius did not introduce a single comic character or incident. As in the prologue to *Asotus* he defends his disregard for the unity of time by professing more respect for his subject matter than for thespian laws. After the call for silence and attention, the prologue closes with the request that the audience not be offended by Aegla's shameless talk or actions because without them Joseph's chaste mind

cannot be shown. Differing from the prudish Crocus, who shunts
the fateful attempt at seduction off-stage between Acts I and II,
Macropedius gives full exposure to the lust of his villainess.

The time is late afternoon as Potiphar dispiritedly trudges
onto the stage to begin Act I. Ranged across the proscenium are
to be envisioned his house, the prison, and the royal palace, in
front of which stands a tribunal. Off-stage behind the palace lies
a military camp. Potiphar is a very busy man, for he is commander
of the army, head of prisons, prophet of Serapis, and priest of
Isis. In the manner of many a Renaissance humanist, he has bitter
words for the life of a courtier, who is subject to the whims of his
lord. Already a stranger to his home like Crocus' Potiphar, he has
been delegated to the ruler of the Ethiopians and has barely man-
aged to delay for a moment of farewell. Aegla (whose name
means "radiance") comes from their house to upbraid him for
neglecting her. Why is it that for a week he scarcely shows himself, she demands to know. Is she so unattractive and unworthy of
his bed that he loathes her? The weary minister tries to make her
understand that his absence results from duty, not indifference;
but in vain. "Again you leave me bereft, disconsolate, and anxious?" she pouts. "You don't love me, to make light of me so often.
You treat the woman you like to call your wife as if you weren't
her husband." Will he not even be able to sleep with her tonight?
He will not, he confesses, and will be away for three weeks. What
solace, what pleasure, what life is she to have with such a mate,
the grass widow mourns. She might as well be married to the
wind. Better to wed a rustic than a nobleman, she sobs. Pharaoh's
minion vows to spend more time with her in the future, but Aegla
is skeptical. Changing the subject somewhat, she inquires who
will supervise the household, since she herself is too tender and
inexperienced. She is consoled to hear that Joseph will remain in
charge as he has been hitherto, although she remarks that she
would rather have Potiphar at home than chattel. Even if she is
telling the truth, despite mutual regard and a still viable affection
she is ripe for infidelity.

The slave is called forth to receive his orders, for which he is
prepared by a reminder that he has been treated like a son [I, 2].
Macropedius was probably thinking here of Terence's *Lady of
Andros*, lines 35–45, and of similar remarks by Potiphar in III, 1
and II, 3 of Crocus' drama. (The latter scene contains an echo

of lines 76–77 from Reuchlin's *Henno*.) Because his master has
been blessed by his God, Joseph will continue to oversee domestic affairs. While Aegla looks on, Potiphar tells him, in keeping
with Genesis 39:9, that she alone will not be subject to his authority and that he must do everything to make her happy. The
steward promises to oblige her completely, not considering the
full import of what he says, and she ominously rejoices to have
him as a substitute. While he is fetching a purse from the house,
harried Potiphar whisks off to his soldiers, not to be back till the
moon is full. Aegla vents both hurt and anger as she gazes after
him. "Am I not to be pitied, married to this man? Could he
justly blame me if he found me unfaithful? Away with shame,
should the opportunity arise!" she cries. Not only does she want
affection; she also seeks revenge. Some extramarital dalliance
would both ease her disquiet and punish her derelict husband.
When Joseph emerges with the money, she sends him to the camp
with it. Having already begun to cast about hungrily for an ap-
petizing lover, she has become enamored of this delicious possibility, whom she will use all her wiles to seduce.

On his return he is surprised at the tears in her eyes, for in
the past she has given evidence, he says, of not loving Potiphar
[I, 3], a hint that she has been ogling him. She asks whether the
commander was really leaving as quickly as he professed, and
Joseph reports seeing horses, chariots, and soldiers ready for departure. At once Aegla begins to talk of loneliness, saying that
there is no one at home with whom she cares to converse. Not
even her daughter Asenath is congenial, resembling Potiphar more.
Like Sephirah in I, 4 of Crocus' play, she avers that her only hope
is Joseph, whom she terms the pillar of her house. After she states
her intention to treat him not as a lackey but as her husband's
surrogate, he again vows to be helpful, though now with the
proviso that he remain honorable at the same time. This Joseph
is no naïve fool, despite his cherished chastity. Aegla is so delighted to find him cooperative that she asks him to dine with her
shortly. While waiting, he can give Asenath and the servants
further religious instruction, she suggests, as Potiphar has re-
quested. She for her part will not be present but goes inside,
probably to deck herself in her most alluring gossamer. "Who can
read this cunning woman's mind," her quarry wonders. "The
truth will out," he sighs, with an inkling of what lies in store. He

closes the act by briefly catechizing Asenath and the domestics concerning false deities, the true God, and the Trinity [I, 4]. When he withdraws for dinner, his converts remain to sing the chorus, which paraphrases in sapphic stanzas with a two-line refrain the story of the creation as told in Genesis 1:1–28.

Act II does not begin until the afternoon of the day when Potiphar is due to return. Throughout the three weeks which have passed, Aegla has persistently tried to coax Joseph into bed with her, as he declares outside in the prayer which constitutes II, 1. Theseus' son Hippolytus was not so importuned by his step-mother as he has been by his mistress, he says.[1] He does not share the cold disdain of the misogynic huntsman, however, for he confesses to God that he has been sorely tempted. Now he fears that after resorting to sophistry and trickery Aegla will arm her-self with threats of death. The thought that it is better to suffer anything than to turn from the Lord leads him to ask for con-stancy, prudence, and tolerance, in the panoply of which he can resist "the fiery darts." Because Aegla is coming outside with her attendants, he goes to the neighboring prison, where he may openly converse with his only friend, Desmophylax ("jailer"). In the manner of Crocus' Joseph (who seems to imitate Euripides' Hippolytus) he nevertheless intends to keep secret the disgraceful conduct of his owner's wife.

Like Sephirah she has grown snappish with frustration. In order to have everything ready for Potiphar, who is expected in the evening, she has a boy named Phronimus ("wise") look for a fellow domestic, Pistus ("faithful"), and for the steward [II, 2]. Before setting out, Phronimus hides nearby to see how she treats the maids, Catharis ("pure") and Agne ("chaste"). Bossily she demands that they make the bedroom spotless and suitably scented for love, while she wants the walls resplendent with tap-estries [II, 3]. Though she says so only later (II, 7), these par-ticular preparations are not so much to welcome her husband as to launch a final assault on Joseph, with the conquest of whom she has become obsessed. Leaving the girls, she paces nervously about, waiting for the Hebrew's return. Behind her back Agne mutters resentfully, shushed by an imploring Catharis. Both of them suspect that their arrogant mistress has designs on Joseph, but they are sure that he will never yield. Stepping from his hid-ing place, Phronimus barely has time to say that he detests the lady's salaciousness when the prison door squeaks open, frightening him away and hastening the maids into the house.

It is the protagonist who emerges. As soon as he spies Aegla on the prowl, he knows that she is looking for him [II, 4]. With a pledge of support and a prayer for endurance from Desmophylax, he approaches her, gritting his teeth over another tug-of-war. Not for nothing is she dressed up, he notes. When he salutes her as mistress, she asks that he call her his friend instead. She even wishes aloud that he were her spouse, moving him to demand at once that she stop pursuing what is pointless, indecorous, and impious. She argues that he should be no less concerned about her than about his God, who prescribes love for one's fellow man. When Joseph is not ensnared by such captiousness, she tries a more direct tactic. "Take this ring," she says, drawing it from her finger, "a token of our love." He refuses, advancing the offense to Potiphar as his reason, which she counters with a reminder of the instructions to make her happy. "If you want to eat gold, as they say, I'll bring you gold," he replies. "If you want me to sing, I'll sing; or to dance, I'll dance. But you'll never lure me into bed with you." Still she does not give up. She offers to be of great benefit to him, and when that maneuver fails she calls him cruel and ungrateful. Exhausting her repertoire of artifices for this occasion and racked with sobs of disappointment, she rushes into the house to recover some composure and to arrange for the ultimate attack.

Joseph is concerned about her unhappiness and tells himself that he would do anything permissible to help her [II, 5]. May God grant him strength, he prays. Asenath and the servants are suddenly chased out for more religious instruction, because Aegla wants to be alone [II, 6]. Joseph generously defends her by implying that she misses her husband. Phronimus mentions that Potiphar is due back in the evening, a point which is stressed through repetition; and in what proves to be an ironic touch the steward hopes for his master's arrival. Now he questions his catechumens on the proper conduct of the godly and dismisses them with the message that adversity is to be accepted with a tranquil mind. As they depart for a stroll, he decides that he must enter the house lest he risk the charge of negligence.

Like a spider Aegla waits. She lures him in by pretending to want his advice regarding her husband's advent [II, 7]. Dispensing with further preliminaries, she then says flatly "Sleep with me." His inevitable rebuff leads to blackmail, as in I, 4 of Crocus' version: She will assert that he violated her. "Is this the flame of love?" he protests, whereupon she immediately reverts to romance, talking of desire, embraces, and nuptials. After trying again to give him a ring, she affirms that the tapestries and incense are for him. Potiphar will not really arrive today, she lies, so that they can revel in passion till morning. Joseph's reaction seems close to boredom when he comments that she is singing the same old song, but he sheds tears in maintaining that his determination to resist has not weakened. She accuses him of feigning and tugs at his cloak. "Must you be dragged to joy?" she taunts. Better to doff his mantle and flee, he murmurs, than to create a tragedy, but a tragedy is precisely what fleeing does create, for true to her threat the jilted vamp shouts "Rape!"

The servants, who have just come back from their walk, are puzzled to see their supervisor plunge uncloaked from the house [II, 8]. With no explanation he strides away, as Aegla staggers forth, trembling and slightly disheveled to make a suitable impression. Exhibiting the mantle, she claims that "the circumcised boy" tried to ravage her. "Am I to be made a fool," she cries, "by this vilest slave?" Well might she be outraged by three weeks of constant humiliation at the hands of a mere retainer, though the fault is her own. To protect herself, as well as to get even, she wants him silenced. "If only Potiphar would come and destroy this pest before our daughter and the household are corrupted!" she rants. Asenath joins the servants in pleading for the accused, whom they privately consider innocent, but her mother refuses to listen. The daughter and the maids follow her in, leaving Phronimus and Pistus to greet the returning steward [II, 9]. Pistus commiserates, fearful of Potiphar's response, but Joseph acts stoic, like his counterpart in IV, 2 of Crocus' drama. "The potter's vessels must be tested in the kiln," he aphorizes, practicing the equanimity which he preached in II, 6. To Phronimus' proposal that they tell the master of his wife's flirtatiousness, he objects. "Better to die than to brand the mistress," he chivalrously pronounces. After sending the two sympathizers into the house, he discloses in a prayer that he is not so unperturbed as he has seemed. "My heart, throbbing with fear of death, is disconsolate," he admits, but all the same he courageously resumes his duties at the conclusion of the act. The chorus, which recapitulates his teachings from II, 6, is not within the framework of the plot, although it is sung by the servants. The meter is trochaic dimeter, alternately acatalectic and catalectic.

Following a time lapse which spans the dinner hour, Act III begins with the arrival of a soldier named "Stratophilus" (meaning "fond of the army"), who tells Aegla that Potiphar has successfully returned, has been well received by Pharaoh, and wants her pretty and happy when she meets him. Pretty she may be, but happy she is not. Even to the herald she complains of mistreatment by the Jew *(verpus)*, and as soon as she sees her husband she runs into the house. This is not at all the welcome which he expected, yet he has more cause for astonishment when she comes back with a cloak, denouncing him for not taking care of his family [III, 2]. Potiphar says exactly what she wants when he asks "Didn't I put Joseph in charge of everything, so you would be free to enjoy yourself?" "This fine fellow," she retorts, "that you brought into our house for your love, did violence to me—oh, shame!" With the expression "for your love" *(tuis amoribus)* Aegla goes so far as to impute homosexual tendencies to Potiphar because of his neglect of her. "Am I not to be pitied, left in the care of such upstanding guardians," the jezebel snivels, playing on her busy husband's conscience. He swears that he has not sinned against Joseph in any way, but if Joseph has sinned against her he himself will correct the miscreant. "You will correct him?" Aegla cynically scoffs, adding "I know how dear he is to you!" She threatens suicide unless the "Apella" (Jew) is executed. In an effort to goad Potiphar to the necessary lengths, she snorts "It grieves me to be stuck with such a spineless man!" He commands her to calm down, repeating words used by Galenus with Mysandra (line 610 of *Petriscus*), and after confessing to affection for Joseph, which he bases on the latter's loyalty and favor with God, he summons him to give account. "What do I hear?" Aegla protests. "Don't you believe your wife?" She wants the offender damned forthwith, holding up the mantle as proof of his guilt, but the judge in this trial insists on a fair hearing, much to her chagrin. When Joseph appears, Aegla again calls him "the pillar of our house," here giving a wry twist to the epithet which she used as a compliment in I, 3 (and which Potiphar utters sarcastically in III, 1 of Crocus' play, where Sephirah also wants the youth killed who can jeopardize her).[2]

Joseph begins the climactic scene [III, 3] by acting guilty, like Crocus' protagonist. "Master, I see you're very wroth at me," he stammers. "I beg you to be merciful in anger." This groveling posture induces Potiphar to believe his wife, with bitter disappointment in his protégé. As in III, 1 of Crocus' version, he reminds Joseph once more that he has treated him like a son, and after establishing that he has not abused the handsome boy, he requests some explanation for the imputed act of ingratitude. The embarrassed innocent denies blame, prompting Aegla to observe that a rapist would not hesitate to lie. She has not only the alleged culprit's cloak but his cap as well to incriminate him, while the servants witnessed his flight and her cries. Despite the evidence, Joseph refuses to defend himself with an explanation of what transpired, preferring silence like Christ before Pilate, except to plead "Have compassion for the guiltless." "Are you still making fun of me?" Potiphar exclaims in vexation. He orders the "guiltless" fellow clapped in chains and locked up until proper chastisement is devised. Aegla is indignant, or perhaps desperate, at this relative lenity and repeats her threat of suicide unless the object of her hate is hanged. Unlike Theseus, however, who precipitately invokes the death of Hippolytus, her husband is not so impetuous or so credulous as to heed her. Even if culpable, Joseph does not deserve to die, he feels, and there is still doubt in the matter. Like Crocus' Potiphar he orders his obstreperous mate into the house and comments, as in III, 2 of the earlier play, that the more she rages the more suspect is her case, particularly since Joseph has so far been pure. Several months of maceration behind bars, he reasons, will certainly cook out any lust, at which time another inquiry will be held. As the hapless steward is led away, his master goes in to check on Aegla, fearing that she may actually carry out her threat.

Outside the jail Joseph is comforted by a guard named Eupolemus ("good at war"), who assures him that even if at fault he will not long be immured [III, 4]. The fellow servants run up, having heard the news, and Desmophylax condoles, harking back to what was said off-stage during the course of II, 2–3. Taking leave of everyone but the jailer, who promises to put him in charge of the other prisoners, Joseph enters his new abode. The

servants stay to discuss his lot [III, 5], and Pistus shares the
optimism of Eupolemus from the preceding scene. The dreams
which Joseph had as a boy, Pistus says, will someday come true,
with his eleven brothers prostrating themselves at his feet. Before returning to their chores, the domestics see two men in the
service of Pharaoh being led to the prison. This pair, whose vicissitudes constitute a subplot, are the butler and the baker of
Genesis 40. Desmophylax commits them to Joseph's care and ex-
patiates on the fickleness of Fortuna, that favorite theme of Renaissance and Baroque [III, 6]. Only a fool, he philosophizes, would
feel secure with the blind goddess' gifts, be they ever so splendid.
After making this observation he retires, as do Potiphar's servants.
The chorus to Act III, in strophes of four glyconics each and
based on Psalm 12 of the Vulgate, is sung by Joseph, with a two-
line refrain rendered by the other inmates and the jailer. A different version of this song was used for III, 4 of *Lazarus*.

Act IV opens early in the morning of the next day. In performance the audience was able to see into the prison, where Pharaoh's
butler and baker both mention that they had dreams during the
night. The baker is disturbed by his, though neither knows what
his vision portends. No sooner do they wish for an interpreter than
Joseph joins them, asking why they are sad, as in Genesis 40:6–7.
The butler explains the circumstances and recounts what he saw
in his sleep. Unhesitatingly Joseph unravels the meaning for him:
In three days he will be restored to his former position. When
this happens, Joseph petitions, he himself as augur of the happy
event and a victim of injustice should be recommended to the
king. The butler gives hearty thanks, promises never to forget the
favor, and vows not to delay in carrying out the request. Cheered
by the prospects of his comrade, the baker tells his dream, but it
proves a portent of disaster. In three days he will be hanged.
Joseph extends perfunctory consolation in the thought that every-
body dies sometime and hastily excuses himself, alleging that he
has other prisoners to attend to.

Between IV, 1 and IV, 2 the three days elapse. Potiphar comes
to the prison with a bad conscience over the treatment of his
steward, for he remembers the young man's unflagging fidelity
and wisdom, without which domstic affairs have deteriorated.
Hopefully the lad will have already been softened enough to acknowledge his transgressions and to beg forgiveness, Potiphar

muses. He chats with Desmophylax for a moment outside and hears the disquieting news that Joseph has steadfastly denied guilt [IV, 3]. After his chief has gone in, the jailer speculates that Potiphar believes in the Hebrew's innocence and needs his help but is kowtowing to Aegla. In this observation Macropedius gives us the key to understanding the commander. He fears his wife more than enemy troops, Desmophylax sneers, adding that the man has in effect given himself in bondage to the woman. So that life can return to normal, Potiphar wants to vindicate his spouse, who would have nothing more to fear if Joseph stated that he really did forget himself and try to rape her. An admission that she brought false charges, however, would entail embarrassment. Unfortunately, the champion of chastity refuses to discredit himself by cooperating.

Potiphar soon returns, irked that his slave is making difficulties [IV, 4]. Desmophylax contends that Joseph's reputation outweighs the circumstantial evidence against him. Potiphar is offended that his wife is thus accused by inference, but the jailer soothes his ruffled boss by sophistically insisting that he is only trying to support a guiltless man. Potiphar postpones further discussion of this controversial subject with the excuse that Pharaoh's birthday is upon them, giving them much to do. After Desmophylax has gone back into the prison, Potiphar admits to himself that it is more honorable, more advantageous, and safer to side with his wife than with his bondsman. At the approach of two royal ministers, Apotomus ("abrupt") and Hyperetes ("assistant"), he hurries to the palace to see what business awaits him.

The officials are coming for the butler and the baker, as the dreams foretold, and Hyperetes surmises that as usual on holidays Pharaoh will demonstrate his clemency and his severity by freeing one prisoner and punishing the other [IV, 5]. In conducting the two from their cell, Joseph reminds the happy butler not to forget him [IV, 6]. The final scene of the act is held in the palace, where the mighty despot squats on his throne, condemning and reprieving as predicted. For the festive occasion he has musicians strike up a melody, and the chorus, based on Apocryphal First Esdras 3:18–4:41, is once again a continuation of the action.[3]

It is unusually long, perhaps as a sign that two years pass. During this time Joseph has remained incarcerated, forgotten by the butler. Since neither he nor Aegla has been willing to yield, Potiphar has left him, preferring peace to justice. It is early morning when Pharaoh summons the commander along with his counselors in Scene 1 to have his dreams (from Genesis 41:1–7) interpreted. He feels that they are highly significant and that prompt explication is imperative. Without equivocating, the wise men confess that his cows and ears of grain have them stumped. Maybe Potiphar, prophet of Serapis and priest of Isis, can decode the symbols, they propose, but he is also baffled and requests a day to ruminate. Grudgingly the tyrant consents, vowing to execute the lot of them should they not have an answer in twenty-four hours. Sounding like Hecastus when Philomathes is preplexed by Hebrew, he thunders "Do I support you at great expense so you can give me empty words in serious affairs, as though I were stupid?"

Outside, Potiphar voices helpless anxiety and wishes for someone at home in whom he might confide [V, 2]. Apostrophizing Joseph, he groans "Too late I regret imprisoning you—you who were always a solace to me." As he leaves to pray and sacrifice to Serapis for revelation, he notices that inside the palace the butler is kneeling before Pharaoh. "Forgive my negligence," the cupbearer begs [V, 3], explaining that a Jew in the prison correctly clarified his and the former baker's dreams and asked to be recommended to the king for release. When questioned about him, the butler briefly recounts the history of Joseph, charging that Potiphar jailed him wrongly to please Aegla. Assured that the young man can be of help, Pharaoh orders him brought as quickly as possible. Hyperetes, who accompanies the butler to the jail, remarks that if the prisoner really is innocent, Potiphar's head is in grave danger.

Desmophylax congratulates the butler on his good luck, though chiding him for forgetting Joseph [V, 4], who also has words of reproof when he appears, as in V, 3 of Crocus' play. Joseph receives an humble apology, however, along with the information that Pharaoh needs his oneirocritical talents. Since he is shaggy, dirty, and ragged, he is escorted off-stage for a trim, a bath, and a change of clothes. Like the jailer at the end of Crocus' *Joseph*, Desmophylax is delighted over his friend's reversal of fortune. He goes next door to inform his superior of what is taking place, surmising like Hyperetes that Potiphar and his wife are in trouble [V, 5]. Joseph's reputation argues his innocence, while Aegla's chasteness has long been suspect. Desmophylax meets Pistus and learns that Potiphar has gone to the temple of Serapis to study entrails [V, 6]. "In vain," he comments, explaining that someone has been found who will really clear up the mysteries. That must be a singular Oedipus, Pistus responds, curious to know who the person is. When he hears that it is Joseph, tears well in his eyes. The jailer relates how the turn of events has come about, and Pistus wishes success for his former supervisor. He will succeed, Desmophylax declares, for he is inspired by the true God. Pistus also foresees catastrophe for his master and mistress, "on account of their impudence and imprudence." The jailer notes that because Joseph was born of free parents he has been improperly held in servitude. As Desmophylax departs for Serapis' temple to warn Potiphar, Pistus descries the butler and Hyperetes conducting their now presentable diviner to the palace. The butler has recounted Pharaoh's dreams and is saying that a full explanation of them will bring a rich reward [V, 7]. Joseph cares nothing for aggrandizement and suggests (as in Genesis 41:16) that he will be only the agent of God, a point which he subsequently reiterates. Leaving him outside with Hyperetes for a moment, the butler goes in to the throne room to announce his arrival. Joseph prays for wisdom.

Welcomed in by Pharaoh, he prostrates himself and begs for liberation [V, 8]. The now avuncular despot magnanimously consents, assuring him that he knows of his mistreatment and guaranteeing protection. If Joseph fulfills expectations, Pharaoh promises, he will be elevated above his superiors and his enemies. After saying that he fell asleep pondering the misfortunes of the poor and the possessions of the rich, Pharaoh relates his dreams— a redundancy in the play which Macropedius my have intended, following the repetition in Genesis 41. Joseph expounds the royal visions and advises the king to seek out an honest, loyal, and industrious man to store up grain against the famine. Pharaoh gratefully pays homage to the true God, sends for Potiphar, and takes Joseph "inside," [4] empowering him to pass judgment on his former master. Thaltibius,[5] the messenger dispatched to the commander, says that Potiphar would be done for if the monarch were not more clement with him than Potiphar has been with his blameless servant.

Accompanied by Desmophylax, the prophet is fretfully walking toward his home from Serapis' temple [V, 9]. He asserts that he has always been fond of his steward and was reluctant to jail him for his "disgraceful deed." "I hope no danger threatens me as a result," he says apprehensively. Desmophylax concedes that his boss has never been averse to Joseph but contends again, as in IV, 4, that he had more reason to believe the young man than his lecherous wife. Potiphar now agrees but asks why Joseph did not defend himself when accused, if he was guiltless. "The faithful servant proves his worth by preferring punishment to betrayal of his mistress' shamefulness," Desmophylax explains, adding that Joseph has tearfully told him this a thousand times. Potiphar is belatedly remorseful over his indiscretion, being imperiled as a consequence of it. When he asks what he is to do, the jailer suggests that he seek pardon without trying to defend himself.

The sight of Thaltibius fills Potiphar with fear. Like Nomodidascalus in II, 7 of *Hecastus*, the messenger reports that the king has ordered him to trial. Potiphar is compliant but wants first to talk to his wife for a moment. Desmophylax asks about Joseph and learns that in all likelihood he has been or will be put in charge of everything, for he has successfully rendered the meaning of the dreams. Potiphar states bravely that nothing pleases him more than this news. When Thaltibius has departed, the priest of Isis and prophet of Serapis cries out to Jupiter, wondering (in language similar to Mysandra's in V, 6 of *Petriscus*) whether Joseph will be propitious. Like Galenus he holds his wife responsible for his troubles. "May the unjust woman be damned who led me into these straits with her lust, guile, and immodesty!" he curses. Desmophylax leaves him with the reassurance that Joseph is gracious. "Woe is me!" whines Potiphar, pitying himself like Galenus and Byrsocopus, as Aegla steps from the house, to climax their subplot.

She has not appeared since III, 3, but she has made her presence felt through her husband and the imprisonment of her erstwhile prey. When she asks Potiphar why he is being so tragic, his wrath erupts [V, 10]. "What do I hear, corrupted pig, about you seducing my virtuous servants with your obscene talk, prostituting yourself, and ruining me?" he roars, as though just becoming aware that she has been false with him. She affects hurt and innocence, asking what she has done wrong. Told that Joseph has suffered because of her lewdness, she complains that she is being vilified. Potiphar informs her that her victim has just been raised to a position from which he can take revenge. Lest she escape unscathed while he himself is executed, he draws his sword, ready to cut her throat. This unexpected ferocity frightens her into an abject confession, but her frenzied husband lacks the mercifulness which he desires in Joseph, reminding us of Thaltibius' remark at the end of V, 8. If Eupolemus, who has been attracted to the scene, did not intervene to save her, Aegla would be murdered. Potiphar leaps from one emotional extreme to the other no less than Byrsocopus or Georgus in *Andrisca*, while his wife is reformed by the menace of death like Dyscolus, Clopicus, Petriscus, and Hecastus, mustering the fortitude of Mysandra to avert tragedy. "I committed the crime," she declares, "and I will bear the consequences." She will beg Joseph and Pharaoh to pardon both of them. If she fails in her effort, Potiphar may then kill her. Pacified somewhat, he sheathes his sword and tows her into the house to discuss the situation, yielding the stage to his former steward. Eupolemus, who has been left outside, sees the court issue from the palace. Since the king will either mount the tribunal to pass judgment or will honor Joseph, Potiphar must hurry, and the soldier goes in to fetch him.

Pharaoh is peeved at his courtier's delay [V, 11]. While waiting, he has Thaltibius summon Joseph. To four satraps who are functioning as advisers he remarks that someone is needed to manage grain storage prior to the famine and that no one seems to him better suited for this position than the interpreter of dreams. Since the counselors would not dare disagree, when Joseph appears in V, 12 Pharaoh places him over all the affairs of Egypt. The young dignitary objects that he lacks the necessary prestige to command respect, particularly having been a slave, but he is assured as in Genesis 41:44 that no one will lift hand or foot without his approval and that he will be second in command. When the satraps pledge their loyalty, he accepts the offer, dedicating energy, care, and his very life to the welfare of Pharaoh and the Egyptian people. The advisers recommend that the appointment be announced to the public so that the viceroy will be universally venerated. After dressing him in a royal robe and hanging a golden chain around his neck, Thaltibius is accordingly sent into the streets with Joseph to proclaim him "savior of the world," conveniently removing him from the stage for the following scene. Later the new minister will be taken from town to town in the second chariot of the kingdom. Seeing Potiphar and Aegla at last approaching, Pharaoh dismisses the satraps, in order to deal privately with his disgraced official.

Throughout V, 13 Joseph is conducted about as Thaltibius chants "By edict of the king this man is to be called the savior of the world and reverenced with genuflection by Egyptians." Such exaltation bodes ill for Potiphar, and he anticipates the worst, whimpering that he is to be sacrificed to a woman's lust. Aegla tries to encourage him by repeating that she will suffer the consequences, but he is scornful and continues to wail, luxuriating in self-pity. "Oh if the ground would open up and swallow me!" he postures tragically. While Thaltibius is heard somewhere broadcasting his proclamation, Aegla flings herself at Pharaoh's feet and makes a clean breast of her trespasses. Not only did she try to seduce the chaste Joseph but she also inveigled her blameless husband into jailing him. She implores that they be pardoned or that only she pay their penalty. Pharaoh rebukes his humiliated general for believing her and thereby tarnishing the splendor of the crown. He holds the man almost as responsible as the woman but reserves judgment for Joseph to pass. When the latter returns [V, 14], Potiphar begs him for mercy, supported by Aegla, who maintains that her husband's only fault was to trust her more than is proper. Because Joseph is benign, Pharaoh restores the commander, chief warden, prophet, and priest to his prior dignities and orders all unpleasantness forgotten. As if to seal the reconciliation, he commands Potiphar to engage Asenath to the new governor. Perhaps he sees this marriage also as a way of insuring the legitimation of the former slave. While Thaltibius goes to bring the girl, Aegla warns in motherly fashion that because of worry Asenath will have forgotten to primp, but Joseph deprecates appearance. "I know the nature of your daughter," he says, "whom I taught from the cradle to fear the Lord."

During the course of her walk toward the tribunal Thaltibius tells Asenath that she has been called by Pharaoh to rejoice with her parents over their restoration to favor [V, 15]. Her father comes to meet her, followed by Joseph and the king himself, and Potiphar relates the royal wish for her marriage. He urges her to consider the proposal, but he does not order her to accept it. "It is improper for a father to betroth his daughter against her will," he says. Fortunately she does not refuse, even though she seems unenthusiastic. "It is right that what pleases the king, all the nobles, and my parents also please me," she murmurs demurely in acquiescing. To her fiancé she swears to be faithful and virtuous and to rear the children correctly, as does he in turn. He gives her "tokens of mutual love and faith," presumably rings like the one which Aegla tried to force upon him in II, 4 and 7. As though remembering it, she tells Asenath that her husband-to-be is "the most pious and by far the chastest of mortals." With tears in her eyes she again expresses remorse and shame over her ignoble conduct. Pharaoh reminds her that the past has been consigned to oblivion and that joy is now in order. Everyone files into the palace, while Thaltibius lingers to inform the audience that what follows will take place in inner chambers. There is nothing more to observe. In a twelve-line epilogue we are told to imitate Joseph, having seen embarrassment, pain, danger, and death as the consequences of lubricity. Honor, praise, and eternal glory, the rewards of chastity, are preferable. Worthy souls who favor sexual restraint are asked to applaud if the cast was pleasing.

Though Macropedius took a motherly pride in *Joseph,* the work is not without faults. At over 2,100 lines in length, it is flaccid with repetitions. Asenath, moreover, is not accorded a prominence early in the play commensurate with her role at the end. In this respect she resemble's Henno's daughter Abra in Reuchlin's farce. After previously appearing only as a mute character, Abra is engaged to Dromo in the closing lines. Instead of having Asenath catechized along with the servants in both I, 4 and II, 6, Macropedius could have devoted the earlier scene to a memorable introduction of this girl later affianced to his title figure. Joseph himself has more personality than Lazarus the beggar, but as a champion of chastity and a prefiguration of Christ ("savior of the world") he is still too straitlaced to preoccupy us. Our interest is drawn from his monotonous high-mindedness to the marital turmoil of his master and mistress.

At first mainly a victim of the circumstances which keep him from hearth and bed, Potiphar shows in Acts III–V that he is also another namby-pamby like Galenus. Only when forced to take a stand does he oppose the wife whom he has for two years appeased. Although he is naturally reluctant to expose her as a false accuser, the consequences at the outset would not be serious.

He is primarily motivated neither by gallantry nor by a desire to preserve intact the honor of his name but simply shies from hurting the vixen who would shatter domestic tranquillity with her snarls. He knows that he would not be assertive enough to muzzle her. In Potiphar's weakness Macropedius gives a better reason for the duration of Joseph's imprisonment than is offered either by Genesis or by Crocus, who adheres more to the sketchy biblical source.

Aegla combines the shrewdness of Mysandra with the sexuality of Porna, yet like Mysandra she comes to demonstrate strength of character. She is a more forgivable jade than Porna, since her transgressions are grounded in her husband's neglect. All of her changing behavior is well motivated. Her vengefulness against the steward results from rejection as well as from the desire to protect herself; and her confession, which Macropedius added to exonerate Joseph and to make reconciliation possible, is wrested from her at sword point. Once the truth is out, her native goodness can reassert itself in contrition and corrective action. She has appeal as an essentially noble woman who has been allowed to succumb to her baser passions. In her, Macropedius' art as a dramatic portraitist reaches its final culmination. The characters that follow are the mediocrities of his senescence.

II   *The Pupil Jesus*

The prologue to his last theatrical work was composed to be spoken by Macropedius himself. He says that he is presenting the pupil Jesus because he wants to imbue his own pupils with the young Christ's conduct. He still considers it indecent to introduce the mature Lord into a comedy (i.e., a play with a happy ending and maybe a few comic touches), but he intimates that he has come to view the Passion as suitable subject matter for stately tragedy, perhaps as treated in Latin by the later Dutchman Hugo Grotius (1583–1645). If this notion is in fact the import of his vague manner of expression, Macropedius contradicts the opinion couched some twenty-five years earlier in the prologue to *Lazarus*. What he states is this: "I would by no means comically portray for you the Man mighty in word and deed. To my mind that would be unseemly. Not all stories are appropriate for comedy. Serious ones are more fitting for tragedy, especially if the characters are heroic and have a sad end." The prologue closes by admonishing lads in the audience to learn attentively from the comportment of both the boy Jesus and His virgin mother.

There is no plot summary to this play, possibly because there is scarcely any plot. The vapid piece is based on Luke 2:41–51, where Christ at age twelve goes about His Father's business with doctors in the temple. The setting is therefore Jerusalem. We are to imagine on the stage the synagogue and the nearby house of young Justus, the future Barsabas of Acts 1:23. The action lasts four days, beginning in the afternoon of the first. Mary, Joseph, and Jesus have come to Jerusalem for the passover, as have Zacharias, Elizabeth, and their son John. The two women and the twelve-year-olds meet, with much weeping and reiteration of lines [I, 1–2]. The husbands join them, and all are about to enter the temple when John the son of Zebedee appears [I, 3]. Mary and Jesus already know him, and the future apostle is introduced to the future baptizer. Stephen, the future martyr, comes from the synagogue to announce that because of uncertainty regarding the Messiah a debate on the subject will be conducted by Gamaliel the following morning [I, 4]. The public is invited to attend, and Jesus longs to do so. Knowing that His parents will not permit, He plans to sneak away from them, in order not to be disobedient. The fact that He is sophistical Macropedius overlooked. In alternately acatalectic and catalectic trochaic dimeters, the meter of all its odes in this play, the chorus sings of raising children to fear the Lord.

Act II opens on the morning of the second day. Jesus is perturbed over the anxiety which He will cause His mother when she discovers that He has stayed behind, but the worry is better than the perishing of mankind, He rationalizes, as though the future of the human race depended on His participation in the imminent discussion. He prays that His mother be comforted, and the angel Gabriel appears with encouragement for Him [II, 2], a touch perhaps suggested by Luke 22:43. After two more days, says Gabriel, Joseph and Mary will be brought back. Despite the reassurance, Jesus sheds tears profusely at His loneliness and His parents' apprehension [II, 3]. He is watched by Gamaliel's sons, Nathaniel and Abibas, and the latter of the two raves over His beauty [II, 4], which signifies divinity, just as Joseph's represents purity. After Jesus has prayed for heavenly support, the pair accost Him, inquiring who He is and why He is here [II, 5–6].

Following a pointless scene break, Nathaniel promises a slice of buttered or honeyed bread in return for being taught how to pray in Jesus' manner [II, 7]. His request is for the time being forgotten in further conversation, however, as Jesus speaks of being taught by His Father. Nathaniel goes to tell Gamaliel of the newcomer, noticing at his departure that young Saul is approaching.

Since Abibas asks about His unusual tunic [II, 8], Jesus explains that His mother made it when He was a baby and that God lets it automatically increase with His size. When He dies it is to pass into foreigners' hands (in keeping with Matthew 27:35 and John 19:23–24). Thinking of His crucifixion makes Him burst into tears again, but Abibas tells Him not to cry, for sardonic Saul might mock. Upon joining them, the future Paul shows great arrogance toward Justus, who also comes up [II, 9]. Stephen, whose martyrdom Jesus foresees, exits from the synagogue to summon the little group to the debate [II, 10]. Though Saul maintains his haughtiness toward Justus, whom he disdains as ignorant, Justus shows that he has both learning and a gift of prophecy in applying to Saul the ravenous wolf of Genesis 49:27, which devours its prey in the morning, sharing its spoils at night. The chorus ends Act II by asking that capable boys be educated.

The first five scenes of Act III take place in the temple. Even though he wonders whether anything good can come out of Nazareth (like Nathaniel in John 1:46), Gamaliel is eager to meet Jesus and gives Him a cordial welcome [III, 1–2]. As in II, 7, Jesus uses some irony in saying that He has been instructed by His Father, seeming to mean the humble carpenter Joseph. Discussion of the Messiah begins as two rabbis disagree over the presence of evidence in the Prophets [III, 3]. Jesus cites Genesis 3:15, Isaiah 53:8, and Deuteronomy 18:18 as proof that a Deliverer will come [III, 4], and after another senseless scene break he quotes Genesis 49:10 as further testimony [III, 5]. Despite the fact that it has hardly begun, Gamaliel adjourns the disputation until the following morning, when the nature of the Messiah will be argued. The high priest observes that Jesus Himself might be the Son of God if He were not lowborn. Gamaliel tells Abibas to take his newfound friend home for lunch, indicating that in the course of this day's brief debate several hours are supposed to have elapsed.

Outside the temple it is Justus who takes Jesus in tow [III, 6].

Before parting, Abibas, who is to lodge the guest tomorrow, remembers to ask again "how the heavenly Father is to be invoked."
What Jesus teaches him is of course the Lord's Prayer, for which
the promised buttered bread is rendered on the spot. On the way
home Justus inquires whether Jesus is accustomed to eat bread
and milk, as he himself is [III, 7]. Jesus says that like His cousin
John, who will live in the desert, He is being raised on an austere
diet. In fact, now He wants to skip lunch lest they be late for the
resumption of the debate—Macropedius having temporarily forgotten that the continuation is not to be held until the next
morning. Justus suggests that they see first whether the meal is
ready, and they end Act III by going into his house. The chorus
reminds us that God takes preference over parents.

Act IV begins early in the third day. Outside and alone, Jesus
prays that His efforts in God's behalf will be blessed and that His
mother will be consoled. With tear-stained cheeks He enters the
synagogue, where Gamaliel receives Him solicitously and repeats
that the nature of the Messiah is the topic for the present session
[IV, 2–3]. Scarcely has the traditional opinion of the Christ as a
conquering hero been stated when the moderator calls for a post-
ponement of debate for fear that "lengthy talk may lead to boredom" [IV, 4], but the high priest insists that Jesus be heard first.
The precocious stripling argues that cogent evidence for the es-
tablished view is wanting and that Zechariah 9:9 shows the
Messiah to be humble rather than regal [IV, 5]. Anticipating
John 18:36, He says "My kingdom is not of this world," whereupon the high priest inquires whether the Messiah is not then to
be God. Jesus' reply that He will be both God and man is rejected as absurd. Again Gamaliel wants to adjourn, but Saul demands a confrontation with the radical, whom he calls "foul"
[IV, 6]. "Saul, Saul, why do you try to persecute me?" Jesus protests, as in Acts 9:4. He defends Himself by referring to Isaiah
53:2–8 and 12, a passage with which the young Pharisee must
confess that he is not familiar. Accordingly, Saul also calls for a
break.

Justus takes Jesus home for lunch again and offers to look for
His mother the next morning, when she is expected to return [IV,
7]. Her tears, he says, will identify her. At mention of tears Jesus
sheds more of His own. While they are eating, Saul joins them,
and Jesus prevails upon Justus to let the greedy intruder share

their food [IV, 8]. Followed by Justus, Jesus soon leaves the table to pray again for His parents, also requesting that an angel direct Him, and one does come to wipe away the inevitable tears. Left alone to gobble what remains, Saul opines that Jesus may be more than He seems, but the traditionalist nevertheless vows to maintain tenaciously the laws and mores of his ancestors, which Jesus, he says, is striving to abrogate. Having sated himself, Saul brutishly comments that he must "lighten his grunting belly." He would also be wise, he decides, not to return to the debate, and we consequently see no more of him. In the temple Gamaliel calls for discussion of Jesus' position and announces that the theme for the disputation to be held the following morning will be the coming of the Messiah [IV, 9]. The chorus says in its chant that Christians, especially little boys, should be honest.

Gamaliel begins Act V early in the fourth day by acknowledging that Jesus' notions have bothered him. The lad arrives at the synagogue and relates that He slept again with Justus (instead of with Abibas), who is now looking for His parents. No sooner does Gamaliel reconvene the disputation than Justus breathlessly interrupts to announce that the mother and father are here [V, 2]. The reunion occasions more weeping, this time for joy [V, 3].

With Mary and Joseph waiting outside, Jesus obliges the rabbis by staying long enough to assert that the Messiah has already come and is gradually to make Himself known [V, 4]. While Jesus then fetches His mother, with whom the high priest requests a few words, Nathaniel suggests that this same youth is Himself the Christ [V, 5]. The high priest demurs in view of Jesus' lowly birth, apparently in Nazareth rather than in Bethlehem, but after Mary reports that her son was actually born in the latter town and that He was instructed by divine grace [V, 6], Nathaniel wins general agreement [V, 7].

Outside, Jesus bids his newfound friends adieu [V, 8], having already thanked the doctors in the temple. Along with Justus and Stephen, whose future martyrdom causes Jesus to cry again, Philip, Prochorus, Nicanor, Timon, and Parmenas of Acts 6:5 are present. Jesus asks about Saul and is informed that he has been temporarily blinded by the north wind, a foretaste of the sightlessness at his conversion and symbolic of his mental state. As Jesus and His parents start for home, the latter are puzzled by what their son must do in years to come [V, 9]. A fifteen-line epilogue reminds schoolboys that they should be humble, upright, and obedient like the young Savior. The speaker begs indulgence for bringing Christ "into this theater" and jokingly warns that anyone disturbed by the word "pupil" in the title will be treated like a pupil. The epilogue concludes with a call for applause.

Macropedius' swan song is, alas, a feeble croak. The best possibility for drama which his subject matter offers—the clash of controversy—he minimized, achieving tension mainly through the conflict between Jesus' duty to God and His concern for His mother. While Jesus is the only figure at all developed, moreover, His lachrymoseness palls. The idea of using Saul as the principal foil is good, but the play would benefit from a more serious and extensive presentation of him in the role of adversary. At the very least Macropedius should have kept his time sequence straight! In the next and last chapter we must succinctly review two other late works which are also no artistic successes. By reviving the sweep of medieval mysteries they are strikingly different, though like *The Pupil Jesus* they might be called colloquies rather than dramas.

CHAPTER 7

The Impatient

IN the period of nine years or more from the completion of *Joseph* (published 1544) to 1553, Macropedius wrote only two more stage works. *Adam* and *Hypomone* were both released in the first volume of his revised and collected plays, the title page of which carries the date 1552, though the preface to *Hypomone* was composed only the following year and the imprimatur was not issued until 1554. In his letter of May 9, 1549, the author acknowledges that his creativity was slack: "Our Muses are languishing, barren and unproductive," he writes, laying the blame at least in part on the torture of his gout.[1] At nearly 2,700 lines, *Adam* is his longest theatrical piece, despite the sterility of his Muses, but its length merely underscores its epic, rather than dramatic, nature. What Macropedius' aging Muses could still bring forth is frail, bearing witness to tenacity more than to talent, as we have discovered with *The Pupil Jesus*.

I *Adam*

In the preface, which is dated October 14, 1551, the author alerts us to a possible disjointedness, particularly in Act V, for at the suggestion of friends, as he relates, he excised some non-biblical material which was felt to be too fictitious for the solemnity of the subject. Despite this soberness, he speaks of the work in the prologue as a comedy. Because it portrays the history of man down to the coming of Christ, it has a happy end after much perturbation. Adam and Eve, who observe the unfolding of events and yearn throughout for redemption from the evil which they have caused, represent all humanity. Though confronted by a serious theme with roughly the structure of a comedy, we are told not to look for either jollity or strutting in the tragic style, as do frivolous men, foolish boys, and women, but rather to expect gentle manners and Christian moderation.

What we mostly find is a great deal of lamentation, starting right at the outset, when Eve (who is to be pictured as wearing more than a fig leaf) bewails her troubles in exile from Eden. The worst of these is Cain's jealousy. Adam joins her in the fields, reciting more from their Iliad of woes, including Cain's threat to murder the more successful Abel [I, 2]. As soon as the parents leave for their abode in hopes of calming the angry son, he steps before us [I, 3]. A churlish Asotus, he chafes at his lack of freedom and vows riddance of the younger brother who might dominate him. The voice of God (Elohim) booms out in a vain attempt at reason, as Abel comes to be bludgeoned on the stage. Seeing his father and mother returning, Cain flees the mangled corpse. Adam and Eve are not surprised to discover it, having expected the worst, though she waxes rhetorically emotional and eventually he cries to the Lord in despair at all their sufferings [I, 4]. After Eve withdraws despondently, her husband's guardian angel appears [I, 5]. Uriel, as he is named, chides Adam for lack of faith in God's promise that the woman's seed will crush the serpent's head (Genesis 3:15), a forecast of Christ that readers of Dutch literature remember from Joost van den Vondel's *Lucifer* (1654). Uriel goes on to announce that Abel will one day be replaced by a person as mild, pious, and just, who will likewise be killed undeservedly, thereby releasing the human race from death. This ransoming will not take place, however, until man has endured enough to appreciate his Savior. Adam hopes to cheer his wife with this news and hurries off to find her, leaving the stage to Cain, who comes with a bad conscience but affects innocence when the voice of God inquires where Abel is [I, 6]. Sentenced to be an outcast, Cain decides to give himself over to temporal pleasures since eternal rewards are denied him, and he sets out at once in order to avoid his parents, who are again wending their way back. Thus Macropedius twice foregoes a potentially dramatic encounter, though one not authorized by his biblical source, Genesis 4:3–15. Eve has been solaced somewhat, but she is still distraught at the prospect of waiting eons to be saved [I, 7]. With a reminder that the dead will ultimately be restored, Adam rouses her to help bury Abel. As they lift up the body and carry it away, they join the chorus in singing praises to God.[2]

For Act II we go to Genesis 22:4–13. The protagonists have not died, contrary to Scripture, and as a result are well up in years.

In the opening scene Adam informs us that nothwithstanding a lapse of three millennia no trace of a Messiah has been detected. High hopes that Noah would bring deliverance never materialized. Like awestruck Thraso sensing the presence of a deity when the angel approaches Laemargus' house in IV, 6 of *Lazarus the Beggar,* Eve is possessed with dread and feels divineness at hand as both Adam's guardian angel and her own draw near. Uriel makes clear that Noah in his ark symbolized man purified by the waters of baptism [II, 2]. Eve asks her angel, Raziel,[3] to allegorize Abraham, who comes onto the stage with Isaac. The boy is given a load of wood to carry, while his tearful sire brings a torch and a sword, observing that the Lord will provide the sacrificial victim [II, 3]. Raziel describes how Abraham, who represents God, prepares to immolate his son, who in turn is analogous to Christ. Eve comments that Isaac reminds her of Abel. As the lad is about to be slaughtered, Elohim's voice resounds once more, staying the upraised knife. The guardian angels depart, and the relieved father greets first Eve [II, 4] then Adam [II, 5], who has been at a distance, conversing with Uriel. Abraham relates that for a surrogate he has just offered up a ram caught in nearby brambles (suggesting that the altar is off-stage). Upon asking him when salvation is due, Adam becomes as distressed as his spouse to hear that they must still be patient for many ages. They decide to retire to a cave to grieve, though they will follow Abraham's descendants into Egypt. After the patriarch has bid them farewell and exited with Isaac, the old couple shuffle out to the funeral strains of an elegy on death and suffering, which they chant with the chorus.

In an apparently short period Act III combines events from Exodus, Leviticus, and Numbers, as the children of Israel are encamped near Mount Horeb in the Sinai peninsula. Adam is heartened by God's graciousness to His chosen people in leading them from Egypt, but Eve is worried about the dangers of the desert [III, 1]. Her husband's comment to the effect that we mortals rightfully suffer because of our sinfulness provokes from her a wish for the promulgation of laws determining what is reprehensible. Adam concedes some justification for this desire but fears that with more statutes will come worse punishment. Unable to keep one commandment, can they expect to abide by many? He longs for Uriel's advice, as well as for clarification of

the Passover. Nadab and Abihu, two of Aaron's sons, approach,
so he questions them regarding the latter point. Abihu relates
what happened on that fateful fourteenth day of Nisan (Exodus
12) but leaves the hidden significance for "Moses or your guardian
angels" to expound.[4] The Levites excuse themselves to proceed
with their duties, and Uriel appears. Adam makes his wife's request for more laws, only to be told contemptuously that man
should rely on his reason and conscience to know what pleases
God and should use his free will to act accordingly [III, 2]. Uriel
repeats his charge's own reservations regarding increased man-
dates, but Adam persists in the demand for them. In immediate
response God issues the Ten Commandments [III, 3], causing
Adam to have second thoughts already. Concerning divine decrees
Eve wants to talk to Moses, whom she sees off-stage with horns,
radiant countenance, and tablets of stone. After his face has been
veiled (Exodus 34:29–35), the liberator of the Hebrews comes to
meet his distinguished visitors, informing them that eventually
God will send a Prophet with new laws [III, 4]. For many gen-
erations, however, a harsher code must be rigidly enforced. Only
after the present covenant has run its course will the new be
made. As proof of just how stringent the prior laws are, a violator
of the sabbath is apprehended [III, 5], and before he can be tried
word is brought that Nadab and Abihu have been burned up for
employing unconsecrated fire, as in Leviticus 10:1–2 [III, 6].
For gathering two or three sticks on the day of rest the prisoner
is sentenced by the voice of Elohim to be stoned, in accordance
with Numbers 15:32–36 [III, 7]. Eve wonders how God can expect to be loved when He treats His people like dogs [III, 8].
Adam, who is not so self-assertive, tells her to be submissively
obedient, and Moses explains that whoever sins against the Lord
deserves to die. Even he, the transmitter of the law, will be punished for his anger and his disbelief, he predicts. As wailing is
is heard from the camp, signaling some disaster, Eve wishes for a
guardian angel to offer consolation and to expound the mystery
of manna. Anticipating John 6:48–51, Uriel obligingly discloses
that manna typifies Christ, "the true bread to come," bestowing
eternal life upon those who partake of Him. Two boys with
baskets of the heavenly food let the elderly pair sample it, though
one of the tykes is reluctant until Eve promises presents in return.
For selling God's gift his outraged friend will see that he is

spanked by his father. On another part of the stage a post from
which a bronze snake dangles has been erected, and people are
grouped about it. As in Numbers 21:4–9, they have been bitten
by fiery serpents because of their grumbling. Now repentant, they
are healed by looking at this brazen replica [III, 9]. Sensing further allegory here, Eve wishes once again for explication, and
Raziel informs her that this viper also prefigures Christ, who will
hang from a cross, saving from Satan's poison those who look to
Him [III, 10]. Moses invites his guests into the camp, where they
will learn about additional decrees, Judaic rites, and symbolism
of the tabernacle [III, 11]. Again dispirited over redemption's
delay, Adam and Eve quit the stage to the plangency of another
sorrowful ode. With the chorus they sing of their fall and ex-
pulsion from Eden.

For Act IV we skip to David's bout with Goliath (I Samuel
17), after which we also meet four prophets. In the first scene Eve
sadly calls the roll of important people who have perished in the
meantime, and Adam warns her not to complain, for God is just.
Together Uriel and Raziel announce that most of the waiting is
over [IV, 2]. They say that from the recently annointed son of
Jesse to Daniel 490 years *(septuaginta hebdomades)* must pass.
Then "the Babylonian boy" will disclose how much time remains.
The two angels also explain that David prefigures Christ by kill-
ing in the Philistine giant a representation of Satan. While the
combat takes place, Adam and Eve give a running commentary in
the manner of modern sportscasters [IV, 3 and 4], but when the
victor emerges from the fray, brandishing the loser's severed head,
there is no interview as with Moses and Abraham. Instead, Uriel
and Raziel immediately present Isaiah, Jeremiah, and Ezekiel,
who foretell the coming of the Messiah, paraphrasing their own
words in the Bible [5] [IV, 5]. No sooner do they depart than the
prophet from Babylon appears [IV, 6], thereby indicating that
the 490 years mentioned in Scene 2 have almost imperceptibly
flashed by.[6] Using language from Daniel 9:24–27, he predicts that
after a period of equal length Christ will be born. To while away
that final interval, Adam and Eve decide to visit the East. Before
taking off, though, they join the chorus for a rendition of Psalm
41 in the Vulgate.

As Act V begins, Daniel's 490 years have all but passed. At one
side of the stage stands Mary's house in Nazareth; at the other,

her cousin Elizabeth's in "a city of Juda" (Luke 1:39). Eve is upset because there is still no sign of a Savior, only corruption in
the world [V, 1]. Raziel scolds her for her lack of faith and calls
attention to two old men who are approaching Nazareth with
word of Christ's imminent birth [V, 2]. One of them, Elizabeth's
husband Zacharias, turns aside temporarily, leaving his companion Simeon to expatiate on the substance of Luke 2:26—that he is
not to die until he has beheld Jesus [V, 3]. Zacharias, struck dumb
until his son John is born, has written out the story of Gabriel's
appearance in the temple (Luke 1:11–20), which Simeon reads
to Adam and Eve, adding that Zacharias and he have come to see
whether the highly reputed virgin Mary is to be the Messiah's
mother [V, 4]. As soon as the two men leave to look for her, Eve
catches sight of a pretty, devout looking, but humbly attired girl
at the open window of her house. The old couple eavesdrop as
she reads aloud Isaiah 7:12–15 and prays for Christ to come, hoping that she might be the virgin to bear him [V, 5]. At once Uriel
and Raziel arrive, escorting Gabriel, who terrifies the former in-
habitants of Eden by reminding them of their banishment. As in
Luke 1:26–38, he informs the pious maiden, who is Mary, that
her wish will come true [V, 6]. He also tells her of Elizabeth,
whom she determines to visit forthwith [V, 7]. Adam and Eve
praise God while she makes ready [V, 8], and they listen as she
takes leaves of her "brother" Joseph, who, like his Old Testament
namesake, is called a champion of chastity [V, 9]. Uriel causes
the primal parents more grief by explaining that Jesus must die
because of their sin, though sinless Himself since not carnally conceived [V, 10]. As Mary and her maid journey across the stage,
they sing a hymn, the refrain of which is chanted by Adam and
Eve [V, 11]. When they finish, they have arrived, and Elizabeth,
like Eumenius in IV, 6 of *Asotus,* has been lured outdoors by the
music. She and Mary meet according to Luke 1:40–45 [V, 12].
Zacharias returns home, bringing Simeon; but Mary, her maid,
and Elizabeth enter the house without greeting him. Adam tells
the two men about Gabriel's announcement of the Incarnation,
adding that the virgin whom they sought is here [V, 13]. Simeon
and Zacharias go inside, leaving the "protoplasts," as Adam and
Eve are frequently called, to wish for their angels. Uriel and
Raziel find them weeping over their wickedness and longing to
talk to Mary, who comes back out with both maid and cousin and

welcomes them [V, 14–15]. Before finally retiring, all laud the Lord in song, joined by Simeon and Zacharias [V, 16], and Elizabeth regrets that Anna of Luke 2:36–38 is not among them [V, 17]. This adumbration of Biblical history from the fall to salvation ends as we are reminded in a ten-line epilogue ("to be spoken, or sung, by anybody," as the directions state) that Adam is each of us in both wrongs and redemption.

The author's apprehensions about incoherence in the last act were unfounded. In fact, the whole work cries for more cutting, yet its verbosity is not its greatest shortcoming. What was previously Macropedius' strength has here become a glaring weakness, for portrayal of the leading figures is inept. Ironically, their prominence, which calls for characterization of them, is not even necessary. By their function Adam and Eve are as peripheral as a Greek chorus. They would illuminate the action more effectively if they briefly questioned their guardian angels as concerned bystanders without being obtrusive and attempting to arouse emotion through their bathos. The author may have intended for them to contribute unity, but his unwieldy throwback to the Middle Ages is not held together so much by their conspicuousness as by its theme, the deliverance of humanity.[7] Having lost his knack for characterization, Macropedius in his old age should have avoided parts which require much of it. In *Hypomone* this is happily what he did. There the leading roles are given to two allegorical figures in a religious play held to fewer than 1,300 lines—less than half the length of rambling and windy *Adam*.

II *Hypomone*

As Uriel and Raziel spur Adam and Eve to bide mankind's redemption, so Hypomone ("patience") and her sister Graphe ("Scripture") urge various disconsolate souls to await better times with hope and faith rather than despair. On the title page Macropedius renders the essence of the play by citing Romans 15:4— "Whatever things were written were written for our learning, that we through patience and comfort of the scriptures might have hope." This morality play has instead of a plot another series of visitations, though not in chronological progression as in *Adam*. Characters both biblical and non-biblical, from both Old Testament and New, both fictional and historical, as well as ancient and modern are jumbled together.

In the prologue, Hypomone introduces herself, declaring that God is her Father and Tribulation her mother. Graphe confirms this parentage by paraphrasing verse six from Psalm 41 of the Vulgate and by quoting from Romans 5:3. Their Father has sent the two of them, Hypomone continues, for the solace of sufferers. We are to see them call on social outcasts (Act I), fugitives (Act II), the physically handicapped (Act III), and paupers (Act IV). Each class will be represented by a few typical figures. Although Hypomone does not say so, Act V will show the rewards of patience, logically completing the simple scheme of the work.

The social outcasts are Job, Lazarus the beggar, and several unnamed lepers. As Hypomone observes Job scrape the pus from his sores with a potsherd, she asks why such a good man should be afflicted [I, 1]. Probably thinking of John 9:3, Graphe replies that the three "comforters," whom they see standing at a distance, are wrong to assume that pain and deprivation are always punishment for sin. Distress may work to the greater glory of God, as with Job, who sets an example of endurance for others. Stricken with the loss of family, property, and health, he can comment "The Lord gave, and the Lord has taken away; blessed be the name of the Lord (Job 1:21), but as in Job 3 he nevertheless wishes that he were dead. The two ladies, whom he no longer even recognizes though they are old acquaintances, accordingly come to bolster his spirits [I, 2]. While he laments his troubles, Lazarus crawls up, together with several diseased companions, and says that dogs grant him more relief than Laemargus does in all his affluence. In response to Hypomone's request that she encourage the whole group, Graphe exhorts them at length to be patient in imitation of Christ and His martyrs [I, 3]. Stirred by her rhetoric, Job becomes ashamed of his despondence and vows to be courageous as long as Hypomone is well disposed [I, 4]. She explains that with Graphe she must visit others but that she will come again. In a forecast of the final act she predicts that on her return she will find him and his fellow sufferers rejoicing. Meanwhile, Graphe adds, the false friends may bring their "cold consolation." The chorus sings about resurrection of the body at the end of time.[8]

In Act II David and the prophet Elijah are hiding from their respective enemies, Saul and Jezebel. David's nephews are with him, and the younger, Abishai, steels Joab to stick by their im-

periled and melancholy uncle [II, 1], who vents his depression
by paraphrasing in glyconics Psalm 87 from the Vulgate [II, 2–3].
After listening sympathetically, Hypomone and her sister cheer
him up [II, 3–5]. In a seventy-six line pep talk Graphe reminds
him of his earlier trust in God by quoting from Psalms 72, 144,
and 32 in the Vulgate. Jacob, Joseph, and Moses she cites as
models for him to follow. He responds enthusiastically in a short
pastiche from several psalms, embracing Hypomone and begging
her not to leave him. With a promise that God will make him
king, she tells him to sing Vulgate Psalms 131:1 and 29:12 while
she and Graphe extend their services to others.

Elijah, who is with several fellow prophets in exile because of
Jezebel's threat to kill him (I Kings 19:2), stops the two ladies in
order to introduce himself [II, 6]. Like Job he prefers to die, and
what follows is rather a perfunctory repeat of the foregoing pro-
cedure. Graphe gives an eighteen-line hortatory speech, stirring
Elijah to patience, whereupon she and Hypomone say good-by.
The chorus closing Act II is a rendering of Psalm 122 in the
Vulgate.

A very short (fifty-five-line) Act III introduces blind Tobit
of the Apocrypha, along with a cripple and a victim of gout. In
Scene 1 Graphe consoles Tobit, who also wishes that he were
dead, by stating that like Job God intends him to be a model of
endurance. Soon his sight will return, she prophesies, seconded by
Hypomone in Scene 2. The other sufferers, Hypomone adds,
should also expect relief. Probably speaking for Macropedius, the
man stricken with podagra says that he prefers to be punished
now for his sins rather than in the life to come, thus contrasting
starkly with the gouty Hieronymus in *Bassarus*. All beg the sisters
to remain, but Graphe insists as before that she and Hypomone
must continue their calls. She advises Tobit and his companions
to lighten their cares in song, as they do with the chorus to this
act, calling for generosity, chastity, humility, and sobriety.

In a hovel the two women find a group of needy schoolboys
[IV, 1–3], including two "sons of the prophets," all of whom
Graphe encourages with another discourse on patience [IV, 4].
The prophets themselves, Christ, and the apostles were all poor,
she says, closing with an allusion to II Kings 4:41. Just as Elisha
cast meal into the pottage of the sons of the prophets to make it
edible, so God will sweeten the lot of these destitute pupils.

Graphe and Hypomone bid them farewell for a time, wanting now to revisit the people whom they strengthened earlier. The chorus to Act IV is a paraphrase of the last five verses in Psalm 9 from the Vulgate, sung by the impoverished boys.

When the sisters begin their rounds once more, Job greets them cheerfully, having been restored to health and prosperity [V, 1]. Lazarus, he relates, has gone to the bosom of Abraham. Promising to return again, Hypomone and Graphe meet David, who is triumphant and regally attired [V, 2]. Like Lazarus, Elijah has passed on, carried home in his chariot of fire. David still paraphrases verses from the Psalms—on this occasion from 142, 29, and 56. Tobit approaches with the good tidings that he has regained his eyesight [V, 3]. His son Tobias and his new daughter-in-law Sara are also present, thanks to the angel who dispelled her demon, as she relates [V, 4]. After Hypomone congratulates her on her good fortune and admonishes her to persevere, Graphe reminds her that marriage and motherhood are fraught with difficulties. As pottery is tested in the fire, so are we in trial and tribulation, Graphe observes in parting.[9] The lot of some of the poor boys, who are visited last, has not improved, but at least their spirits have, so that they welcome the women in song [V, 5]. Hypomone is pleased at their sustenance and abstinence, as she says, alluding to the motto of Epictetus which Thraso quotes in *Lazarus* II, 1. God will not desert them, Graphe solemnly declares. To close the play, the cast joins in singing an extra chorus (from Psalm 40:1–5 of the Vulgate), after which in a four-line epilogue the author comes to ask for applause.[10]

Although our survey has drawn to a close with the three least effective of Macropedius' plays, *Hypomone* is at any rate the best of the trio, if only because it is the least pretentious. In its utter simplicity it is unbotched, since its lack of plot and its scant need for characterization leave little to go awry. Its modest demands could still be met by the author's faltering ability. To have omitted *Adam, Hypomone,* and *The Pupil Jesus* with scarcely a word of comment would have been kinder to Macropedius, but his failures do not cancel his triumphs. Though in releasing all his plays he unwittingly sowed the seed of critical censure as well as of praise, the good grain in his harvest is not diminished by the tares.

CHAPTER 8

Conclusion

THE quality of Macropedius' dramas curves upward from the apprentice work *Asotus* to *Petriscus, Andrisca,* and *Bassarus.* Starting with *Hecastus,* which has traditionally been considered his masterpiece, a decline sets in, though deterioration becomes marked only after *Joseph.* The result is at least half a dozen good plays, even if *Asotus, The Rebels,* and *Aluta* are excluded. The most remarkable aspect of the author's development is his rejection of secular comedy just after demonstrating virtuosity in handling it. *Hecastus, Lazarus,* and *Joseph* reveal an atrophying of comic elements altogether. Ultimately the earnestness of his moral message led Macropedius to disregard the demands of his dramatic medium, as is clearly shown by his appendages to *The Rebels* in the 1553 edition, as well as by *Adam, Hypomone,* and *The Pupil Jesus.* Already in the plodding last act of *Hecastus* this trend begins to appear.

The twelve plays might be grouped in an order somewhat different from the arrangement used in this study. They can be divided according to the five matters which they emphasize rather than with regard to dominant characters. *Asotus, The Rebels,* and *Petriscus* warn boys not to leave home and school for the will-o'-the-wisp of pleasure. *Aluta, Andrisca,* and *Bassarus* stress entertainment in a context of social commentary. *Hecastus* stands in a category by itself as a dramatization of the theology of justification. *Lazarus, Joseph,* and *The Pupil Jesus* inculcate virtue, while *Adam* and *Hypomone* teach forbearance. Though we might wish that the class of *Aluta, Andrisca,* and *Bassarus* were enlarged, what we do have is considerable diversification.

If, instead of compartmentalizing the dramas, we try to gather as many as possible over a common denominator, we can say that Macropedius' world is typically one of failings and transgressions which end happily in reform. Even *Adam* may be called a case in point, though *Lazarus, Hypomone,* and *The Pupil Jesus* are sure exceptions. A more basic feature is the greater concern for characterization than for plot, and Macropedius is the first significant creator of character on either Netherlandish or German stages. Because he was forced to compose quickly, he facilitated the portrayal of his figures by modifying those from previous plays. Asotus is an ancestor of Hecastus and Laemargus as well as of the rebels and Petriscus. The bibulous Aluta foreshadows Andrisca, who is also a shrew like Mysandra and Cacolalia. Aegla's large debt to both Porna and Mysandra is clear, along with variations in the figure of the meek husband. The result is not jejune repetition, as we have seen, but rich variety in a company of sharply delineated personages infused with vitality. Regarding this second point of comparison, however, there are still exceptions. *Adam* and *Hypomone,* if not also *The Pupil Jesus,* lack characterization. The lowest common denominator in all of Macropedius' theatrical pieces is the fact that he wrote them as Latin school plays.

This rather humble and, with regard to language, alien nature has limited their appeal since the Renaissance. Even then it was only in Germany, where especially the near-Protestant *Hecastus* was popular, that any of them had much influence. Macropedius is nevertheless the foremost Dutch stage writer before the seventeenth century. In the Germany of his day he was rivaled only by the rabid anti-Catholic Thomas Naogeorgus (1511–63), whose Aristophanic *Merchant* (*Mercator,* 1540), is a work derived from *Hecastus.* His status as one of Europe's first notable dramatists since antiquity should earn for Macropedius a simple niche in any pantheon of playwrights to enjoy, to profit from, and to remember.

Notes and References

Chapter One

1. For source material see Georgius Macropedius, *Bassarus,* ed. Rudolphus Cornelis Engelberts, Diss. Utrecht 1968 (Tilburg: Drukkerij-Uitgeverij H. Gianotten N.V., 1968), pp. 7–22. To Engelberts goes the credit for discovering the year of Macropedius' birth, which was previously thought to have been about 1475.

2. The passage in question reads in rather literal translation as follows: "I cannot, my Bruno [one Georgius Bruno, to whom the preface is addressed], after the Italian plays shared with me, after the antiquities of the city of Rome shown to me, after some difficulties (which gave me trouble) settled through your skill, and several other signs of your favor toward me—I cannot, I say, help seeking to gratify you somehow in return."

Daniel Jacoby, *Georg Macropedius, Ein Beitrag zur Litteraturgeschichte des sechzehnten Jahrhunderts* (Berlin: R. Gaertners Verlagsbuchhandlung, 1886), pp. 7–8, states that Macropedius never left his fatherland and cites as evidence part of an elegy by one of the playwright's colleagues, Arnold van Tricht. This person writes that Macropedius never saw Paris, Cologne, or "those cities which Italy cherishes on account of learning." The import is not that Macropedius never traveled but only that he did not study at a university.

3. In the prologue to *Adam* he states that he returned to biblical subjects because his Shrovetide comedies offended pious ears. In the prologue to *Lazarus* he remarks that because many souls in his audiences prefer sacred plays he has taken this one from the Bible.

4. In the chorus to the second act of his last play, *The Pupil Jesus,* he still demands that all capable boys be educated. "Take away the school and you'll destroy both church and state" is the essence of the third strophe.

5. In the preface to the appendix of his *Kalendarius* (1541) Macropedius states that he decided not to publish "quae ante annos .12. auditoribus meis de Numeris et Cantu ecclesiastico dictaveram. . . ." Cf. Engelberts, *Bassarus,* p. 27.

6. For various editions see Jacoby, *Macropedius,* p. 13. Number 4

listed by him *(Nominum et verborum . . .)* is not by Macropedius but is a catalogue of nouns and verbs, with Dutch equivalents, from the *Institutiones grammaticae,* compiled by Ioannes Henricus Scoendervuordanus. Number 8 *(Textus evangelicarum et apostolicarum lectionum . . .* as the no longer extant first edition was titled) is also not actually a work by Macropedius. The 's-Hertogenbosch, 1605 edition (titled *Evangelia et lectiones sacrae epistolae dictae . . .)* is a collection of New Testament passages with only explanations of word meanings by Macropedius. A different version, with commentary also by Hermannus Torrentinus, was printed at Antwerp in 1576 (copy at the Bibliothèque Nationale in Paris) and at Utrecht in 1606, under the title *Evangelia et epistolae.* Number 11b listed by Jacoby *(Methodus de conscribendis epistolis . . .)* is a reprint of the *Epistolica . . . ,* number 11a.

7. The copy of these two songs (with a transcription of the "Ode on the Image of Death") which was formerly in the Collection Duc d'Arenberg of the Bibliothèque Royale de Belgique is now in the Houghton Library of Harvard University.

8. See Jacoby, *Macropedius,* pp. 11–12, whose case against imputing these two dramas to Macropedius has been followed here.

9. Georgius Macropedius, *Rebelles und Aluta,* Lateinische Litteraturdenkmäler des XV. und XVI. Jahrhunderts, 13, ed. Johannes Bolte (Berlin: Weidmannsche Buchhandlung, 1897), p. xi, note 1.

10. *D. Martin Luthers Werke,* Tischreden, I (Weimar: Hermann Böhlaus Nachfolger, 1912), 431.

11. See George E. Duckworth, *The Nature of Roman Comedy* (Princeton: Princeton University Press, 1952), p. 82.

12. Expeditus Schmidt, in *Die Bühnenverhältnisse des deutschen Schuldramas und seiner volkstümlichen Ableger im sechzehnten Jahrhundert* (Berlin: Verlag von Alexander Duncker, 1903), p. 120, shared this assumption, writing "Macropedius spielte wohl meist in seiner Schule. . . ."

13. In a letter dated November 24, 1548, his pupil and friend Cornelius Valerius van Auwater writes that Macropedius often wished to retire from his administrative position in order to have more time for his literary concerns. See Henry de Vocht, ed., *Cornelii Valerii ab Auwater Epistolae et Carmina,* Humanistica Lovaniensia, 14 (Louvain: Librairie Universitaire, 1957), p. 119.

Chapter Two

1. In the preface to the 1535 edition of *The Rebels* and *Aluta* Macropedius refers to this statement by Gnapheus, showing that he definitely was acquainted with *Acolastus.* He says "A certain person wonders

(and I myself grieve) that among so many very learned men of our age no Menanders, no Terences are to be found. . . ."

2. Franz Spengler, *Der Verlorene Sohn im Drama des XVI. Jahrhunderts* (Innsbruck: Verlag der Wagner'schen Universitäts-Buchhandlung, 1888), passim. Cf. Wilhelm Creizenach, *Geschichte des neueren Dramas*, II (Halle a.S.: Verlag von Max Niemeyer, 1918), 114.

3. Macropedius used this verse again in the eighth strophe of the chorus to the second act of *Petriscus*:

> Although it is impossible
> To set whom God contemns aright,
> The impious should still be whipped,
> In order that the rest take fright.

In *Adam* I, 2 the father applies it to Cain.

4. Adolf Schweckendiek, *Bühnengeschichte des Verlorenen Sohnes in Deutschland*, Theatergeschichtliche Forschungen, 40 (Leipzig: Verlag von Leopold Voss, 1930), pp. 46–52, assumes that Macropedius used the so-called *Terenzbühne* and that the prison and the brothel were indicated on the stage together with Eumenius' house. The barn Schweckendiek does not mention. His evidence for the prison, the phrase "huic phylacae" in III, 8, was changed to "hinc phylacae" in the revised 1552 edition, and regarding the brothel he ignores the fact that in IV, 6 Tribonius, who has been on the stage watching Asotus and the prostitutes, says he *thinks* they went there ("in ganeum ut conijcio"). If the brothel were in sight, Tribonius would know without a doubt. Also, Comasta in I, 3 would not have to send Colax for the girls if they were merely next door. The "intus hic" of IV, 7 which Schweckendiek cites as partial proof of his interpretation may refer to Eumenius' house rather than the brothel, or it may be an inconsistency resulting from the earlier revision.

5. All the choral odes of *Asotus* are in iambic dimeters.

6. Cf. Plautus' *Mostellaria* 233 and Creizenach II, 117, and 251.

7. These verses Macropedius used again in the fifth strophe of the chorus to the first act of *Hecastus*:

> Don't let the prime of life pass by.
> We should crown ourselves with roses of spring
> Collected from every meadow and way
> Before we find them withering.

In different form they appear in the chorus to Act III of *Lazarus the Beggar*, and the first line of the stanza just quoted recurs in a speech by Tryphera in I, 2 of *Lazarus*.

8. In the 1552 edition Eumenius is given an added line in this scene, stating that his wife is dead.

Chapter Three

1. *Geschichte des neueren Dramas* II, 153.

2. This name, from the founder of the Cyrenaic school of philosophy, is supposed to connate sternness. In I, 3 of *Asotus* Colax refers to Eumenius as "so crabbed [*tetricus*] that he clearly surpasses Aristippus or Diogenes."

3. Cornelius Schonaeus from Gouda (1540–1611), schoolmaster in Haarlem, crossed Macropedius' *Rebels* with *Acolastus* to produce a comedy called *Dyscoli,* first published in 1603. In V, 4 of this work he has the teacher Eugenius argue that the judge should defer to him for the punishment of guilty pupils, "according to an old and praiseworthy custom."

4. The situation is analogous to Judgment Day as depicted in the *cantilena* of 1539, where (in the ninth strophe) Macropedius writes that there will be no one to oppose God's arbitrary decree.

5. All the choral odes of *Petriscus* are in iambic dimeters.

6. Johannes Bolte, *Rebelles und Aluta,* pp. viii–ix and xvii–xxiii, cites a number of works sharing farcical motifs with the Shrovetide plays of Macropedius. On "smoke," see p. ix, note 1.

Chapter Four

1. Bolte, *ibid.,* p. xix, note 4, rejects this possibility for no reason.

2. On the international popularity of the peasant robbed by city dwellers, see Creizenach, *Geschichte des neueren Dramas,* III (Halle a.S.: Verlag von Max Niemeyer, 1923), 112, including note 2 there, and 199.

3. In addition to Bolte, *Rebelles und Aluta,* p. xix, see Stith Thompson, *Motif-Index of Folk-Literature,* IV (Bloomington: Indiana University Press, 1957), 176, no. J2086, where a cow is pawn.

4. All the choruses of this play are in iambic dimeters.

5. In IV, 1 of Plautus' *Pseudolus* the slave Simia feels that he can frighten Harpax, whom he is impersonating, into denying his identity.

6. See Bolte, *Rebelles und Aluta,* pp. xx–xxi.

7. All the choral odes of *Andrisca* are in iambic dimeters.

8. The text here reads simply "haec" ("these things"), but the bread and cheese mentioned earlier in the scene by Andrisca seem to be meant. Less clear is how Georgus comes to have them, for they were presumably in the house and we have no indication that Georgus has gone inside. Later, in IV, 5, he informs Byrsocopus that Andrisca handed him some dry bread, so that early in II, 3, just before she tells him to eat it, she must quickly fetch the bread and cheese from the

house. What she says at that point in the original is "Ibi panis est, ibi caseus./ Ede, atque abi ocyus, redito vesperi."

9. On folklore used in *Bassarus* see Bolte, *Rebelles und Aluta,* pp. viii–ix, note 3, though the references to Erasmus' *Convivium fabulosum* and to *Deutsche Volksmärchen aus Schwaben,* no. 66, are inappropriate. See also Thompson, *Motif-Index,* IV, 227 (J2618), 278 (K343.2.1), and V, 510 (X424).

10. Greta's malapropism may have been suggested by Guillemette's confusion of *grammaire* with *grimaire (grimoire)* in Scene 1 of *Pathelin.*

11. Thompson, *Motif-Index,* IV, 418 (K1655).

12. The meter of these odes is basically iambic dimeter, with the refrain alternating between iambic trimeter and iambic tetrameter.

13. Engelberts, *Bassarus,* p. 77, says that Macropedius was thinking here of hams, and we are referred to Janus Hartelust, *De dictione Georgii Macropedii,* Diss. Utrecht 1902 (Traiecti ad Rhenum: J. Van Boekhoven, 1902), p. 32, where Hartelust cites Plautus' *Captivi* 908 as the source. Because the Latin word *fumarium* used by Macropedius means "a smoke chamber for wine," Plautus' *Poenulus* 311–12 is a likelier source. The image is rather one of grapes hung to dry, as indicated by Ganymede, Jupiter's cup-bearer.

14. Engelberts, *Bassarus,* p. 91, interprets the word *taberna* here to mean Bassarus' own house, making the sexton also an innkeeper. Evidence in his favor is the fact that the coppersmith calls Bassarus a *caupo* ("taverner") in IV, 7, yet Macropedius may have intended that merely as synonymous with *hospes* ("host") in the same scene (lines 789–90).

15. Both Creoborus and the coppersmith repeat their question in Dutch, indicating a Dutch source, says Engelberts, *Bassarus,* p. 38.

16. See R. C. Engelberts and W. P. Gerritsen, "De dobbelscène in Macropedius' *Bassarus,*" *De Nieuwe Taalgids,* 61 (1968), 391–96.

17. In III, 2, line 460, Hieronymus says that a goose was taken along with the pig, but it is not otherwise mentioned. Macropedius must have momentarily confused the goose with the sausages.

Chapter Five

1. "Hisecastus" is from εἰς ἕχαστος, "everyone." The messenger seems unsure of the exact form of the name.

2. The verses paraphrased from Ecclesiasticus are Chapter 41:1–2, also used to begin the complaint in II, 10.

3. Philocrates says that he is crying even though he and his brother have both reached manhood ("tametsi uterque modo ex ephebis cessimus"). This implies that each of them is older than twenty, despite the fact that Hecastus is only thirty! Epicuria may be thirty-five.

4. The meter here is trochaic dimeters in four-line strophes, the last line of each being catalectic.

5. "Aphron" is probably taken from Luke 12:20 of the Greek New Testament.

6. Macropedius paraphrases verses 18–19 of this parable, and the angel who soon appears replaces God, who in verse 20 says "Fool! This night your soul is required of you. . . ."

7. Abraham indicates his relative position by using the verb *conscendere* ("climb up") to indicate how he would be reached from where Laemargus is.

Chapter Six

1. Jacoby, *Macropedius,* p. 30, points out that the names "Phaedra" and "Aegla" have the same meaning. In part Seneca's Phaedra, from what Creizenach II, 394 calls "die Lieblingstragödie der Frührenaissance," served Macropedius as a model, being also neglected, lovesick, and furious when scorned.

2. In line 287 of Terence's *Phormio* Demipho wryly calls his slave Geta "pillar of the household." Crocus uses Terence's exact words, "columen vero familiae," which Macropedius alters to "domus columen meae" (I, 3) and "domus nostrae columen" (III, 2).

3. This ode is in iambic dimeters grouped into five-line strophes with a five-line refrain.

4. Pharaoh's words are "Sequere intro me. . . ." At the beginning of the scene he is definitely already inside, however. Regarding Joseph, he says "Cur stat foris?/ Quin' introducitur?" and the butler replies "Introduxero. . . ." Either the king walks outside with Joseph during the course of their conversation or the two go into an inner chamber at the end. The former choice is likelier. Since the scene is 101 lines long, Macropedius may have wanted a little movement to combat tedium, and he may have wished to bring the two actors into fuller view of the audience for their extended discourse.

5. In Seneca's *Troades* there is a herald named Talthybius.

Chapter Seven

1. De Vocht, *Cornelii Valerii ab Auwater Epistolae et Carmina,* p. 141.

2. All the choral odes of *Adam* are in anapestic dimeters.

3. Actually Macropedius confuses Raziel with Uriel here.

4. Macropedius subsequently forgot this matter, which is never dealt with.

5. Isaiah 9:6–7; 11:1–2; 7:14; 53:2–8 and 12; Jeremiah 31:22; and Ezekiel 44:2–3.

6. Already in Scene 5 Solomon—as a man of peace another fore-shadowing of Jesus—is spoken of in the past tense.

7. In 1538 the German Lutheran Valten Voith (1487–after 1558) published a 3,068-line vernacular drama in the same vein, suggested by an allegorical painting in the Madgeburg council chamber. In this *Schön, Lieblich Spiel von dem herlichen ursprung . . . des Menschen,* the figures Law, Sin, Death, and Satan conspire against mankind as Adam and Eve err (Act I) and are expelled from Eden (Act II); Cain kills Abel (Act III); Isaac is born and nearly sacrificed (Act IV); and David has Uriah killed (Act V). The four onlookers chronicle history between these events and up to the advent of Christ (V, 6), who triumphs over them as predicted. Regarding medieval Dutch mysteries on the theme of man's deliverance, see J. A. Worp, *Geschiedenis van het Drama en van het Tooneel in Nederland,* I (Groningen: J. B. Wolters, 1904), 28.

8. All the choruses of *Hypomone* are in iambic dimeters.

9. Her cliché is also uttered by the title figure in *Joseph,* II, 9.

10. Among the *dramatis personae* is listed *Poeta seu Epilogus.* Presumably Macropedius himself is meant.

5. Isaiah 9:6–7; 11:1–2; 7:14; 53:2–8 and 12; Jeremiah 31:22; and Ezekiel 44:2–3.

6. Already, in Scene 5 Solomon—as a man of peace another foreshadowing of Jesus—is spoken of in the past tense.

7. In 1526 the German Lutheran Valten Voith (1487–after 1558) published a 3,068-line vernacular drama in the same vein, [illegible] by an allegorical painting in the Magdeburg council chamber. In this [illegible], the figures Law, Sin, Death, and Satan conspire against [illegible] Adam and Eve (Act I) and are expelled from Eden (Act II); Cain kills Abel (Act III); [illegible] and nearly sacrificed (Act IV); and David has Goliath killed (Act V). The four [illegible] between [illegible] into the advent of [illegible] drama over [illegible]. Regarding medieval Old Testament [illegible], see J. A. Wynn, [illegible] and [illegible] (Chapel Hill, [illegible]), 23.

8. The chorus of Hypocrisy [illegible].

9. [illegible]

10. [illegible]

Selected Bibliography

I. Best editions of Macropedius' plays

A. *Adam: Omnes Georgii Macropedii Fabulae Comicae, Denuo recognitae, et iusto ordine (prout editae sunt) in duas partes divisae.* Ultraiecti: H. Borculous, 1552–54.

B. *Aluta:* Georgius Macropedius. *Rebelles und Aluta*, Lateinische Litteraturdenkmäler des XV. und XVI. Jahrhunderts, 13, ed. JOHANNES BOLTE. Berlin: Weidmannsche Buchhandlung, 1897.

C. *Andrisca: Georgii Macropedii Andrisca fabula lepidissima.* Busciducis: G. Hatardus, 1538.

D. *Asotus: Asotvs Evangelicus, seu euangelica de filio prodigo parabola, a Georgio Macropedio comice descripta.* Busciducis: G. Hatardus, 1537.

E. *Bassarus:* Georgius Macropedius. *Bassarus*, ed. RUDOLPHUS CORNELIS ENGELBERTS, Diss. Utrecht, 1968. Tilburg: Drukkerij-Uitgeverij H. Gianotten N.V., 1968.

F. *Hecastus:* JOHANNES BOLTE, ed. *Drei Schauspiele vom sterbenden Menschen.* Bibliothek des literarischen Vereins in Stuttgart, 269–70. Leipzig: W. Hiersemann, 1927.

G. *Hypomone:* See "A" above.

H. *Joseph: Iosephus Macropedii, Fabula sacra, pietatis et pudicitiae cultoribus perlegenda.* Antverpiae: M. Hillenius, 1544.

I. *Lazarus the Beggar: Lazarus Mendicus Georgii Macropedii.* Ultraiecti: H. Borculous, 1541.

J. *Petriscus:* Pp. 143–204 in JANUS HARTELUST. *De dictione Georgii Macropedii.* Diss. Utrecht, 1902. Traiecti ad Rhenum: J. Van Boekhoven, 1902.

K. *Pupil Jesus: Iesus Scholasticus Georgii Macropedii.* Ultraiecti: H. Borculous, 1556.

L. *Rebels:* See "B" above

II. Some correspondence to and from Macropedius

DE VOCHT, HENRY, ed. *Cornelii Valerii ab Auwater Epistolae et Carmina*, Humanistica Lovaniensia, 14. Louvain: Librairie Universitaire, 1957.

III. Specialized literature on Macropedius

ENGELBERTS, RUDOLPHUS CORNELIS, ed. *Bassarus*. Diss. Utrecht, 1968. Tilburg: Drukkerij-Uitgeverij H. Gianotten N.V., 1968. Best biographical source.

ENGELBERTS, R. C. and W. P. GERRITSEN. "De dobbelscène in Macropedius' *Bassarus*," *De Nieuwe Taalgids*, 61 (1968), 391–96. A clarification of the gambling scene in *Bassarus*.

HARTELUST, JANUS. *De dictione Georgii Macropedii*. Diss. Utrecht, 1902. Traiecti ad Rhenum: J. Van Boekhoven, 1902. Detailed study of Macropedius' style.

JACOBY, DANIEL. *Georg Macropedius, Ein Beitrag zur Litteraturgeschichte des sechzehnten Jahrhunderts*. Berlin: R. Gaertners Verlagsbuchhandlung, 1886. Outdated but still valuable presentation of Macropedius' life and works.

IV. General literature

CREIZENACH, WILHELM. *Geschichte des neueren Dramas*, vols. I–III. Halle a.S.: Verlag von Max Niemeyer, 1911–23. Basic survey of European drama through the early Renaissance.

DUCKWORTH, GEORGE E. *The Nature of Roman Comedy*. Princeton: Princeton University Press, 1952. Detailed analysis of Plautine and Terentian comedy.

GOEDEKE, KARL. *Every-man, Homulus und Hekastus*. Hannover: Carl Rümpler, 1865. Classic history of the Everyman-theme.

LILIENCRON, ROCHUS VON. "Die Chorgesänge des lateinisch-deutschen Schuldramas," *Vierteljahrsschrift für Musikwissenschaft*, 6 (1890), 309–387. Standard study of the chorus in Dutch and German school drama.

NAHDE, ERNST. *Der reiche Mann und der arme Lazarus im Drama des 16. Jahrhunderts*. Diss. Jena, 1928. Borna-Leipzig: Universitätsverlag von Robert Noske, 1928. Shows Macropedius' importance for German dramatizations of the Lazarus parable.

SCHMIDT, EXPEDITUS. *Die Bühnenverhältnisse des deutschen Schuldramas und seiner volkstümlichen Ableger im sechzehnten Jahrhundert*. Berlin: Verlag von Alexander Duncker, 1903. A partly questionable but still useful source of information on school drama.

SPENGLER, FRANZ. *Der verlorene Sohn im Drama des 16. Jahrhunderts*. Innsbruck: Verlag der Wagner'schen Universitäts-Buchhandlung, 1888. Best survey of Dutch and German plays reflecting the prodigal-son parable.

WEILEN, ALEXANDER VON. *Der ägyptische Joseph im Drama des 16. Jahrhunderts*. Wien: Alfred Hölder, 1887. Briefly describes and analyzes Dutch and German dramatizations of the Joseph story.

WORP, J.A. *Geschiedenis van het Drama en van het Tooneel in Nederland.* 2 vols. Groningen: J. B. Wolters, 1904–8. Standard history of Dutch drama.

Index

Acts of the Apostles, 69, 154, 156-57
Aeschylus, 95
  Seven against Thebes, 95
Antwerp, 24, 172
Apostles' Creed, 122
Ariosto, Ludovico, 11
Aristophanes, 119
Aristotle, 28

Bidermann, Jacob, 11
Bolte, Johannes, 5, 17, 172, 174-75
Brethren of the Common Life, 11-12
Bruno, Georgius, 171
Brussels, 6

Charles V, 116-17
Cologne, 171
Creizenach, Wilhelm, 5, 42, 173-74, 176
Crocus, Cornelius, 136, 138-40, 142, 144, 147, 153
  Joseph, 136, 138-40, 142, 144, 147

Daniel, Book of, 118, 163
Delfius, Jacobus, 137
Deuteronomy, 155
De Vocht, Henry, 172, 176
De Volder, Willem, see Gnapheus
Dorlandus, Petrus, 111
Duckworth, George E., 172

Eberhard VI, 90
Ecclesiastes, 29, 129
Ecclesiasticus, 118, 175
Elckerlijc, 111-12, 115, 117
Enfans de Maintenant, 42-44, 49
Engelberts, R. C., 6, 15, 21, 171, 175

England, 11, 16
Epictetus, 127, 168
Erasmus, 5, 12, 35-36, 175
  Convivium fabulosum, 175
Esdras, First Book of, 146
Euripides, 35, 140
  Iphigenia in Aulis, 35-36
Everyman, 111-12, 115, 117, 119
Exodus, 162
Ezekiel, Book of, 177

Ferrara, 11
France, 11
Frischlin, Nicodemus, 18
  Julius Redivivus, 18

Gemert, 11
Genesis, 136, 139-40, 145, 147-48, 150, 153, 155, 160
Gennep, Jaspar von, 111
Gent, 6
Germany, 11-12, 15, 18-19
Gerritsen, W. P., 175
Gesner, Conrad, 15
  Bibliotheca, universalis, 15
Gesta Romanorum, 90
Gnapheus, Gulielmus, 15, 24-25, 28-29, 31, 40, 48, 172-73
  Acolastus, 15-16, 24-30, 37, 40, 44, 48, 172-74
Goedeke, Karl, 5
Göttingen, 6
Gouda, 24, 174
Grimmelshausen, H. J. C. von, 88
  Courasche, 88
Grimms' *Fairy Tales,* 74, 104
Groote, Geert, 11-12

Grotius, Hugo, 153
Gryphius, Andreas, 11

Haarlem, 174
Hadrian, 132
Hague, The, 6, 136
Hartelust, Janus, 175
Hatard, Gerard, 23
Heidelberg, 90
Hofmannsthal, Hugo von, 119
Horace, 17, 19, 24, 32, 37
    Ars poetica, 32, 37

Ischyrius, Christianus, 111-13
    Homulus, 20, 111-12, 115
Isaiah, Book of, 118, 132, 155-56,
    164, 177
Italy, 171

Jack Juggler, 74
Jacoby, Daniel, 171-72, 176
James, Epistle of, 121
Jeremiah, Book of, 177
Job, Book of, 166
John, Gospel of, 155-56, 162, 166
Jonson, Ben, 109
    Volpone, 16

Kempis, Thomas a, 12
    Imitation of Christ, 12
Kings, First Book of, 167
Kings, Second Book of, 167

Lamentations of Jeremiah, 120
Leviticus, 162
Liège, 12
Louvain, 6
Luke, Gospel of, 16, 24, 93, 124,
    131-32, 134-35, 154, 164-65, 176
Luther, Martin, 19

Maastricht, 20
Machiavelli, Niccolò, 108
    Mandragola, 108
    Prince, 108
Macropedius
    Adam, 15, 17, 20-21, 159-65, 169-
    71, 173, 176

Aluta, 15, 17, 19-24, 66-77, 90,
    96, 104, 130, 137, 169, 172
Andrisca, 14-16, 18, 21, 23, 57,
    66-67, 76-90, 108, 150, 169,
    174-75
Asotus, 13, 15-16, 21-25, 28-41,
    43, 45, 53, 76, 106, 114, 122,
    130, 132, 136-37, 160, 164, 169,
    173-74
Bassarus, 6, 15-17, 21-23, 66-67,
    76-77, 89-110, 112, 124, 167,
    169, 175
Dimulla, 15
Hecastus, 12-16, 20, 76, 89, 100,
    110-27, 134-35, 147, 149-50,
    169, 170, 173
Hypomone, 15, 20-22, 126, 159,
    165-70, 177
Joseph, 15-16, 20-22, 135-53, 159,
    169, 177
Lazarus the Beggar, 12, 15, 20-22,
    91, 100, 110, 124-36, 145, 153,
    161, 168-71, 173
Passion of Christ, 15
Petriscus, 13-16, 19-24, 29, 41-42,
    52-68, 70, 76-77, 79, 84, 89, 95,
    99, 124, 143, 149-50, 169, 173-
    74
Pupil Jesus, 15, 21, 137, 153-59,
    169-71
Rebels, 13-15, 18-20, 22-24, 29,
    41-53, 56, 59-60, 62-63, 65-68,
    76, 90, 113, 124, 150, 169, 172,
    174
Susanna, 15
Mariken van Nimmegen, 18
Matthew, Gospel of, 105, 155
Medici, Lorenzino de', 75
    Aridosia, 75
Menander, 40
Molière, 108
Moorkensvel, 90

Naogeorgus, Thomas, 170
    Merchant, 170
Netherlands, 11-12, 15, 18-19, 50, 93
Nu noch, 75
Numbers, 162-63

Index

Paris, 6, 171
Pathelin, 91-92, 98, 175
Peter of Diest, 111
Plaijerwater, 89
Plautus, 11, 16-17, 20, 24, 28-31,
   40-41, 48, 74, 91, 106, 113, 136,
   173-75
   Amphitruo, 74
   Aulularia, 91
   Captivi, 28, 30, 32, 38, 40, 106,
     136, 175
   Curculio, 30
   Miles gloriosus, 30
   Mostellaria, 40, 173
   Poenulus, 175
   Pseudolus, 174
   Rudens (Rope), 48, 113
Pliny, 137
Proverbs, Book of, 42
Psalms, Book of, 118, 127, 129-30,
   132, 145, 163, 166-68

Ralph Roister Doister, 16
Reuchlin, Johann, 17, 90-93, 100,
   107, 109, 125, 139, 152
   Henno, 91-92, 96, 100, 109, 125,
     139, 152
   Sergius, 90-91
Revelations, Book of, 118, 122
Romans, Epistle to, 165-66
Rome, 12, 15, 110, 124, 171
Ruwet, J., 6

Sacher-Masoch, Leopold von, 27
Sachs, Hans, 60, 75, 90, 119
   Bös Rauch, 60, 90
   Kälberbrüten, 75
Samuel, First Book of, 163

Schmidt, Expeditus, 172
Schonaeus, Cornelius, 174
   Dyscoli, 174
Schweckendiek, Adolf, 173
Scoendervuordanus, Ioannes, 172
Seneca, 176
   Troades, 176
Shakespeare, William, 75
   Twelfth Night, 75
's-Hertogenbosch, 11, 12, 23
Snoy, Reynier, 24
Spengler, Franz, 173
Sterck, see Ischyrius

Terence, 11, 17, 20, 25-27, 36, 42,
   47, 56, 124, 138, 176
   Andria, 42, 138
   Eunuchus, 26, 47, 56, 124
   Heauton Timorumenos, 36, 136
   Phormio, 176
Thirty Years' War, 88
Thompson, Stith, 174-75
Tobit, Book of, 167

Utrecht, 6, 12, 17, 21, 23, 90, 172

Van Auwater, C. V., 172
Van den Boll, Goeyert, 23
Van den Vondel, Joost, 160
   Lucifer, 160
Van Tricht, Arnold, 171
Voith, Valten, 177

Waldis, Burkard, 24
Wisdom of Solomon, 35, 115
Worp, J. A., 177

Zechariah, Book of, 156